ROBERT G. BELL, ARCHITECT
10025 E. WATFORD WAY
SUN LAKES, AZ 85248

Frank Lloyd Wright:
Writings and Buildings

SELECTED BY EDGAR KAUFMANN AND BEN RAEBURN

Frank Lloyd Wright:
Writings and Buildings

HORIZON PRESS
NEW YORK

Contents

CONTENTS

Index to Illustrations

Roots

to 1893

While Frank Lloyd Wright was growing up in the 1870s and 80s his mind was directed by his progressive parents toward architecture, literature and music. The story is told superbly in AN AUTOBIOGRAPHY, which also deals with Wright's dramatic struggle to find his way of life and his way to a living architecture. The passages that follow here, describing events in the architect's early life, are taken from A TESTAMENT, published in 1957; fortunately Wright was able to recall the past with exceptional, detailed vitality.

Wright's professional training, limited to engineering since no school of architecture was at hand, was interrupted when he left home to find his fate in Chicago. Skilled in rendering, Wright soon was accepted in the office of Adler and Sullivan where he became chief assistant to Louis H. Sullivan and thus took an active part in some of the great achievements of Chicago commercial architecture. Sullivan, who was eloquent in ideas as well as forms, remained one of Wright's great admirations (along with Beethoven, his father's favorite musician, and the Japanese print makers he discovered in the early 1890s).

17

Wright was the office expert on domestic architecture, and when his financial burdens led him to enter independent practice, houses and apartment blocks were naturally enough the first commissions received. Wright set up on his own in 1893, the year of the Chicago World's Fair, the most massive promotion of academic classicism ever attempted; progressive designers throughout the United States were hard put to hold their place in the community. Most domestic architects up till the Fair were satisfied with reminiscences of Tudor or Pilgrim buildings; some homes even boasted two-story "halls" open to subsidiary spaces; emphasis was placed on hearths, inglenooks and bay windows; materials were given a handicraft look wherever possible. In this world of stucco grandeur and contrived coziness, Wright's designs introduced a dissenting note; he was in search of an architecture based not on effect but on principle.

Roots

Mother's intense interest in the Froebel system was awakened at the Philadelphia Centennial, 1876. In the Frederick Froebel Kindergarten exhibit there, mother found the "Gifts." And "gifts" they were. Along with the gifts was the system, as a basis for design and the elementary geometry behind all natural birth of Form.

Mother was a teacher who loved teaching; Father a preacher who loved and taught music. He taught me to see great symphony as a master's *edifice of sound.* Mother learned that Frederick Froebel taught that children should not be allowed to draw from casual appearances of Nature until they had first mastered the basic forms lying hidden behind appearances. Cosmic, geometric elements were what should first be made visible to the child-mind.

Taken East at the age of three to my father's pastorate near Boston, for several years I sat at the little kindergarten table-top ruled by lines about four inches apart each way making four-inch squares; and, among other things, played upon these "unit-lines" with the square (cube), the circle (sphere) and the triangle (tetrahedron or tripod)—these were smooth maple-wood blocks. Scarlet cardboard triangle (60°-30°) two inches on the short side, and one side white, were smooth triangular sections with which to come by pattern—design—by my own imagination. Eventually I was to construct designs in other mediums. But the smooth cardboard triangles and maple-wood blocks were most important. All are in my fingers to this day.

In outline the square was significant of integrity; the circle—infinity; the triangle—aspiration; all with which to "design" significant new forms. In the third dimension, the smooth maple blocks became the cube, the sphere and the tetrahedron; all mine to "play" with.

To reveal further subordinate, or encourage composite, forms these simple elemental blocks were suspended from a small gibbet by little wire inserts at the corners and whirled. On this simple unit-system ruled on the low table-top all these forms were combined by the child into imaginative pattern. Design was recreation!

Also German papers, glazed and matte, beautiful soft color qualities, were another one of the "gifts"—cut into sheets about twelve inches each way, these squares were slitted to be woven into gay colorful checkerings as fancy might dictate. Thus color sense awakened. There were also ingenious "constructions" to be made with straight, slender, pointed sticks like toothpicks or jack-straws, dried peas for the joinings, etc., etc. The virtue of all this lay in the awakening of the child-mind to rhythmic structure in Nature—giving the child a sense of innate cause-and-effect otherwise far beyond child-comprehension. I soon became susceptible to constructive pattern *evolving in everything I saw.* I learned to "see" this way and when I did, I did not care to draw casual incidentals of Nature. I wanted to *design.*

Later, when I was put to work as a teen-ager on my Uncle James' farm in the valley where I now live, this early habit of *seeing into and seeing from within* outward went on and on way beyond until at the age of nineteen when I presented myself as a novice to Mr. Sullivan I was already, and naturally, a potential designer with a T-square and triangle technique on a unit-system; the technique that could grow intimate with and master the rapacious characteristics of the Machine in consistent straight-line, flat-plane effects natural to machine technology, which then, as now, confronted all who were to build anything for modern life in America.

Victor Hugo, in the most illuminating essay on architecture yet written, declared European Renaissance "the setting sun all Europe mistook for dawn." During 500 years of elaborate reiteration of restatements by classic column, entablature and pediment—all finally became moribund. Victor Hugo, greatest modern of his time, went on to prophesy: the great mother-art, architecture, so long formalized, pictorialized by way of man's intellect could and would come spiritually alive again. In the latter days of the nineteenth or early in the twentieth century man would see architecture revive. The soul of man would by then, due to the changes wrought upon him, be awakened by his own critical necessity.

I was fourteen years old when this usually expurgated chapter in *Notre Dame* profoundly affected my sense of the art I was born to live with—lifelong; architecture. His story of the tragic decline of the great mother-art never left my mind.

The University of Wisconsin had no course in architecture. As civil-engineer, therefore, several months before I was to receive a degree, I ran away from school (1888) to go to work in some real architect's office in Chicago. I did not want to be an engineer. A visit to the pawnbroker's—"old man Perry"— made exodus possible. My father's Gibbon's *Rome* and Plutarch's *Lives* (see Alcibiades) and the mink cape collar my mother had sewed to my overcoat financed the enterprise.

There, in Chicago, so many years after Victor Hugo's remarkable prophecy, I found Naissance had already begun. The sun—architecture—was rising!

As premonition, then, the pre-Raphaelites had appeared in England but they seemed sentimentalist reformers. Beside the mark. Good William Morris and John Ruskin were much in evidence in Chicago intellectual circles at the time. The Mackintoshes of Scotland; restless European protestants also—Van de Velde of Belgium, Berlage of Holland, Adolph Loos and Otto Wagner of Vienna: all were genuine protestants, but then seen and heard only in Europe. Came Van de Velde with *Art Nouveau,* himself predecessor of the subsequent Bauhaus. Later, in 1910 when I went to Germany by instigation of Professor Kuno Francke, there I found only the rebellious "Secession" in full swing. I met no architects.

But more important than all, a great protestant, grey army engineer, Dankmar Adler, builder and philosopher, together with his young partner, a genius, rebel from the Beaux-Arts of Paris, Louis H. Sullivan, were practising architecture there in Chicago, about 1887.

After tramping the Chicago streets for some days I got in with Cecil Corwin, foreman for J. L. Silsbee, then Chicago's foremost resident architect. He was a minister's son—as I was

—and so were Cecil and the other four draughtsmen there at the time. One year later I was accepted by Mr. Sullivan and went to work for "Adler and Sullivan" then the only moderns in architecture, and with whom, for that reason, I wanted to work. Adler and Sullivan were then building the Chicago Civic Auditorium, still the greatest room for opera in the world.

The tragedy befallen beloved architecture was still with me, Victor Hugo's prophecy often in mind. My sense of the tragedy had already bred in me hatred of the pilaster, the column for its own sake, the entablature, the cornice; in short all the architectural paraphernalia of the Renaissance. Only later did I come to know that Victor Hugo in the sweeping arc of his great thought had simply affirmed the truth: *Art can be no restatement.*

The great poet had foreseen that new uses of new materials by new inventions of new machine-methods would be devised and therefore great social changes become inevitable in the life of mankind. The poet saw that inherited styles and customs would undergo fundamental change in life and so in architecture: to make man ready to face reality anew in accord with "the great becoming." The inexorable Law of Change, by way of which the very flow of human life provides fresh inspiration, would compel new architecture, based upon Principle, to come alive.

The poet's message at heart, I wanted to go to work for the great moderns, Adler and Sullivan; and finally I went, warned by the prophecy and equipped, in fact armed, with the Froebel-kindergarten education I had received as a child from my mother. Early training which happened to be perfectly suited to the T-square and triangle technique now to become a characteristic, natural to the machine-age . . .

Let us look back. I remember how, as a boy, primitive American architecture—Toltec, Aztec, Mayan, Inca—stirred my wonder, excited my wishful admiration. I wished I might someday have money enough to go to Mexico, Guatemala and Peru to join in excavating those long slumbering remains of lost cultures; mighty, primitive abstractions of man's nature—ancient arts of the Mayan, the Inca, the Toltec. Those great American abstractions were all earth-architectures: gigantic masses of masonry raised up on great stone-paved terrain, all planned as one mountain, one vast plateau lying there or made into the great mountain ranges themselves; those vast areas of paved earth walled in by stone construction. These were human creations, cosmic as sun, moon, and stars! Nature?

Yes, but the nature of the human being as he was, then. *Entity even more cosmic* had not yet been born. The machine then was but a simple lever in the hand of the slave: man himself a menial, subject to the cruel despotisms of high authority; priests imposing "divine" mysteries upon his lack of a better sense of himself. This he called "divinity" by equally mysterious authority. By the will of despots his hands were thus tied behind his back. He was himself but an obedient tool. His magnificent masonry was architecture beyond conceivable human need; truly monumental. Monuments to the gods of temporal power were laid out and built upon the great man-made stone-paved earth-levels of South American plateau. Architectural grandeur was thus made one with the surrounding features of mountainous land; made by wasting away the mountains; mountains moved at will by the simple persistent might of the human being multiplied, a man's own strength multiplied by the strength of multitudes of his kind. By such direct and simple multiplication of strength his buildings grew to be man-mountains. All were built as and for grandiloquent religious rituals to stand forever in the eye of the sun as the earthly embodiment of the mystery of human majesty, honoring deity. Thus man was made into, built into, living harmony with surrounding mountains by the physical might of primitive man. Reverence for authority was thus made manifest and mighty by the nature of manpower thus animated. All this great, man-building took place with a splendid human sense of primitive resources and the majesty of what was then apprehended as Man's place in Nature. All was exponent of great nature and, as we have called civilization, an abstraction. There was architecture by powerful primitive manpower. Basic it was, but based upon glorified abnegation of man to authority because of what he himself did not know. Such was his worship. His sense of beauty as a mighty son of Earth! Man's God involved with the worship of means to ends then—as now? A grandeur arose in the scale of total building never since excelled, seldom equalled by man either in truth of plan or simple primitive integrity of form. Architecture intrinsic to Time, Place, and Man.

But now the man, potent lever of primitive authority in architecture, has been given even more powerful means with which to build. The science of the Machine. Already a power grown to dominant world-power. Worship of this power has grown by means of the man of science. But science in true human civilization is but a tool. Science is inventive but creative never.

So many centuries later, American man begins to build again. Something has happened to his buildings. Notwithstanding his new sciences, nor due to them, a more powerful vision has come to him, the higher sense of his own soul. This is his own sovereignty—his freedom as native American. Interior vision far greater now even in grandeur of construction, himself therefore more deeply creative as an individual, there comes to him this concept of "might" as spiritual. The dignity and worth to himself of the soul of individual man—a man no longer a tool of power or of a monarch or of any exterior authority, a man not bowed down to sacrificial mysticism but man free. Kingship now of his own soul ruled by conscience and increasingly cultured intelligence. This man has risen: himself gradually coming awake to power even greater than man's primitive power because it is power of the spirit. A new ideal of civilization arises based upon freedom of man's mind guided by his conscience. In view of this new abstraction the past subsides. Ever higher come new interpretations of old power by man's new might. Spirit is man's new power if he is to be truly mighty in his civilization. Only Art and Religion can bring this new vision as reality to a nation. Only the free man brings freedom. This new sense of life comes to his own nation and to the modern world as well. So Art and Architecture, soon his Religion too, must be new. The spiritual dignity of this new humane life for mankind, is the Spirit of Man himself sacrosanct. America has made this commitment. How are we to live up to the promise of that commitment? Where find the true sacrifices by and for this new man in this new world we call the United States of America?

. . . Among the architects practising in America when I entered Adler and Sullivan's offices, Richardson had the high honor of the field; Beaux-Arts graduate, Bostonian well-connected with the better elements of society, the Adamses, etc. But Richardson had robust appetite for romance. His Romanesque soon overthrew prevailing preferences for Renaissance. Eventually he became the most productive and successful of those men, the great eclectics of their time. Many of them fell in love with his love of the Romanesque. Yes, his Romanesque soon amounted to something wherever his fellow architects were concerned with a style.

Louis Sullivan himself kept an eye upon Richardson's superb use of stone in the arch. H. H. Richardson's use of the arch in early days, "but not his ornament," had a visible effect upon Lieber Meister. Richardson disciples were legion; his success was tremendous. Henry Hobson Richardson, though an artist

23

and giving signs of emerging as modern, was just what America deserved most but should have had least—a powerful romantic eclectic. Gone now.

McKim, Mead and White, Richardson's elite running competition, were also Beaux-Arts men. Their eclecticism was of another more elegant order, faithful to the more choice effects of early Italian (moyen-age or better-day) Renaissance. In their affected cultivated stride they took the ancient buildings verbatim. Whenever they found the buildings they admired, they copied them, enlarging the details by lantern slide. Used them straight. Their following was, of course, automatically more socially elite than Richardson's but extensive. Gone now.

Richard M. Hunt, darling of New York's four hundred, head of their procession on Fifth and other American avenues, was a good technician with a finished preference for the French-Gothic ensemble. He was fashionable, too, his eclecticisms immensely popular and profitable to him. But not to America. Gone now.

There was another much less idolized group, to which Adler and Sullivan, Major Jenney, John Root, Cass Gilbert, Van Brunt and Howe and several others, belonged. Of them the only men indicating genius above engineering ability and the capabilities of front-men were Louis Sullivan and John Root. Of Root it might be said that Sullivan was slightly envious because the two firms, Adler and Sullivan and Burnham and Root, were in direct competition, the latter firm having the best of it. Then Root's office building, the Monadnock of Chicago, might be put against Louis Sullivan's Wainwright of St. Louis. Although the Monadnock arose later, it was vital too, but an unsuitable forcing of the material: brick. See the unbricklike molded corners.

The strain of genius in Root was far less than the miracle of genius in Sullivan. Unfortunately Root barely survived the Chicago World's Fair, in the planning of which he had a major hand, supported as he was by the great master-manager, his partner Daniel H. Burnham, head architect of the Fair. He, "Uncle Dan" ("make no little plans") would have been equally great in the hat, cap or shoe business.

Of young aspirants at the time there were many, mostly head-draughtsmen like myself. There were also independents like S. S. Beman, J. L. Silsbee and many other talented men in the offices of the Middle West and of the East, such men as the Beaux-Arts Carrère and Hastings, etc., etc.

24

The Chicago World's Fair was a procession of this talent that brought these leaders of their profession out into the open. Their merits and defects might be there seen and appraised. Due largely to "Uncle Dan" Burnham's ("Frank, the Fair shows our people the beauty of the Classic—they will never go back") ability to promote ideas of Charles McKim et al, the Fair reopened wide the case for European Renaissance, and America had a memorable field day à la Paris Beaux-Arts. The "Classic" easily won and the more pertinacious and influential among the more successful architects of the A.I.A. were for the time being almost totally in command. "The eye of the vox-populi" (as a popular Fourth of July orator once put it) opened wide in dreamy-eyed wonder at the Chicago World's Fair. The ambitious ignoramus in the architectural profession throughout America was captivated. The old, old story! By this overwhelming rise of grandomania I was confirmed in my fear that a native architecture would be set back at least fifty years.

But Louis Sullivan's Transportation Building was the only picture building at the Fair presented by the Paris Beaux-Arts itself with its distinguished gold medal; which must have astonished the Beaux-Arts society of America. A society of which the original French Beaux-Arts seemed not to think highly, as I learned long years later, 1940.

Such in broad outline was the rough contour of the A.I.A. during my apprenticeship with Adler and Sullivan. There in the Adler and Sullivan offices high in the Chicago Auditorium Tower I worked for nearly seven years—George Elmslie alongside—occasionally looking out through the romantic Richardsonian Romanesque arches over Lake Michigan or often, after dark, watching the glow of giant Bessemer Steel converters reddening the night sky down towards South Chicago. I looked from those high-up arches down upon the great, growing city of Chicago as the Illinois Central trains puffed along the lake front. . . .

Among most of the architects I soon saw the great mother-art, architecture, completely confused when not demoralized. I saw their work as hackneyed or sentimentalized travesty of some kind; some old or limited eclecticism or the so-called "classic" of Beaux-Arts training encouraged by too many influential American Beaux-Arts graduates. The pilaster again!

But of the *Naissance* needed to replace moribund Renaissance I saw little or nothing outside the offices of Adler and

Sullivan to take the place of the futility of restatement at least. Awakening was to come. Whoever then acknowledged the importance of art did not seem to know so well as we now know that art cannot be restatement. Against all this face-down servile perversion by education, encouraged by my early training at the kindergarten table and subsequent work on the farm in the valley, I came to feel that in the nature of Nature —if from within outward—I would come upon nothing not sacred. Nature had become my Bible.

Man the spiritual being, I now saw continually defeating himself—confusing his spiritual power with his mentality; his own beauty lost by his own stupidity or cupidity simply because he could not see from inside by his intellect alone: could not see the nature of his own intrinsic values: see his own genius, therefore. So during those days of early apprenticeship to Adler and Sullivan I found that when I talked about Nature I was not talking about the same thing those around me meant when they used the term. I could not fail to see (nearby was the Chicago Art Institute) each noble branch of the fine-arts family driven to filch what might be from the great wreck of architecture—the head of the regal family of art—and trying to make a go of it.

To survive, our American art was cheating itself of life. This consequent spread of the tragic Renaissance, I saw largely due to outworn but desperate reliance upon a dated formal professionalism: the Classic. This not alone in architecture but in all the arts; partly, perhaps mostly, due to the fearfully efficient tools, invented by Science, so abusing artists and abused by them. These new tools I saw wrecking the "classic" imitation of ancient formalism, called modern art but founded upon a philosophy completely false to modern life.

Human life itself was being cheated.

All was the same dire artificiality. Nature thus denied was more than ever revenging itself upon human life! The very soul of man was endangered. The Machine thus uncontrolled enlarged, and was living upon, these abuses. Already machine systems had done deadly harm—and more harm, as things were then. Modern machine-masters were ruling man's fate in his manufactures as in his architecture and arts. His way of life was being sterilized by marvelous power-tools and even more powerful machine-systems, all replacing hand labor by multiplying—senselessly—his activity and infecting his spirit. Everywhere these inventions of science by ignorant misuse of a new technique were wiping out the artist. He was himself now becoming a slave. The new chattel. I saw in these new "masters" no great motive above the excess of necessity-for-profit; all likely themselves by way of their own assembly lines to become machines. The kind of slavery that now loomed was even more monstrous and more devastating to our culture now dedicated to senseless excess, so it seemed to me, than ever before. Slavery more deadly to human felicity than any yet devised. Unless in the competent artist's hand.

The pole-and-wire men in the name of social necessity had already forged a mortgage on the landscape of our beautiful American countryside while all our buildings, public and private, even churches, were senseless commitments to some kind of expediency instead of the new significances of freedom we so much needed. In the name of necessity, false fancy fronts hung with glaring signs as one trod along the miles of every urban sidewalk—instead of freedom, license—inextricable confusion. Trimmings and embellishments of trimmings pressed on the eye everywhere, made rampant by the casual taste of any ignoramus. These were all social liabilities forced upon American life by the misconception, or no conception at all, of the mother-art—architecture. Man, thus caricatured by himself—nature thus violated—invaded even the national forest-parks by a clumsy rusticity false to nature and so to architecture. The environment of civilized mankind was everywhere insulted by such willful stupidity.

But soon this saving virtue appeared to me in our disgraceful dilemma: Realization that any true cultural significance our American free society could know lay in the proper use of *the machine as a tool and used only as a tool.* But the creative-artist's use of mechanical systems, most beneficial miracles, was yet wholly missing.

Steel and glass themselves seemed to have come to use only to be misunderstood and misused, put to shame by such abuses as might be seen anywhere because they were everywhere.

In the plans and designs here presented in much detail may be seen the appropriate uses of the properties of steel in tension in relation to concrete (concrete the new-old plastic). With glass and the growing sheet-metal industries, these were, it seemed to me, only awaiting creative interpretation to become the body of our new democratic world: the same being true of new uses of the old materials—wood, brick and stone.

Often I sat down to write about this as well as continue to design new forms for these new methods and materials. Occasionally, when invited, I went out to speak on the subject of the proper use of all these—always to say "we must know better the here and now of *our own* life in its Time and Place. In all we must learn to see ourselves as we are, as *modern* man—and this be our true culture." As architects young and old we owed this to ourselves, and certainly to our people. In this country of ours we were free now to abandon outdated idiosyncrasy in the name of taste, or arbitrary academic formalisms without thought or feeling—and learn to show, by our own work, our love and consequent understanding of the principles of Nature. Life *indigenous* was now to be embodied in new forms and more significant uses; new forms of materials by the inevitable new machine-methods yet missing or misunderstood. A natural heretic, I declared these materials and methods to be in themselves a new potential needed in the culture of modern life. Because of the machine itself, architecture was now bound by its own nature to be prophetic. The architect's interpretations would show the way to the right use of these great new organic resources. Our new facilities were already capable of inspiring and enriching human life if provided with true forms, instead of perpetually inciting American life to folly and betrayal of its own nature by ignorant or silly eclecticism or any of the 57 fashionable Varieties of the day. Despite artificial limitations, a new beauty would be ours. Thus awakening to action, we architects had to become effective soon—or our civilization would destroy its chances for its own culture. Instead of by the handle, man had taken this dangerous new tool by the blade!

In this sense I saw the architect as savior of the culture of modern American society; his services the mainspring of any future cultural life in America—savior now as for all civilizations heretofore. Architecture being inevitably the basis of an indigenous culture, American architects must become emancipators of senselessly conforming human beings imposed upon by mediocrity and imposing mediocrity upon others in this sanitary but soulless machine-age. Architecture, I believed, was bound to become more humanely significant because of these vast new facilities. Therefore not only special but social knowledge of the nature of architecture as presenting man himself, must be greatly expanded. Architecture was to be liberated from all formalistic stylizing by any elite, especially from that perpetuated by scholastic architects or by the criteria of insolent criticism. Architecture of the machine-age should become not only fundamental to our culture but natural to the happiness of our lives in it as well. All this was rank heresy at the time. We have made some progress since because it does not seem so heretical now.

Young heretic, then, I freely spoke but steadily planned all the time: hope of realization firmly at heart — pretty well in mind now, as poetry. I loved architecture as romantic and prophetic of a true way of life; life again coming beautifully alive today as before in the greatest ancient civilizations. We were free men now? The architect among us then should qualify as so inspired; be free leader of free human beings in our new free country. All buildings built should serve the liberation of mankind, liberating the lives of *individuals*. What amazing beauty would be ours if man's spirit, thus organic, should learn to characterize this new free life of ours in America as natural!

But soon I saw the new resources not only shamefully wasted by machinesters but most shamefully wasted by our influential architects themselves; those with the best educations were most deadly. Our resources were being used to ruin the significance of any true architecture of the life of our own day by ancient ideas imposed upon modern building or ancient building ruined by so-called "modern" ideas. Thus played upon, some better architects, then called modern, were themselves desperately trying to reorganize American building and themselves as well. The A.I.A., then composed of architects who came down the hard way, was inclined to be sincere, but the plan-factory was already appearing as public enemy number one.

I had just opened my own office in the Schiller Building, 1893, when came disaster—Chicago's first World's Fair. The fair soon appeared to me more than ever tragic travesty: florid countenance of theoretical Beaux-Arts formalisms; perversion of what modern building we then had achieved by negation; already a blight upon our progress. A senseless reversion. Nevertheless at that time—now more than sixty years ago—I was myself certain that awakening in our own architecture was just around the turn of the corner of the next year. That year I wrote *The Art and Craft of the Machine,* delivering the essay at Hull House by Jane Addams' invitation. Next day a Chicago Tribune editorial announced that an American artist had said the first word for the appropriate use of the machine as an artist's tool. I suspect that Jane Addams wrote the editorial herself.

By this time the American people had become sentimentally enamored of the old-lace, nervous artificiality of the "classic"

grandomania endorsed by the A.I.A. at the fair. It was everywhere in evidence: excess—as usual—mistaken for exuberance.
Owing to this first World's Fair, recognition of organic American architecture would have to wait at least another half-
century.

No school exists without something to teach; and until the
phrase "Chicago School" appeared so many years later, I was
not aware that anything like a "school" had existed. At the
time, there was a small group composed of my own adherents
and of contemporary dissenters by nature. The work of Adler
and Sullivan was in constant contrast to the work of Richardson and Root; later, Shepley, Rutan and Coolidge (heirs of
Richardson), but few of the architects, young or old, then
admitted the Adler and Sullivan influence.

Because I was, so far as they were concerned, Sullivan's
"alter ego," a small clique soon formed about me, myself
naturally enough the leader. Friendships were formed in those
early days, especially after the gold letters ARCHITECT were
put upon the plate glass door of my office in The Schiller Building. The "followers" were not many: first among them Cecil
Corwin and Robert C. Spencer, Jr. (Bob)—first converts to the
new architecture. Bob was regarded by his "classic" comrades
as apostate because his employers—Shepley, Rutan and Coolidge—had gone "classic'" soon after the romantic Richardson's
death. Bob and I were often seen together; later he took the
office next mine in the Schiller. Chicago conformists working
in other offices, seeing us arm in arm down the street, would
say in derision, "There goes God-almighty with his Jesus
Christ." Bob didn't mind. He stuck. Some others began to
"come around": George Dean, Hugh Garden, Myron Hunt,
Dwight Perkins, Dick Schmidt and Howard Shaw; all were
friendly but not willing to cut their umbilical cord to the
Colonial or the French chateau, the English manor house or
the grandomania of Beaux-Arts days.

Before long a little luncheon club formed, comprised of
myself, Bob Spencer, Gamble Rogers, Handy and Cady, Dick
Schmidt, Hugh Garden, Dean, Perkins and Shaw, several
others; eighteen in all. We called the group the "Eighteen."

The "Eighteen" often wanted to know how I convinced my
clients that the new architecture was the right thing. "Do you
hypnotize them?" was a common question. The idea of an
American architecture fascinated them to a certain degree according to the nature of their understanding. Almost all admired what I was doing though they were not yet willing to
say it was the right thing.

Gamble Rogers never left the Gothic; Howard Shaw never dared leave colonial English. But most of the others fell in with the idea of some sort of modern architecture. I became original advisory exemplar to the group.

The little luncheon round-table broke up after a year or two. I with those nearest me rented a vacant loft in Steinway Hall: a building Dwight Perkins had built. But Spencer, Perkins, Hunt and Birch Long (clever boy renderer) moved in with me. Together we subdivided the big attic into studio-like draughting rooms. We felt the big attic especially appropriate for our purpose. We each had a share in a receptionist and stenographer in common as "office force" on the floor below, trying to please us all. The entrance door panel was a single sheet of clear plate glass, the second one in existence, like the entrance door to the Schiller offices, with all our names thereon in the same kind of gold letters.

By this time an increasing number of young draughtsmen, like Max Dunning et al, began to come around. I got Lieber Meister to address the Chicago Architectural Sketch-Club, which he did with great effect. Dankmar Adler was dean of the A.I.A. at the time, and he also wrote valuable papers on the subject of skyscraper construction, and the effect of steel on modern life. Meantime, buildings were going up under "the Adler and Sullivan influence." A little of the new was worked in by others here and there. But all in all, from my impatient standpoint, weak if not impotent or cowardly. On occasion, I did say so, but patiently worked on their plans when I could be helpful. My most enthusiastic advocate, young Myron Hunt, was first among them to set up in Evanston, Illinois, as a "modern," with the building of the "White" house. That was a characteristic instance. I believed myself helpful to them all.

I remember an ebullient Italian, Boari by name, who won the competition to build the National Grand Opera House in Mexico City. He came into our attic space, temporarily, to make plans for that edifice. He was far from all of us but observing, curious and humorous. He would look at something I was doing and say with a good natured grunt, "Huh, temperance-architecture!" turn on his heel with another grunt and go back to his Italian Renaissance "gorge" as I called it in retaliation. What he was then doing is now there in Mexico City but badly affected by the universal settlements going on because of the lowering of the water-level beneath the city.

Other work went on in our studio-loft for several more years. But when I had left Adler and Sullivan to settle down in Oak Park, Bob had moved out to River Forest, the next suburb to the west. I—the amateur still with Adler and Sulli-van—was able to build a little house on Chicago Avenue; and, on my own, built a studio adjoining my home, where the work I had then to do enabled me to take in several draughtsmen and a faithful secretary, Isabel Roberts, for whom I later built a dwelling in River Forest, now owned by and revised for the Scotts.

But by that time at Oak Park I had lost touch with most of the original group. Into the now flourishing Oak Park studio had come Walter Griffin, Marion Mahoney (later married to Walter), William Drummond, George Willis, Andrew Willatzen, Frank Byrne, Albert McArthur. Others came and went as time went along.

By that time, 1894–5, architecture so-called "modern" had made sporadic appearances here and there around Chicago; reminiscent of Lieber Meister's ornament or something I had myself done or was doing as a dwelling.

George Elmslie—I had brought George from Silsbee's as my understudy (lasting the seven years I remained with Adler and Sullivan and staying on for many more years)—would sometimes come out to lend us a hand in the Oak Park studio, putting in overtime when pressure of work would keep us all up all night, and the dawn would find the boys asleep on their draughting boards.

But, now independent, I didn't use the fascinating ornament, had struck out a new line in a field of my own—the American dwelling: the nature of materials and steel in tension. Of what was going on abroad at this time I had no knowledge nor any interest in. Nor was there any Japanese architectural influence, as may be seen in these illustrations.

Schools of thought, to and fro, soon arose in America—one of them misled by the dictum "Art is art precisely in that it is not nature"; misunderstanding the word "nature." This was

1908   A version of the Isabel Roberts house, *River Forest, Ill.*

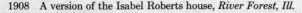

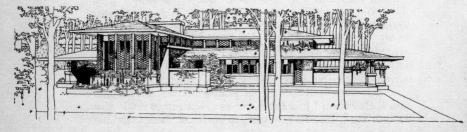

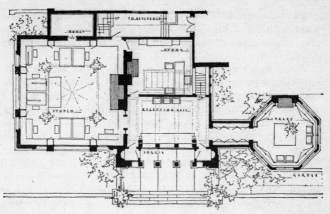

1895   Frank Lloyd Wright studio, *Oak Park, Ill.* Plan. (Photograph on page 112.)

really art for art's sake? "Form follows function" came along now also to become the new slogan (also misunderstood). But art was not as yet transferred to the region of the mere nervous system; the nervous system had not yet been mistaken for the soul. But little men were using little brains and little-finger sensibility to confect semblances that "tasted" to them like inspiration, confections mistaken for architecture. All but several architects seemed to be trying to annul the idea of architecture as noble organic expression of nature; the Form-Follows-Function group seeing it as a physical raw-materialism instead of the spiritual thing it really is: the idea of life itself—bodily and spiritually—intrinsic *organism.* Form and function as one.

Well—Daniel H. Burnham was right. The Chicago World's Fair became the occasion of modern architecture's grand relapse. The nature of man was there reduced to the level of a clever trained animal: Architecture contrived as a hackneyed ruse to cheat modern life of its divine due instead of serving to glorify it. Beaux-Arts intellectualism was the aesthetic that could only eventuate as some kind of menial to the monumental. Therefore "classic" misuse of the "Classic" slandered the noble idea of art as organic, and I was compelled to see that it would go on so long as man had no true sense of his own dignity as a free man. Only if his intellect, which had been stimulated but pauperized by education, again became subject to the inner laws of his own being, could he be a valid force in Architecture, Art or in Religion: only so could he ever rise creative above our inventive sciences in the grasp of the Expedient. Otherwise his life in America would remain helplessly afloat upon a sea of corrupted taste; no realization would be possible.

When man's pride in his own intellect was set up as an anti-nature-formalism in art, he became responsible for the dictum: "where every prospect pleases and only man is vile."

Different were the Orientals and different were Jesus, Shakespeare, Milton, Blake, Wordsworth, Coleridge, Keats, Shelley, Beethoven, Bach, Brunelleschi, Goethe, Rembrandt, Dante, Cervantes, Giotto, Mantegna, Leonardo, Bramante, Angelo. Different were the prophets of the human soul. All masters of the Nature of Man and the hosts they have inspired. No longer trying to lift himself by his boot-straps or busy cutting out the head of his drum to see whence comes the sound, man by nature still creative may grow.

As Victor Hugo wrote also in *Notre Dame,* Gutenberg's invention of shifting-type *was* the beginning of the great triumph of the machine over all the fine-arts and crafts of architecture. By way of the machine came the soulless monstrosities now so far out of human scale as to be out of hand. Death came to handicraft and to any corresponding culture in the world, blindly inherited by us. As for America, cultural confusion had already come upon us in our new "house," almost before we were born. Buildings, business, education—all were

1902   Hillside Home School, *Spring Green, Wis.*

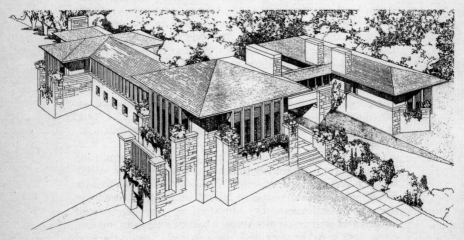

becoming great enterprises stimulated by infatuations with science and sentimentality concerning the past. The inventive engineering of mechanization lacked the insight—creative poetic imagination, let's say—to recognize the power of interpretation by architecture of these vast new facilities. As they came fresh from science, they but stimulated the cupidity of commerce. As for the architects, they were either silent or huddled in the lap of overpowering change. Our capitalism was a kind of piracy, our profit-system tended to encourage low forms of avaricious expansion. American culture, such as it was, wore a false face, a hideous masquerade. Success was misunderstood as essential to progress. Really success was worse than failure. Wanton denials of humanity were made by machine-power, abetted by the impotence of artists and architects, themselves blind to the fresh opportunities, really their duties. Such failures as they were making of life, then as now, were a standardized slander upon the liberated individual rather than any true reflection of his innate power. Thus doomed to spiritual sterility, art and architecture were facing extinction in all the hell there was.

Well, nevertheless—rather more—I kept on planning, preaching, presenting the real social need for the creative artist-architect—the competent, conscientious interpreter of his kind and time! But where were such architects? Was the A.I.A. alive to the new ideals? The story by now might have been different if the A.I.A. had not been more interested in architects than in architecture. In such circumstances how could the architect's vision become effective action? Could action come to grips with selfish forces to humanize their excesses by rejecting their power, to evolve the new forms modern man needed to sustain the freedom he had declared, 1776? This was up to the greater architect we had neither inherited nor cultivated. Because of this default I kept trying to gather together the dangling, loose ends, so twisted by this confusion; gather them little by little into organic synthesis of means to ends, thus showing with all my might the idea and purpose of organic character and proportions in building, if made appropriate to life under American Democracy.

New architecture was fundamental necessity. But it seemed impossible for architecture to rise without deeper knowledge of the poetic principle involved. The slide-rule of the engineer could not diminish, but only cherish and confirm, all this damnation—and did so.

The needed interpretation had arrived in my own mind as

organic and, being true to nature would naturally, so I thought, be visible to my fellow architects. In spite of myself, because becoming more and more articulate, I became a kind of troublesome reminder—a reproach to my fellows. Naturally enough I would not join the profession to help make a harbor of refuge for the incompetent? So, deemed arrogant even by those who might have been expected to go a little deeper and go to work themselves, I had to go it pretty much alone— Lieber Meister gone.

from A TESTAMENT, *1957*

Prairie Architecture

1893-1910

Frank Lloyd Wright's earliest independent work contains conventional elements that can readily be traced to stylistic currents of the times. But in his own day from the start he was considered a revolutionary, as he proved to be throughout a very long career. Before the turn of the century, young Wright was the leader of insurgent Midwest architects, men less interested in dogmas than in vital ideas. They were designers of homes as a rule, since an older generation pre-empted commercial and industrial commissions. Between them, the two generations of Chicago architects were part of an original cultural manifestation, today less famous than the earlier "flowering of New England" in literature, but perhaps even more creative, certainly as enduring and influential.

Wright's leadership and phenomenal talent brought him clients and fame. Two established groups contended for his allegiance: the academic classicists in the person of the great Daniel Burnham, chief architect of the Fair, vainly offered him a Beaux-Arts training in Paris and an assured future; a few years later the English arts and crafts leader, C. R. Ashbee, persuaded Wright to become the first secretary of a com-

mittee for the preservation of historic architecture in Chicago. But Wright never became academic nor classical, despite a command of the style, and never believed in reviving hand craftsmanship, as his famous early paper, THE ART AND CRAFT OF THE MACHINE, demonstrates.

Wright—and some contemporary colleagues—started the style known as Prairie Architecture, thus called because it was designed to fit the broad expanses of middle western terrain. This architecture was predominantly horizontal under heavy sheltering roofs; the planning was compact and practical for small, often servantless families; the details were suited to the skills, equipment and materials ready to hand. In Wright's own works exceptionally open plans evolved that led to an expression of outside walls as sheltering screens; outside and inside began to relate. Wright now also built churches and office buildings as radical and as clearly presented as his homes and mansions. A strong new style was evolving, and some Europeans who came to look went away enthusiastic. In 1910 Wright had the unusual honor of seeing a large, beautiful portfolio of his works published in Germany, that was followed by a smaller book with an introduction by Ashbee. Wright's influence abroad spread rapidly and struck deep.

Prairie Architecture

The cardboard house needs an antidote. The antidote is far more important than the house. As antidote—and as practical example, too. of the working out of an ideal of organic simplicity that has taken place here on American soil, step by step, under conditions that are your own—could I do better than to take apart for your benefit the buildings I have tried to build, to show you how they were, long ago, dedicated to the ideal of organic simplicity? It seems to me that while another might do better than that, I certainly could not—for that is, truest and best, what I know about the subject. What a man *does, that* he has.

When, "in the cause of architecture," in 1893, I first began to build the houses, sometimes referred to by the thoughtless

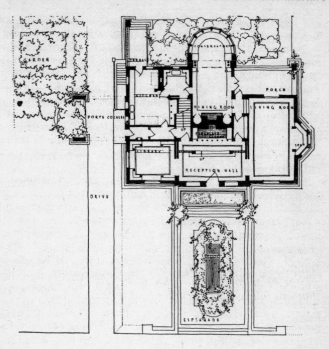

1893   W. H. Winslow house and plan, *River Forest, Ill.*

as "The New School of the Middle West" (some advertiser's slogan comes along to label everything in this our busy woman's country), the only way to simplify the awful building in vogue at the time was to conceive a finer entity—a better building—and get it built. The buildings standing then were all tall and all tight. Chimneys were lean and taller still, sooty fingers threatening the sky. And beside them, sticking up by way of dormers through the cruelly sharp, saw-tooth roofs, were the attics for "help" to swelter in. Dormers were elaborate devices, cunning little buildings complete in themselves, stuck to the main roof slopes to let "help" poke heads out of the attic for air.

Invariably the damp sticky clay of the prairie was dug out for a basement under the whole house, and the rubble-stone walls of this dank basement always stuck up above the ground a foot or more and blinked, with half-windows. So the universal "cellar" showed itself as a bank of some kind of masonry running around the whole house, for the house to sit up on—like a chair. The lean, upper house walls of the usual two floors above this stone or brick basement were wood, set on top of this masonry-chair, clapboarded and painted, or else shingled and stained, preferably shingled and mixed, up and down, all together with moldings crosswise. These overdressed wood house walls had, cut in them—or cut out of them, to be precise —big holes for the big cat and little holes for the little cat to get in and out or for ulterior purposes of light and air. The house walls were be-corniced or bracketed up at the top into the tall, purposely profusely complicated roof, dormers plus. The whole roof, as well as the roof as a whole, was scalloped and ridged and tipped and swanked and gabled to madness before they would allow it to be either shingled or slated. The whole exterior was be-deviled—that is to say, mixed to puzzle-pieces, with corner-boards, panel-boards, window-frames, corner-blocks, plinth-blocks, rosettes, fantails, ingenious and jigger work in general. This was the only way they seemed to have, then, of "putting on style." The scroll-saw and turning-lathe were at the moment the honest means of this fashionable mongering by the wood-butcher and to this entirely "moral" end. Unless the householder of the period were poor indeed, usually an ingenious corner-tower on his house eventuated into a candle-snuffer dome, a spire, an inverted rutabaga or radish or onion or—what is your favorite vegetable? Always elaborate bay-windows and fancy porches played "ring around a rosy" on this "imaginative" corner feature. And all this the building of the period could do equally well in brick or stone. It was an impartial society. All material looked pretty much alike in that day.

Simplicity was as far from all this scrap pile as the pandemonium of the barnyard is far from music. But it was easy for the architect. All he had to do was call: "Boy, take down No. 37, and put a bay-window on it for the lady!"

So—the first thing to do was to get rid of the attic and, therefore, of the dormer and of the useless "heights" below it. And next, get rid of the unwholesome basement, entirely— yes, absolutely—in any house built on the prairie. Instead of lean, brick chimneys, bristling up from steep roofs to hint at "judgment" everywhere, I could see necessity for one only, a

1902   W. W. Willitts house and plan, *Highland Park, Ill.*

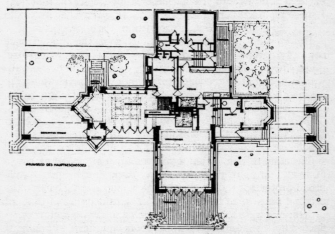

broad generous one, or at most, for two, these kept low down on gently sloping roofs or perhaps flat roofs. The big fireplace below, inside, became now a place for a real fire, justified the great size of this chimney outside. A real fireplace at that time was extraordinary. There were then "mantels" instead. A mantel was a marble frame for a few coals, or a piece of wooden furniture with tiles stuck in it and a "grate," the whole set slam up against the wall. The "mantel" was an insult to comfort, but the *integral* fireplace became an important part of the building itself in the houses I was allowed to build out there on the prairie. It refreshed me to see the fire burning deep in the masonry of the house itself.

Taking a human being for my scale, I brought the whole house down in height to fit a normal man; believing in no other scale, I broadened the mass out, all I possibly could, as I brought it down into spaciousness. It has been said that were I three inches taller (I am 5′ 8½″ tall), all my houses would have been quite different in proportion. Perhaps.

House walls were now to be started at the ground on a cement or stone water table that looked like a low platform under the building, which it usually was, but the house walls were stopped at the second story window-sill level, to let the rooms above come through in a continuous window-series, under the broad eaves of a gently sloping, overhanging roof. This made enclosing screens out of the lower walls as well as light screens out of the second story walls. Here was true *enclosure of interior space*. A new sense of building, it seems.

The climate, being what it was, a matter of violent extremes of heat and cold, damp and dry, dark and bright, I gave broad protecting roof-shelter to the whole, getting back to the original purpose of the "cornice." The undersides of the roof projections were flat and light in color to create a glow of reflected light that made the upper rooms not dark, but delightful. The overhangs had double value, shelter and preservation for the walls of the house as well as diffusion of reflected light for the upper story, through the "light screens" that took the place of the walls and were the windows.

At this time, a house to me was obvious primarily as interior space under fine *shelter*. I liked the sense of shelter in the "look of the building." I achieved it, I believe. I then went after the variegate bands of material in the old walls to eliminate odds and ends in favor of one material and a single surface from grade to eaves, or grade to second story sill-cope, treated as simple enclosing screens—or else made a plain screen band around the second story above the window-sills, turned up over on to the ceiling beneath the eaves. This screen band was of the same material as the under side of the eaves themselves, or what architects call the "soffit." The planes of the building parallel to the ground were all stressed, to grip the whole to earth. Sometimes it was possible to make the enclosing wall below this upper band of the second story, from the second story window-sill clear down to the ground, a heavy "wainscot" of fine masonry material resting on the cement or stone platform laid on the foundation. I liked that wainscot to be of masonry material when my clients felt they could afford it.

As a matter of form, too, I liked to see the projecting base, or water table, set out over the foundation walls themselves— as a substantial preparation for the building. This was managed by setting the studs of the walls to the inside of the foundation walls, instead of to the outside. All door and window tops were now brought into line with each other with only comfortable head-clearance for the average human being. Eliminating the sufferers from the "attic" enabled the roofs to lie low. The house began to associate with the ground and become natural to its prairie site. And would the young man in architecture ever believe that this was all "new" then? Not only new, but destructive heresy—or ridiculous eccentricity. So new that what little prospect I had of ever earning a livelihood by making houses was nearly wrecked. At first, "they" called the houses "dress-reform" houses, because society was just then excited about that particular "reform." This simplification looked like some kind of "reform" to them. Oh, they called them all sorts of names that cannot be repeated, but "they" never found a better term for the work unless it was "horizontal Gothic," "temperance architecture" (with a sneer), etc., etc. I don't know how I escaped the accusation of another "renaissance."

What I have just described was all on the *outside* of the house and was there chiefly because of what had happened *inside*. Dwellings of that period were "cut-up," advisedly and completely, with the grim determination that should go with any cutting process. The "interiors" consisted of boxes beside or inside other boxes, called *rooms*. All boxes inside a complicated boxing. Each domestic "function" was properly box to box. I could see little sense in this inhibition, this cellular sequestration that implied ancestors familiar with the cells of penal institutions, except for the privacy of bedrooms on the upper floor. They were perhaps all right as "sleeping boxes."

So I declared the whole lower floor as one room, cutting off the kitchen as a laboratory, putting servants' sleeping and living quarters next to it, semi-detached, on the ground floor, screening various portions in the big room, for certain domestic purposes—like dining or reading, or receiving a formal caller. There were no plans like these in existence at the time and my clients were pushed toward these ideas as helpful to a solution of the vexed servant-problem. Scores of doors disappeared and no end of partition. They liked it, both clients and servants. The house became more free as "space" and more livable, too. Interior spaciousness began to dawn.

Having got what windows and doors there were left lined up and lowered to convenient human height, the ceilings of the rooms, too, could be brought over on to the walls, by way of the horizontal, broad bands of plaster on the walls above the windows, the plaster colored the same as the room ceilings. This would bring the ceiling-surface down to the very window tops. The ceilings thus expanded, by extending them downward as the wall band above the windows, gave a generous overhead to even small rooms. The sense of the whole was broadened and made plastic, too, by this expedient. The enclosing walls and ceilings were thus made to flow together.

Here entered the important element of plasticity—indispensable to successful use of the machine, the true expression of modernity. The outswinging windows were fought for because the casement window associated the house with out-of-doors —gave free openings, outward. In other words the so-called "casement" was simple and more human. In use and effect, more natural. If it had not existed I should have invented it. It was not used at that time in America, so I lost many clients because I insisted upon it when they wanted the "guillotine" or "doublehung" window then in use. The guillotine was not simple nor human. It was only expedient. I used it once in the Winslow House—my first house—and rejected it thereafter— forever. Nor at that time did I entirely eliminate the wooden trim. I did make it "plastic," that is, light and continuously flowing instead of the heavy "cut and butt" of the usual carpenter work. No longer did the "trim," so called, look like carpenter work. The machine could do it perfectly well as I laid it out. It was all after "quiet."

This plastic trim, too, with its running "back-hand" enabled poor workmanship to be concealed. It was necessary with the field resources at hand at that time to conceal much. Machinery versus the union had already demoralized the workmen. The machine resources were so little understood that extensive drawings had to be made merely to show the "mill-man" what to leave off. But the "trim" finally became only a single, flat, narrow, horizontal wood band running around the room, one at the top of the windows and doors and another next to the floors, both connected with narrow, vertical, thin wood bands that were used to divide the wall surfaces of the whole room smoothly and flatly into folded color planes. The trim merely completed the window and door openings in this same plastic sense. When the interior had thus become wholly plastic, instead of structural, a new element, as I have said, had entered architecture. Strangely enough an element that had not existed in architectural history before. Not alone in the trim, but in numerous ways too tedious to describe in words, this revolutionary sense of the plastic whole, an instinct with me at first, began to work more and more intelligently and have fascinating, unforeseen consequences. Here was something that began to organize itself. When several houses had been finished and compared with the house of the period, there was very little of that house left standing. Nearly every one had stood the house of the period as long as he could stand it, judging by appreciation of the change. Now all this probably tedious description is intended to indicate directly in bare outline how thus early there *was* an ideal of organic simplicity put to work, with historical consequences, here in your own country. The main motives and indications were (and I enjoyed them all):

FIRST—To reduce the number of necessary parts of the house and the separate rooms to a minimum, and make all come together as enclosed space—so divided that light, air and vista permeated the whole with a sense of unity.

SECOND—To associate the building as a whole with its site by extension and emphasis of the planes parallel to the ground, but keeping the floors off the best part of the site, thus leaving that better part for use in connection with the life of the house. Extended level planes were found useful in this connection.

THIRD—To eliminate the room as a box and the house as another by making all walls enclosing screens—the ceilings and floors and enclosing screens to flow into each other as one large enclosure of space, with minor subdivisions only.

Make all house proportions more liberally human, with

45

less wasted space in structure, and structure more appropriate to material, and so the whole more livable. *Liberal* is the best word. Extended straight lines or streamlines were useful in this.

FOURTH—To get the unwholesome basement up out of the ground, entirely above it, as a low pedestal for the living portion of the home, making the foundation itself visible as a low masonry platform on which the building should stand.

FIFTH—To harmonize all necessary openings to "outside" or to "inside" with good human proportions and make them occur naturally—singly or as a series in the scheme of the whole building. Usually they appeared as "light-screens" instead of walls, because all the "architecture" of the house was chiefly the way these openings came in such walls as were grouped about the rooms as enclosing screens. The *room* as such was now the essential architectural expression, and there were to be no holes cut in walls as holes are cut in a box, because this was not in keeping with the ideal of "plastic." Cutting holes was violent.

SIXTH—To eliminate combinations of different materials in favor of mono-material so far as possible; to use no ornament that did not come out of the nature of materials to make the whole building clearer and more expressive as a place to live in, and give the conception of the building appropriate revealing emphasis. Geometrical or straight

1902   Yahara Boat Club, project for Lake Mendota, *Madison, Wis.*

lines were natural to the machinery at work in the building trades then, so the interiors took on this character naturally.

SEVENTH—To incorporate all heating, lighting, plumbing so that these systems became constituent parts of the building itself. These service features became architectural and in this attempt the ideal of an organic architecture was at work.

EIGHTH—To incorporate as organic architecture—so far as possible—furnishings, making them all one with the building and designing them in simple terms for machine work. Again straight lines and rectilinear forms.

NINTH—Eliminate the decorator. He was all curves and all efflorescence, if not all "period."

This was all rational enough so far as the thought of an organic architecture went. The particular forms this thought took in the feeling of it all could only be personal. There was nothing whatever at this time to help make them what they were. All seemed to be the most natural thing in the world and grew up out of the circumstances of the moment. Whatever they may be worth in the long run is all they are worth.

Now *simplicity* being the point in question in this early constructive effort, organic simplicity I soon found to be a matter of true coordination. And beauty I soon felt to be a matter of the sympathy with which such coordination was effected. Plainness was not necessarily simplicity. Crude furniture of the Roycroft-Stickley-Mission Style, which came along later, was offensively plain, plain as a barn door—but never was simple in any true sense. Nor, I found, were merely machine-made things in themselves simple. To think "in simple," is to deal in simples, and that means with an eye single to the altogether. This, I believe, is the secret of simplicity. Perhaps we may truly regard nothing at all as simple in itself. I believe that no one thing in itself is ever so, but must achieve simplicity (as an artist should use the term) as a perfectly realized part of some organic whole. Only as a feature or any part becomes an harmonious element in the harmonious whole does it arrive at the estate of simplicity. Any wild flower is truly simple, but double the same wild flower by cultivation, it ceases to be so. The *scheme* of the original is no longer clear. Clarity of design and perfect significance both are first essentials of the spontaneously born simplicity of the lilies of the field who neither toil nor spin, as contrasted with Solomon who had "toiled and spun"—that is to say, no doubt had put on himself and had put on his temple, properly "composed," everything in the category of good things but the cook-stove.

Five lines where three are enough is stupidity. Nine pounds where three are sufficient is stupidity. But to eliminate expressive words that intensity or vivify meaning in speaking or writing is not simplicity; nor is similar elimination in architecture simplicity—it, too, may be stupidity. In architecture, expressive changes of surface, emphasis of line and especially textures of material, may go to make facts eloquent, forms more significant. Elimination, therefore, may be just as meaningless as elaboration, perhaps more often is so. I offer any fool, for an example.

To know what to leave out and what to put in, just where and just how—ah, *that* is to have been educated in knowledge of simplicity.

As for objects of art in the house even in that early day they were the "bête noir" of the new simplicity. If well chosen, well enough in the house, but only if each was properly digested by the whole. Antique or modern sculpture, paintings, pottery, might become objectives in the architectural scheme and I accepted them, aimed at them, and assimilated them. Such things may take their places as elements in the design of any house. They are then precious things, gracious and good to live with. But it is difficult to do this well. Better, if it may be done, to design all features together. At that time, too, I tried to make my clients see that furniture and furnishings, not built in as integral features of the building, should be designed as attributes of whatever furniture was built in and should be seen as minor parts of the building itself, even if detached or kept aside to be employed on occasion. But when the build-

1902   Richard Bock studio house, project, *Maywood, Ill.*

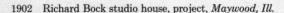

ing itself was finished, the old furniture the clients already possessed went in with them to await the time when the interior might be completed. Very few of the houses were, therefore, anything but painful to me after the clients moved in and, helplessly, dragged the horrors of the old order along after them.

But I soon found it difficult, anyway, to make some of the furniture in the "abstract"; that is, to design it as architecture and make it "human" at the same time—fit for human use. I have been black and blue in some spot, somewhere, almost all my life from too intimate contacts with my own furniture. Human beings must group, sit or recline—confound them—and they must dine, but dining is much easier to manage and always was a great artistic opportunity. Arrangements for the informality of sitting comfortably, singly or in groups, where it is desirable or natural to sit, and still to belong in disarray to the scheme as a whole—that is a matter difficult to accomplish. But it can be done now, and should be done, because only those attributes of human comfort and convenience, made to belong in this digested or integrated sense to the architecture of the home as a whole, should be there at all, in modern architecture. For that matter about four-fifths of the contents of nearly every home could be given away with good effect to that home. But the things given away might go on to poison some other home. So why not at once destroy undesirable things . . . make an end of them?

Here then, in foregoing outline, is the gist of America's contribution to modern American architecture as it was already under way in 1893. But the gospel of elimination is one never preached enough. No matter how much preached, simplicity is a spiritual ideal seldom organically reached. Nevertheless, by assuming the virtue by imitation—or by increasing structural makeshifts to get superficial simplicity—the effects may cultivate a taste that will demand the reality in course of time, but it may also destroy all hope of the real thing.

Standing here, with the perspective of long persistent effort in the direction of an organic architecture in view, I can again assure you out of this initial experience that repose is the reward of true simplicity and that organic simplicity is sure of repose. Repose is the highest quality in the art of architecture, next to integrity, and a reward for integrity. Simplicity may well be held to the fore as a spiritual ideal, but when actually achieved, as in the "lilies of the field," it is something that comes of itself, something spontaneously born out of the nature of the doing whatever it is that is to be done. Simplicity, too, is a reward for fine feeling and straight thinking in working a principle, well in hand, to a consistent end. Solomon knew nothing about it, for he was only wise. And this, I think, is what Jesus meant by the text we have chosen for this discourse—"Consider the lilies of the field," as contrasted, for beauty, with Solomon.

Now, a chair *is* a machine to sit in.

A home *is* a machine to live in.

The human body *is* a machine to be worked by will.

A tree *is* a machine to bear fruit.

A plant *is* a machine to bear flowers and seeds.

And, as I've admitted before somewhere, a heart *is* a suction pump. Does that idea thrill you?

Trite as it is, it may be as well to think it over because the *least* any of these things may be, *is* just that. All of them are that before they are anything else. And to violate that mechanical requirement in any of them is to finish before anything of higher purpose can happen. To ignore the fact is either sentimentality or the prevalent insanity. Let us acknowledge in this respect, that this matter of mechanics is just as true of the work of art as it is true of anything else. But, were we to stop with that trite acknowledgment, we should only be living in a low, rudimentary sense. This skeleton rudiment accepted, *understood,* is the first condition of any fruit or flower we may hope to get from ourselves. Let us continue to call this flower and fruit of ourselves, even in this machine age, art. Some architects, as we may see, now consciously acknowledge this "machine" rudiment. Some will eventually get to it by circuitous mental labor. Some *are* the thing itself without question and already in need of "treatment." But "Americans" (I prefer to be more specific and say "Usonians") have been educated "blind" to the higher human uses of it all—while actually in sight of this higher human use all the while.

Therefore, now let the declaration that "all is machinery" stand nobly forth for what it is worth. But why not more profoundly declare that "form follows function" and let it go at that? Saying, "form follows function," is not only deeper, it is clearer, and it goes further in a more comprehensive way to say the thing to be said, because the implication of this saying includes the heart of the whole matter. It may be that function follows form, as, or if, you prefer, but it is easier thinking with the first proposition just as it is easier to stand on your feet and nod your head than it would be to stand on your head and nod your feet. Let us not forget that the simplicity of the universe is very different from the simplicity of a machine.

1908 Avery Coonley house, *Riverside, Ill.* Living room. (Photographs on pages 107, 108.)

New significance in architecture implies new materials qualifying form and textures, requires fresh feeling, which will eventually qualify both as "ornament." But "decoration" must be sent on its way or now be given the meaning that it has lost, if it is to stay. Since "decoration" became acknowledged as such, and ambitiously set up for itself as decoration, it has been a makeshift, in the light of this ideal of organic architecture. Any house decoration, as such, is an architectural makeshift, however well it may be done, unless the decoration, so-called, is part of the architect's design in both concept and execution.

Since architecture in the old sense died and decoration has had to shift for itself more and more, all so-called decoration is become *ornamental,* therefore no longer *integral.* There can be no true simplicity in either architecture or decoration under any such condition. Let decoration, therefore, die for architecture, and the decorator become an architect, but not an "interior architect."

Ornament can never be applied to architecture any more than architecture should ever be applied to decoration. All ornament, if not developed within the nature of architecture and as organic part of such expression, vitiates the whole fabric no matter how clever or beautiful it may be as something in itself.

Yes—for a century or more decoration has been setting up for itself, and in our prosperous country has come pretty near to doing very well, thank you. I think we may say that it is pretty much all we have now to show as domestic architecture,

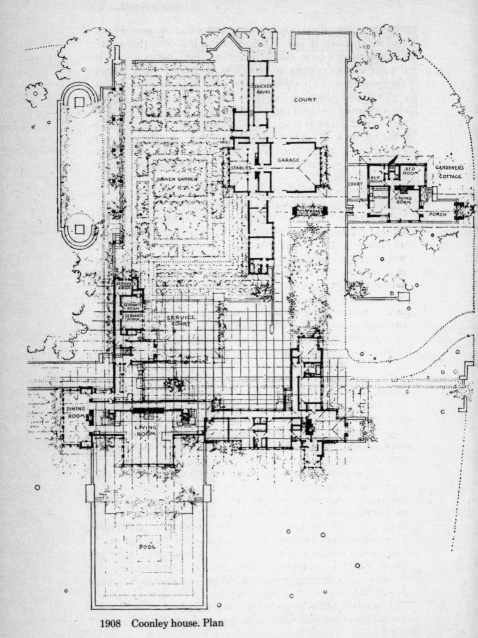

1908   Coonley house. Plan

52

as domestic architecture still goes with us at the present time. But we may as well face it. The interior decorator thrives with us because we have no architecture. Any decorator is the natural enemy of organic simplicity in architecture. He, persuasive doctor-of-appearances that he *must* be when he becomes architectural substitute, will give you an imitation of anything, even an imitation of imitative simplicity. Just at the moment, he is expert in this imitation. France, the born decorator, is now engaged with Madame, owing to the good fortune of the French market, in selling us this ready-made or made-to-order simplicity. Yes, imitation simplicity is the latest addition to imported "stock." The decorators of America are now equipped to furnish *especially* this. Observe. And how very charming the suggestions conveyed by these imitations sometimes are!

Would you have again the general principles of the spiritual ideal of organic simplicity at work in our culture? If so, then let us reiterate: first, simplicity is constitutional order. And it is worthy of note in this connection that 9×9 equals 81 is just as simple as $2 + 2$ equals 4. Nor is the obvious more simple necessarily than the occult. The obvious is obvious simply because it falls within our special horizon, is therefore easier for us to *see;* that is all. Yet all simplicity near or far has a countenance, a visage, that is characteristic. But this countenance is visible only to those who can grasp the whole and enjoy the significance of the minor part, as such, in relation to the whole when in flower. This is for the critics.

This characteristic visage may be simulated—the real complication glossed over, the internal conflict hidden by surface and belied by mass. The internal complication may be and usually is increased to create the semblance of and get credit for—simplicity. This is the simplicity-lie usually achieved by most of the "surface and mass" architects. This is for the young architect.

Truly ordered simplicity in the hands of the great artist may flower into a bewildering profusion, exquisitely exuberant, and render all more clear than ever. Good William Blake says exuberance is *beauty,* meaning that it is so in this very sense. This is for the modern artist with the machine in his hands. False simplicity—simplicity as an affectation, that is, simplicity constructed as a decorator's *outside* put upon a complicated, wasteful engineer's or carpenter's "structure," outside or inside—is not good enough simplicity. It cannot be simple at all. But that is what passes for simplicity, now that startling simplicity-effects are becoming the *fashion*. That kind of simplicity is *violent*. This is for "art and decoration."

1901   Lexington Terrace, project, *Chicago, Ill.*

54

Soon we shall want simplicity inviolate. There is one way to get that simplicity. My guess is, there is *only* one way really to get it. And that way is, on principle, by way of *construction* developed as architecture. That is for us, one and all.

from MODERN ARCHITECTURE, 1931

The Art and Craft of the Machine

As we work along our various ways, there takes shape within us, in some sort, an ideal—something we are to become—some work to be done. This, I think, is denied to very few, and we begin really to live only when the thrill of this ideality moves us in what we will to accomplish. In the years which have been devoted in my own life to working out in stubborn materials a feeling for the beautiful, in the vortex of distorted complex conditions, a hope has grown stronger with the experience of each year, amounting now to a gradually deepening conviction that in the Machine lies the only future of art and craft—as I believe, a glorious future; that the Machine is, in fact, the metamorphosis of ancient art and craft; that we are at last face to face with the machine—the modern Sphinx —whose riddle the artist must solve if he would that art live— for his nature holds the key. For one, I promise "whatever gods may be" to lend such energy and purpose as I may possess to help make that meaning plain; to return again and again to the task whenever and wherever need be; for this plain duty is thus relentlessly marked out for the artist in this, the Machine Age, although there is involved an adjustment to cherished gods, perplexing and painful in the extreme; the fire of many long-honored ideals shall go down to ashes to reappear, phœnix like, with new purposes.

The great ethics of the Machine are as yet, in the main, beyond the ken of the artist or student of sociology; but the artist mind may now approach the nature of this thing from experience, which has become the commonplace of his field, to suggest, in time, I hope, to prove, that the machine is capable of carrying to fruition high ideals in art—higher than the world has yet seen!

Disciples of William Morris cling to an opposite view. Yet William Morris himself deeply sensed the danger to art of the transforming force whose sign and symbol is the machine, and though of the new art we eagerly seek he sometimes despaired, he quickly renewed his hope.

He plainly foresaw that a blank in the fine arts would follow the inevitable abuse of new-found power, and threw himself body and soul into the work of bridging it over by bringing into our lives afresh the beauty of art as she had been, that the new art to come might not have dropped too many stitches nor have unraveled what would still be useful to her.

That he had abundant faith in the new art his every essay will testify.

That he miscalculated the machine does not matter. He did sublime work for it when he pleaded so well for the process of elimination its abuse had made necessary; when he fought the innate vulgarity of theocratic impulse in art as opposed to democratic; and when he preached the gospel of simplicity.

All artists love and honor William Morris.

He did the best in his time for art and will live in history as the great socialist, together with Ruskin, the great moralist: a significant fact worth thinking about, that the two great reformers of modern times professed the artist.

The machine these reformers protested, because the sort of luxury which is born of greed had usurped it and made of it a terrible engine of enslavement, deluging the civilized world with a murderous ubiquity, which plainly enough was the damnation of their art and craft.

It had not then advanced to the point which now so plainly indicates that it will surely and swiftly, by its own momentum, undo the mischief it has made, and the usurping vulgarians as well.

Nor was it so grown as to become apparent to William Morris, the grand democrat, that the machine was the great forerunner of democracy.

The ground plan of this thing is now grown to the point where the artist must take it up no longer as a protest: genius must progressively dominate the work of the contrivance it has created; to lend a useful hand in building afresh the "Fairness of the Earth."

That the Machine has dealt Art in the grand old sense a death-blow, none will deny.

The evidence is too substantial.

Art in the grand old sense—meaning Art in the sense of structural tradition, whose craft is fashioned upon the handicraft ideal, ancient or modern; an art wherein this form and that form as structural parts were laboriously joined in such a way as to beautifully emphasize the manner of the joining: the million and one ways of beautifully satisfying bare structural necessities, which have come down to us chiefly through the books as "Art."

For the purpose of suggesting hastily and therefore crudely wherein the machine has sapped the vitality of this art, let us assume Architecture in the old sense as a fitting representative of Traditional-art, and Printing as a fitting representation of the Machine.

What printing—the machine—has done for architecture—the fine art—will have been done in measure of time for all art immediately fashioned upon the early handicraft ideal.

With a masterful hand Victor Hugo, a noble lover and a great student of architecture, traces her fall in "Notre Dame."

The prophecy of Frollo, that "The book will kill the edifice," I remember was to me as a boy one of the grandest sad things of the world.

After seeking the origin and tracing the growth of architecture in superb fashion, showing how in the middle ages all the intellectual forces of the people converged to one point—architecture—he shows how, in the life of that time, whoever was born poet became an architect. All other arts simply obeyed and placed themselves under the discipline of architecture. They were the workmen of the great work. The architect, the poet, the master, summed up in his person the sculpture that carved his façades, painting which illuminated his walls and windows, music which set his bells to pealing and breathed into his organs—there was nothing which was not forced in order to make something of itself in that time, to come and frame itself in the edifice.

Thus down to the time of Gutenberg architecture is the principal writing—the universal writing of humanity.

In the great granite books begun by the Orient, continued by Greek and Roman antiquity, the middle ages wrote the last page.

So to enunciate here only summarily a process, it would require volumes to develop; down to the fifteenth century the chief register of humanity is architecture.

In the fifteenth century everything changes.

Human thought discovers a mode of perpetuating itself, not

only more resisting than architecture, but still more simple and easy.

Architecture is dethroned.

Gutenberg's letters of lead are about to supersede Orpheus' letters of stone.

The book is about to kill the edifice.

The invention of printing was the greatest event in history.

It was the first great machine, after the great city.

It is human thought stripping off one form and donning another.

Printed, thought is more imperishable than ever—it is volatile, indestructible.

As architecture it was solid; it is now alive; it passes from duration in point of time to immortality.

Cut the primitive bed of a river abruptly, with a canal hollowed out beneath its level, and the river will desert its bed.

See how architecture now withers away, how little by little it becomes lifeless and bare. How one feels the water sinking, the sap departing, the thought of the times and people withdrawing from it. The chill is almost imperceptible in the fifteenth century, the press is yet weak, and at most draws from architecture a superabundance of life, but with the beginning of the sixteenth century, the malady of architecture is visible. It becomes classic art in a miserable manner; from being indigenous, it becomes Greek and Roman; from being true and modern, it becomes pseudo-classic.

It is this decadence which we call the Renaissance.

It is the setting sun which we mistake for dawn.

It has now no power to hold the other arts; so they emancipate themselves, break the yoke of the architect, and take themselves off, each in its own direction.

One would liken it to an empire dismembered at the death of its Alexander, and whose provinces become kingdoms.

Sculpture becomes statuary, the image trade becomes painting, the canon becomes music. Hence Raphael, Angelo, and those splendors of the dazzling sixteenth century.

Nevertheless, when the sun of the middle ages is completely set, architecture grows dim, becomes more and more effaced. The printed book, the gnawing worm of the edifice, sucks and devours it. It is petty, it is poor, it is nothing.

Reduced to itself, abandoned by other arts because human thought is abandoning it, it summons bunglers in place of artists. It is miserably perishing.

Meanwhile, what becomes of printing?

All the life, leaving architecture, comes to it. In proportion as architecture ebbs and flows, printing swells and grows. That capital of forces which human thought had been expending in building is hereafter to be expended in books; and architecture, as it was, is dead, irretrievably slain by the printed book; slain because it endures for a shorter time; slain because human thought has found a more simple medium of expression, which costs less in human effort; because human thought has been rendered volatile and indestructible, reaching uniformly and irresistibly the four corners of the earth and for all.

Thenceforth, if architecture rise again, reconstruct, as Hugo prophesies she may begin to do in the latter days of the nineteenth century, she will no longer be mistress, she will be one of the arts, never again *the* art; and printing—the Machine—remains the second Tower of Babel of the human race.

So the organic process, of which the majestic decline of Architecture is only one case in point, has steadily gone on down to the present time, and still goes on, weakening the hold of the artist upon the people, drawing off from his rank poets and scientists until architecture is but a little, poor knowledge of archeology, and the average of art is reduced to the gasping poverty of imitative realism; until the whole letter of Tradition, the vast fabric of precedent, in the flesh, which has increasingly confused the art ideal while the machine has been growing to power, is a beautiful corpse from which the spirit has flown. The spirit that has flown is the spirit of the new art, but has failed the modern artist, for he has lost it for hundreds of years in his lust for the *letter,* the beautiful body of art made too available by the machine.

So the artist craft wanes.

Craft that will not see that human thought is stripping off one form and donning another, and artists are everywhere, whether catering to the leisure class of old England or ground beneath the heel of commercial abuse here in the great West, the unwilling symptoms of the inevitable, organic nature of the machine, they combat, the hell-smoke of the factories they scorn to understand.

And, invincible, triumphant, the machine goes on, gathering force and knitting the material necessities of mankind ever closer into a universal automatic fabric; the engine, the motor, and the battle-ship, the works of art of the century!

The Machine is Intellect mastering the drudgery of earth that the plastic art may live; that the margin of leisure and strength by which man's life upon the earth can be made beautiful, may immeasurably widen; its function ultimately to emancipate human expression!

It is a universal educator, surely raising the level of human intelligence, so carrying within itself the power to destroy, by its own momentum, the greed which in Morris' time and still in our own time turns it to a deadly engine of enslavement. The only comfort left the poor artist, side-tracked as he is, seemingly is a mean one; the thought that the very selfishness which man's early art idealized, now reduced to its lowest terms, is swiftly and surely destroying itself through the medium of the Machine.

The artist's present plight is a sad one, but may he truthfully say that society is less well off because Architecture, or even Art, as it was, is dead, and printing, or the Machine, lives?

Every age has done its work, produced its art with the best tools or contrivances it knew, the tools most successful in saving the most precious thing in the world—human effort. Greece used the chattel slave as the essential tool of its art and civilization. This tool we have discarded, and we would refuse the return of Greek art upon the terms of its restoration, because we insist now upon a basis of Democracy.

Is it not more likely that the medium of artistic expression itself has broadened and changed until a new definition and new direction must be given the art activity of the future, and that the Machine has finally made for the artist, whether he will yet own it or not, a splendid distinction between the Art of old and the Art to come? A distinction made by the tool which frees human labor, lengthens and broadens the life of the simplest man, thereby the basis of the Democracy upon which we insist.

To shed some light upon this distinction, let us take an instance in the field naturally ripened first by the machine—the commercial field.

The tall modern office building is the machine pure and simple.

We may here sense an advanced stage of a condition surely entering all art for all time; its already triumphant glare in the deadly struggle taking place here between the machine and the art of structural tradition reveals "art" torn and hung upon the steel frame of commerce, a forlorn head upon a pike, a solemn warning to architects and artists the world over.

We must walk blindfolded not to see that all that this magnificent resource of machine and material has brought us so far is a complete, broadcast degradation of every type and form sacred to the art of old; a pandemonium of tin masks, huddled deformities, and decayed methods; quarreling, lying, and cheating, with hands at each other's throats—or in each other's pockets; and none of the people who do these things, who pay for them or use them, know what they mean, feeling only—when they feel at all—that what is most truly like the past is the safest and therefore the best; as typical Marshall Field, speaking of his new building, has frankly said: "A good copy is the best we can do."

A pitiful insult, art and craft!

With this mine of industrial wealth at our feet we have no power to use it except to the perversion of our natural resources? A confession of shame which the merciful ignorance of the yet material frame of things mistakes for glorious achievement.

We half believe in our artistic greatness ourselves when we toss up a pantheon to the god of money in a night or two, or pile up a mammoth aggregation of Roman monuments, sarcophagi and Greek temples for a postoffice in a year or two—the patient retinue of the machine pitching in with terrible effectiveness to consummate this unhallowed ambition—this insult to ancient gods. The delicate, impressionable facilities of terra cotta becoming imitative blocks and voussoirs of tool-marked stone, badgered into all manner of structural gymnastics, or else ignored in vain endeavor to be honest; and granite blocks, cut in the fashion of the followers of Phidias, cunningly arranged about the steel beams and shafts, to look "real"—leaning heavily upon an inner skeleton of steel for support from floor to floor, which strains beneath the "reality" and would fain, I think, lie down to die of shame.

The "masters"—ergo, the fashionable followers of Phidias—have been trying to make this wily skeleton of steel seem seventeen sorts of "architecture" at once, when all the world knows—except the "masters"—that it is not one of them.

See now, how an element—the vanguard of the new art—has entered here, which the structural-art equation cannot satisfy without downright lying and ignoble cheating.

This element is the structural necessity reduced to a skeleton, complete in itself without the craftsman's touch. At once the million and one little ways of satisfying this necessity beautifully, coming to us chiefly through the books as the traditional art of building, vanish away—become history.

The artist is emancipated to work his will with a rational freedom unknown to the laborious art of structural tradition

—no longer tied to the meagre unit of brick arch and stone lintel, nor hampered by the grammatical phrase of their making—but he cannot use his freedom.

His tradition cannot think.

He will not think.

His scientific brother has put it to him before he is ready.

The modern tall office building problem is one representative problem of the machine. The only rational solutions it has received in the world may be counted upon the fingers of one hand. The fact that a great portion of our "architects" and "artists" are shocked by them to the point of offense is as valid an objection as that of a child refusing wholesome food because his stomach becomes dyspeptic from over-much unwholesome pastry—albeit he be the cook himself.

We may object to the mannerism of these buildings, but we can take no exception to their manner nor hide from their evident truth.

The steel frame has been recognized as a legitimate basis for a simple, sincere clothing of plastic material that idealizes its purpose without structural pretense.

This principle has at last been recognized in architecture, and though the masters refuse to accept it as architecture at all, it is a glimmer in a darkened field—the first sane word that has been said in Art for the Machine.

The Art of old idealized a Structural Necessity—now rendered obsolete and unnatural by the Machine—and accomplished it through man's joy in the labor of his hands.

The new will weave for the necessities of mankind, which his Machine will have mastered, a robe of ideality no less truthful, but more poetical, with a rational freedom made possible by the machine, beside which the art of old will be as the sweet, plaintive wail of the pipe to the outpouring of full orchestra.

It will clothe Necessity with the living flesh of virile imagination, as the living flesh lends living grace to the hard and bony human skeleton.

The new will pass from the possession of kings and classes to the every-day lives of all—from duration in point of time to immortality.

This distinction is one to be felt now rather than clearly defined.

The definition is the poetry of this Machine Age, and will be written large in time; but the more we, as artists, examine into this premonition, the more we will find the utter helplessness of old forms to satisfy new conditions, and the crying need of the machine for plastic treatment—a pliant, sympathetic treatment of its needs that the body of structural precedent cannot yield.

To gain further suggestive evidence of this, let us turn to the Decorative Arts—the immense middle-ground of all art now mortally sickened by the Machine—sickened that it may slough the art ideal of the constructural art for the plasticity of the new art—the Art of Democracy.

Here we find the most deadly perversion of all—the magnificent prowess of the machine bombarding the civilized world with the mangled corpses of strenuous horrors that once stood for cultivated luxury—standing now for a species of fatty degeneration simply vulgar.

Without regard to first principles or common decency, the whole letter of tradition—that is, ways of doing things rendered wholly obsolete and unnatural by the machine—is recklessly fed into its rapacious maw until you may buy reproductions for ninety-nine cents at "The Fair" that originally cost ages of toil and cultivation, worth now intrinsically nothing—that are harmful parasites befogging the sensibilities of our natures, belittling and falsifying any true perception of normal beauty the Creator may have seen fit to implant in us.

The idea of fitness to purpose, harmony between form and use with regard to any of these things, is possessed by very few, and utilized by them as a protest chiefly—a protest against the machine!

As well blame Richard Croker for the political iniquity of America.

As "Croker is the creature and not the creator" of political evil, so the machine is the creature and not the creator of this iniquity; and with this difference—that the machine has noble possibilities unwillingly forced to degradation in the name of the artistic; the machine, as far as its artistic capacity is concerned, is itself the crazed victim of the artist who works while he waits, and the artist who waits while he works.

There is a nice distinction between the two.

Neither class will unlock the secrets of the beauty of this time.

They are clinging sadly to the old order, and would wheedle the giant frame of things back to its childhood or forward to its second childhood, while this Machine Age is suffering for the artist who accepts, works, and sings as he works, with the joy of the *here* and *now!*

We want the man who eagerly seeks and finds, or blames

himself if he fails to find, the beauty of this time; who distinctly accepts as a singer and a prophet; for no man may work while he waits or wait as he works in the sense that William Morris' great work was legitimately done—in the sense that most art and craft of to-day is an echo; the time when such work was useful has gone.

Echoes are by nature decadent.

Artists who feel toward Modernity and the Machine now as William Morris and Ruskin were justified in feeling then, had best distinctly wait and work sociologically where great work may still be done by them. In the field of art activity they will do distinct harm. Already they have wrought much miserable mischief.

If the artist will only open his eyes he will see that the machine he dreads has made it possible to wipe out the mass of meaningless torture to which mankind, in the name of the artistic, has been more or less subjected since time began; for that matter, has made possible a cleanly strength, an ideality and a poetic fire that the art of the world has not yet seen; for the machine, the process now smooths away the necessity for petty structural deceits, soothes this wearisome struggle to make things seem what they are not, and can never be; satisfies the simple term of the modern art equation as the ball of clay in the sculptor's hand yields to his desire—comforting forever this realistic, brain-sick masquerade we are wont to suppose art.

William Morris pleaded well for simplicity as the basis of all true art. Let us understand the significance to art of that word —SIMPLICITY—for it is vital to the Art of the Machine.

We may find, in place of the genuine thing we have striven for, an affectation of the naïve, which we should detest as we detest a full-grown woman with baby mannerisms.

English art is saturated with it, from the brand-new imitation of the old house that grew and rambled from period to period to the rain-tub standing beneath the eaves.

In fact, most simplicity following the doctrines of William Morris is a protest; as a protest, well enough; but the highest form of simplicity is not simple in the sense that the infant intelligence is simple—nor, for that matter, the side of a barn.

A natural revulsion of feeling leads us from the meaningless elaboration of to-day to lay too great stress on mere platitudes, quite as a clean sheet of paper is a relief after looking at a series of bad drawings—but simplicity is not merely a neutral or a negative quality.

64

Simplicity in art, rightly understood, is a synthetic, positive quality, in which we may see evidence of mind, breadth of scheme, wealth of detail, and withal a sense of completeness found in a tree or a flower. A work may have the delicacies of a rare orchid or the stanch fortitude of the oak, and still be simple. A thing to be simple needs only to be true to itself in organic sense.

With this ideal of simplicity, let us glance hastily at a few instances of the machine and see how it has been forced by false ideals to do violence to this simplicity; how it has made possible the highest simplicity, rightly understood and so used. As perhaps wood is most available of all homely materials and therefore, naturally, the most abused—let us glance at wood.

Machinery has been invented for no other purpose than to imitate, as closely as possible, the wood-carving of the early ideal—with the immediate result that no ninety-nine cent piece of furniture is salable without some horrible botchwork meaning nothing unless it means that art and craft have combined to fix in the mind of the masses the old hand-carved chair as the *ne plus ultra* of the ideal.

The miserable, lumpy tribute to this perversion which Grand Rapids alone yields would mar the face of Art beyond repair; to say nothing of the elaborate and fussy joinery of posts, spindles, jig sawed beams and braces, butted and strutted, to outdo the sentimentality of the already over-wrought antique product.

Thus is the wood-working industry glutted, except in rarest instances. The whole sentiment of early craft degenerated to a sentimentality having no longer decent significance nor commercial integrity; in fact all that is fussy, maudlin, and animal, basing its existence chiefly on vanity and ignorance.

Now let us learn from the Machine.

It teaches us that the beauty of wood lies first in its qualities as wood; no treatment that did not bring out these qualities all the time could be plastic, and therefore not appropriate—so not beautiful, the machine teaches us, if we have left it to the machine that certain simple forms and handling are suitable to bring out the beauty of wood and certain forms are not; that all wood-carving is apt to be a forcing of the material, an insult to its finer possibilities as a material having in itself intrinsically artistic properties, of which its beautiful markings is one, its texture another, its color a third.

The machine, by its wonderful cutting, shaping, smoothing,

65

1898   River Forest Golf Club, *River Forest, Ill.* (Enlarged 1901)

and repetitive capacity, has made it possible to so use it without waste that the poor as well as the rich may enjoy to-day beautiful surface treatments of clean, strong forms that the branch veneers of Sheraton and Chippendale only hinted at, with dire extravagance, and which the middle ages utterly ignored.

The machine has emancipated these beauties of nature in wood; made it possible to wipe out the mass of meaningless torture to which wood has been subjected since the world began, for it has been universally abused and maltreated by all peoples but the Japanese.

Rightly appreciated, is not this the very process of elimination for which Morris pleaded?

Not alone a protest, moreover, for the machine, considered only technically, if you please, has placed in artist hands the means of idealizing the true nature of wood harmoniously with man's spiritual and material needs, without waste, within reach of all.

And how fares the troop of old materials galvanized into new life by the Machine?

Our modern materials are these old materials in more plastic guise, rendered so by the Machine, itself creating the very quality needed in material to satisfy its own art equation.

We have seen in glancing at modern architecture how they fare at the hands of Art and Craft; divided and sub-divided in orderly sequence with rank and file of obedient retainers awaiting the master's behest.

Steel and iron, plastic cement and terra-cotta.

Who can sound the possibilities of this old material, burned clay, which the modern machine has rendered as sensitive to the creative brain as a dry plate to the lens—a marvelous simplifier? And this plastic covering material, cement, another simplifier, enabling the artist to clothe the structural frame with a simple, modestly beautiful robe where before he dragged in, as he does still drag, five different kinds of material to compose one little cottage, pettily arranging it in an aggregation supposed to be picturesque—as a matter of fact, millinery, to be warped and beaten by sun, wind, and rain into a variegated heap of trash.

There is the process of modern casting in metal—one of the perfected modern machines, capable of any form to which fluid will flow, to perpetuate the imagery of the most delicately poetic mind without let or hindrance—within reach of everyone, therefore insulted and outraged by the bungler forcing it to a degraded seat at his degenerate festival.

Multitudes of processes are expectantly awaiting the sympathetic interpretation of the master mind; the galvano-plastic and its electrical brethren, a prolific horde, now cheap fakirs imitating real bronzes and all manner of the antique, secretly damning it in their vitals.

Electro-glazing, a machine shunned because too cleanly and delicate for the clumsy hand of the traditional designer, who depends upon the mass and blur of leading to conceal his lack of touch.

That delicate thing, the lithograph—the prince of a whole reproductive province of processes—see what this process becomes in the hands of a master like Whistler. He has sounded but one note in the gamut of its possibilities, but that product is intrinsically true to the process, and as delicate as the butterfly's wing. Yet the most this particular machine did for us, until then in the hands of Art and Craft, was to give us a cheap, imitative effect of painting.

So spins beyond our ability to follow to-night, a rough, feeble thread of the evidence at large to the effect that the machine has weakened the artist; all but destroyed his hand-made art, if not its ideals, although he has made enough miserable mischief meanwhile.

These evident instances should serve to hint, at least to the thinking mind, that the Machine is a marvelous simplifier; the emancipator of the creative mind, and in time the regenerator of the creative conscience. We may see that this destructive process has begun and is taking place that Art might awaken to the power of fully developed senses promised by dreams of its childhood, even though that power may not come the way it was pictured in those dreams.

Now, let us ask ourselves whether the fear of the higher artistic expression demanded by the Machine, so thoroughly grounded in the arts and crafts, is founded upon a finely guarded reticence, a recognition of inherent weakness or plain ignorance?

Let us, to be just, assume that it is equal parts of all three, and try to imagine an Arts and Crafts Society that may educate itself to prepare to make some good impression upon the Machine, the destroyer of their present ideals and tendencies, their salvation in disguise.

Such a society will, of course, be a society for mutual education.

Exhibitions will not be a feature of its programme for years, for there will be nothing to exhibit except the short-comings of the society, and they will hardly prove either instructive or amusing at this stage of proceedings. This society must, from the very nature of the proposition, be made up of the people who are in the work—that is, the manufacturers—coming into touch with such of those who assume the practice of the fine arts as profess a fair sense of the obligation to the public such assumption carries with it, and sociological workers whose interests are ever closely allied with art, as their prophets Morris, Ruskin, and Tolstoy evince, and all those who have as personal graces and accomplishment perfected handicraft, whether fashion old or fashion new.

Without the interest and co-operation of the manufacturers, the society cannot begin to do its work, for this is the cornerstone of its organization.

All these elements should be brought together on a common ground of confessed ignorance, with a desire to be instructed, freely encouraging talk and opinion, and reaching out desperately for any one who has special experience in any way connected, to address them.

I suppose, first of all, the thing would resemble a debating society, or something even less dignified, until some one should suggest that it was time to quit talking and proceed to do something, which in this case would not mean giving an exhibition, but rather excursions to factories and a study of processes in place—that is, the machine in processes too numerous to mention, at the factories with the men who organize and direct them, but not in the spirit of the idea that these things are all gone wrong, looking for that in them which would most nearly approximate the handicraft ideal; not looking into them with even the thought of handicraft, and not particularly looking for craftsmen, but getting a scientific ground-plan of the process in mind, if possible, with a view to its natural bent and possibilities.

Some processes and machines would naturally appeal to some, and some to others; there would undoubtedly be among us those who would find little joy in any of them.

This is, naturally, not child's play, but neither is the work expected of the modern artist.

I will venture to say, from personal observation and some experience, that not one artist in one hundred has taken pains to thus educate himself. I will go further and say what I believe to be true, that not one educational institution in America has as yet attempted to forge the connecting link between Science and Art by training the artist to his actual tools, or, by a process of nature-study that develops in him the power of independent thought, fitting him to use them properly.

Let us call these preliminaries then a process by which artists receive information nine-tenths of them lack concerning the tools they have to work with to-day—for tools to-day are processes and machines where they were once a hammer and a gouge.

The artist to-day is the leader of an orchestra, where he once was a star performer.

Once the manufacturers are convinced of due respect and appreciation on the part of the artist, they will welcome him and his counsel gladly and make any experiments having a grain of apparent sense in them.

They have little patience with a bothering about in endeavor to see what might be done to make their particular machine mediaeval and restore man's joy in the mere work of his hands —for this once lovely attribute is far behind.

This proceeding doubtless would be of far more educational value to the artist than to the manufacturer, at least for some time to come, for there would be a difficult adjustment to make on the part of the artist and an attitude to change. So many artists are chiefly "attitude" that some would undoubtedly disappear with the attitude.

But if out of twenty determined students a ray of light should come to one, to light up a single operation, it would have been worth while, for that would be fairly something; while joy in mere handicraft is like that of the man who played the piano for his own amusement—a pleasurable personal accomplishment without real relation to the grim condition confronting us.

Granting that a determined, dauntless body of artist material could be brought together with sufficient persistent enthusiasm to grapple with the Machine, would not some one be found who would provide the suitable experimental station (which is what the modern Arts and Crafts shop should be)—an experimental station that would represent in miniature the elements of this great pulsating web of the machine, where each pregnant process or significant tool in printing, lithography, galvano-electro processes, wood and steel working machinery, muffles and kilns would have its place and where the best young scientific blood could mingle with the best and truest artistic inspiration, to sound the depths of these things, to accord them the patient, sympathetic treatment that is their due?

Surely a thing like this would be worth while—to alleviate the insensate numbness of the poor fellows out in the cold, hard shops, who know not why nor understand, whose dutiful obedience is chained to botch work and bungler's ambition; surely this would be a practical means to make their dutiful obedience give us something we can all understand, and that will be as normal to the best of this machine age as a ray of light to the healthy eye; a real help in adjusting the *Man* to a true sense of his importance as a factor in society, though he does tend a machine.

Teach him that that machine is his best friend—will have widened the margin of his leisure until enlightenment shall bring him a further sense of the magnificent ground plan of progress in which he too justly plays his significant part.

If the art of the Greek, produced at such cost of human life, was so noble and enduring, what limit dare we now imagine to an Art based upon an adequate life for the individual?

The machine is his!

In due time it will come to him!

Meanwhile, who shall count the slain?

From where are the trained nurses in this industrial hospital to come if not from the modern arts and crafts?

Shelley says a man cannot say—"I will compose poetry." "The greatest poet even cannot say it, for the mind in creation is as a fading coal which some invisible influence, like an inconstant wind awakens to transitory brightness; this power arises from within like the color of a flower which fades and changes as it is developed, and the conscious portions of our nature are unprophetic either of its approach or its departure"; and yet in the arts and crafts the problem is presented as a more or less fixed quantity, highly involved, requiring a surer touch, a more highly disciplined artistic nature to organize it as a work of art.

The original impulses may reach as far inward as those of Shelley's poet, be quite as wayward a matter of pure sentiment, and yet after the thing is done, showing its rational qualities, is limited in completeness only by the capacity of whoever would show them or by the imperfection of the thing itself.

This does not mean that Art may be shown to be an exact Science.

"It is not pure reason, but it is always reasonable."

It is a matter of perceiving and portraying the harmony of organic tendencies; is originally intuitive because the artist nature is a prophetic gift that may sense these qualities afar.

To me, the artist is he who can truthfully idealize the common sense of these tendencies in his chosen way.

So I feel conception and composition to be simply the essence of refinement in organization, the original impulse of which may be registered by the artistic nature as unconsciously as the magnetic needle vibrates to the magnetic law, but which is, in synthesis or analysis, organically consistent, given the power to see it or not.

And I have come to believe that the world of Art, which we are so fond of calling the world outside of Science, is not so much outside as it is the very heart quality of this great material growth—as religion is its conscience.

A foolish heart and a small conscience.

A foolish heart, palpitating in alarm, mistaking the growing pains of its giant frame for approaching dissolution, whose sentimentality the lusty body of modern things has outgrown.

Upon this faith in Art as the organic heart quality of the scientific frame of things, I base a belief that we must look to the artist brain, of all brains, to grasp the significance to society of this thing we call the Machine, if that brain be not blinded, gagged, and bound by false tradition, the letter of precedent. For this thing we call Art is it not as prophetic as a primrose or an oak? Therefore, of the essence of this thing we call the Machine, which is no more or less than the principle of organic growth working irresistibly the Will of Life through the medium of Man.

Be gently lifted at nightfall to the top of a great down-town office building, and you may see how in the image of material man, at once his glory and menace, is this thing we call a city.

There beneath, grown up in a night, is the monster leviathan, stretching acre upon acre into the far distance. High overhead hangs the stagnant pall of its fetid breath, reddened with the light from its myriad eyes endlessly everywhere blinking. Ten thousand acres of cellular tissue, layer upon layer, the city's flesh, outspreads enmeshed by intricate network of veins and arteries, radiating into the gloom, and there with muffled, persistent roar, pulses and circulates as the blood in your veins, the ceaseless beat of the activity to whose necessities it all conforms.

Like to the sanitation of the human body is the drawing off of poisonous waste from the system of this enormous creature; absorbed first by the infinitely ramifying, thread-like ducts gathering at their sensitive terminals matter destructive to its life, hurrying it to millions of small intestines, to be collected in turn by larger, flowing to the great sewer, on to the drainage canal, and finally to the ocean.

This ten thousand acres of flesh-like tissue is again knit and inter-knit with a nervous system marvelously complete, delicate filaments for hearing, knowing, almost feeling the pulse of its organism, acting upon the ligaments and tendons for motive impulse, in all flowing the impelling fluid of man's own life.

Its nerve ganglia!—The peerless Corliss tandems whirling their hundred ton fly-wheels, fed by gigantic rows of water tube boilers burning oil, a solitary man slowly pacing backward and forward, regulating here and there the little feed valves controlling the deafening roar of the flaming gas, while beyond, the incessant clicking, dropping, waiting—lifting, waiting, shifting of the governor gear controlling these modern Goliaths seems a visible brain in intelligent action, registered infallibly in the enormous magnets, purring in the giant embrace of great induction coils, generating the vital current meeting with instant response in the rolling cars on elevated tracks ten miles away, where the glare of the Bessemer steel converter makes a conflagration of the clouds.

More quietly still, whispering down the long, low rooms of factory buildings buried in the gloom beyond, range on range of stanch, beautifully perfected automatons, murmur contentedly with occasional click-clack, that would have the American manufacturing industry of five years ago by the throat to-day; manipulating steel as delicately as a mystical shuttle of the modern loom manipulates a silk thread in the shimmering pattern of a dainty gown.

And the heavy breathing, the murmuring, the clangor, and the roar!—how the voice of this monstrous thing, this greatest of machines, a great city, rises to proclaim the marvel of the units of its structure, the ghastly warning boom from the deep throats of vessels heavily seeking inlet to the waterway below, answered by the echoing clangor of the bridge bells growing nearer and more ominous as the vessel cuts momentarily the flow of the nearer artery, warning the current from the swinging bridge now closing on its stately passage, just in time to receive in a rush of steam, as a streak of light, the avalanche of blood and metal hurled across it and gone, roaring into the night on its glittering bands of steel, ever faithfully encircled by the slender magic lines tick-tapping its invincible protection.

Nearer, in the building ablaze with midnight activity, the wide white band streams into the marvel of the multiple press, receiving unerringly the indelible impression of the human hopes, joys, and fears throbbing in the pulse of this great activity, as infallibly as the gray matter of the human brain receives the impression of the senses, to come forth millions of neatly folded, perfected news sheets, teeming with vivid appeals to passions, good or evil; weaving a web of intercommunication so far reaching that distance becomes as nothing, the thought of one man in one corner of the earth one day visible to the naked eye of all men the next; the doings of all the world reflected as in a glass, so marvelously sensitive this wide white band streaming endlessly from day to day becomes in the grasp of the multiple press.

If the pulse of activity in this great city, to which the tremor of the mammoth skeleton beneath our feet is but an awe-inspiring response, is thrilling, what of this prolific, silent obedience?

And the texture of the tissue of this great thing, this Forerunner of Democracy, the Machine, has been deposited particle by particle, in blind obedience to organic law, the law to which the great solar universe is but an obedient machine.

Thus is the thing into which the forces of Art are to breathe the thrill of ideality! A SOUL!

An address by Frank Lloyd Wright to the Chicago Arts and Crafts Society, at Hull House, March 6, and to the Western Society of Engineers, March 20, 1901. Here reprinted in full for the first time

Designing Unity Temple

Had Doctor Johonnot, the Universalist pastor of Unity Church, been Fra Junipero the "style" of Unity Temple would have been predetermined. Had he been Father Latour it would have been Midi-Romanesque. Yes, and perhaps being what he was, he was entitled to the only tradition he knew—that of the little white New England Church, lean spire pointing to heaven—"back East." If sentimentality were sense this might be so.

But the pastor was out of luck. Circumstances brought him to yield himself up "in the cause of architecture." The straight line and the flat plane were to emerge as the cantilever slab.

And to that cause every one who undertakes to read what follows is called upon to yield. It should only be read after studying the plans and perspective of Unity Temple. Constant reference to the plan will be necessary if the matter is to come clear.

Our building committee were all "good men and true." One of them, Charles E. Roberts, a mechanical engineer and inventor, enlightened in creation.

One, enlightened, is leaven enough in any Usonian lump. The struggle . . . it is always a struggle in architecture for the architect where "good men and true" are concerned—began.

First came the philosophy of the building.

Human sensibilities are the strings of the instrument upon

1906 Unity Church and Parish House, *Oak Park, Ill.* (Photograph on page 115.)

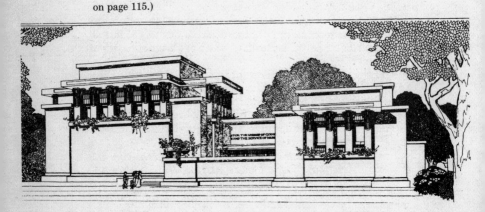

which the true artist plays . . . "abstract" . . . ? But why not avoid the symbol, as such? The symbol is too literal. It is become a form of Literature in the Arts.

Let us abolish, in the art and craft of architecture, literature in any "symbolic" form whatsoever. The sense of inner rhythm, deep planted in human sensibility, lives far above other considerations in Art.

Then why the steeple of the little white church? Why *point* to heaven?

I told the committee a story. Did they not know the tale of the holy man who, yearning to see God, climbed up and up the highest mountain—up and up on and to and up the highest relic of a tree there was on the mountain too? Ragged and worn, there he lifted up his eager perspiring face to heaven and called on "God." A voice . . . bidding him get down . . . go back!

Would he really see God's face? Then he should go back, go down there in the valley below where his own people were —there only could *he* look upon God's countenance.

Was not that "finger," the church steeple, pointing on high like the man who climbed on high to see HIM? A misleading symbol perhaps. A perversion of sentiment—sentimentality.

Was not the time come now to be more simple, to have more faith in man on his Earth and less anxiety concerning his Heaven about which he could *know* nothing. Concerning this heaven he had never received any testimony from his own senses.

Why not, then, build a temple, not to GOD in that way— more sentimental than sense—but build a temple to man, appropriate to his uses as a meeting place, in which to study man himself for his God's sake? A modern meeting-house and good-time place.

Build a beautiful ROOM proportioned to this purpose. Make it beautiful in this *simple* sense. A *natural* building for natural Man.

The pastor was a "liberal." His liberality was thus challenged, his reason piqued and the curiosity of all aroused.

What would such a building be like? They said they could imagine no such thing.

"That's what you came to me for," I ventured. "I can imagine it and will help you create it."

Promising the building committee something tangible to look at soon—I sent them away, they not knowing, quite, whether they were foolish, fooled, or fooling with a fool.

That ROOM; it began to be that same night.

Enter the realm of architectural ideas.

The first idea—to keep a noble ROOM in mind, and let the room shape the whole edifice, let the room inside be the architecture outside.

What shape? Well, the answer lay, in what material? There was only one material to choose as the church funds were $45,000, to "church" 400 people in 1906. Concrete was cheap.

Concrete alone could do it. But even concrete as it was in use at that time meant wood "forms" and some other material than concrete for outside facing. They were in the habit of covering the concrete with brick or stone, plastering and furring the inside of the walls. Plastering the outside would be cheaper than brick or stone but wouldn't stick to concrete in our climate. Why not make the wooden boxes or forms so the concrete could be cast in them as separate blocks and masses, these separate blocks and masses grouped about an interior space in some such way as to preserve this desired sense of the interior space in the appearance of the whole building? And the block-masses be left as themselves with no "facing." That would be cheap and permanent.

Then, how to cover the separate features and concrete masses as well as the sacrosanct space from the extremes of northern weather. What roof?

What had concrete to offer as a cover shelter? The slab—of course. The reinforced slab. Nothing else if the building was to be thoroughbred, meaning built in character out of one material.

Too monumental, all this? Too forthright for my committee I feared. Would a statement so positive as that final slab over the whole seem irreligious to them? Profane in their eyes? Why?

The flat slab was direct. It would be "nobly" simple. The wooden forms or molds in which concrete buildings must at that time be cast were always the chief item of expense, so to repeat the use of a single one as often as possible was desirable, even necessary. Therefore a building all four sides alike looked like the thing. This, in simplest terms, meant a building square in plan. That would make their temple a cube, a noble form.

The slab, too, belonged to the cube by nature. "Credo simplicitatem."

That form is most imaginative and "happy" that is most radiant with the "aura" or overtone of superform.

Geometric shapes through human sensibility have thus acquired to some extent human significance as, say, the cube or square, integrity; the circle or sphere, infinity; the straight line, rectitude; if long drawn out . . . repose; the triangle . . . aspiration, etc.

There was no money to spend in working on the concrete mass outside or with it after it was once cast.

Good reason, this, if no other, for getting away from any false facing. Couldn't the surface be qualified in the casting process so this whole matter of veneered "Facade" could be omitted with good effect? This was later the cause of much experiment, with what success may be seen.

Then the Temple itself—still in my mind—began to take shape. The site was noisy, by the Lake Street car tracks. Therefore it seemed best to keep the building closed on the three front sides and enter it from a court at the center of the lot.

Unity Temple itself with the thoughts in mind I have just expressed, arrived easily enough, but there was a secular side to Universalist church activities—entertainment—Sunday school, feasts, etc. . . .

To embody these latter with the temple would spoil the simplicity of the room—the noble ROOM—in the service of MAN for the worship of GOD.

So finally I put the space as "Unity House," a long free space to the rear of the lot, as a separate building to be sub-divided by moveable screens, on occasion. It thus became a separate building but harmonious with the Temple—the entrance to both to be the connecting link between them. (See the plan.) That was that.

To go back to the Temple itself. What kind of "square room"? How effect the cube and best serve the purpose of audience room?

Should the pulpit be put toward the street and let the congregation come in and go out at the rear in the usual disrespectful church fashion so the pastor missed contact with his flock? And the noise of the street cars on Lake Street come in?

No. Why not put the pulpit at the entrance side at the rear of the square Temple entirely cut off from the street and bring the congregation into the room at the sides and on a lower level so those entering would be imperceptible to the audience? This would make the incomers as little a disturbance or challenge to curiosity as possible. This would preserve the quiet and the dignity of the room itself. Out of that thought came the depressed foyer or "cloister" corridor either side leading from the main entrance lobby at the center to the stairs in the near and far corners of the room. Those entering the room in this way could see into the big room but not be seen by those already seated within it.

And when the congregation rose to disperse here was opportunity to move forward toward their pastor and by swinging wide doors open beside the pulpit let the flock pass out by the minister and find themselves directly in the entrance loggia from which they had first come in. They had gone into the depressed entrances at the sides from this same entrance to enter the big room. But it seemed more respectful to let them go out thus toward the pulpit than turn their backs upon their minister to go out as is usual in most churches. This scheme gave the minister's flock to him to greet. Few could escape. The position of the pulpit in relation to the entrance made this reverse movement possible.

So this was done. (See the plan.)

The room itself—size determined by comfortable seats with leg-room for four hundred people—was built with four interior free standing posts to carry the overhead structure. These concrete posts were hollow and became free-standing ducts to insure economic and uniform distribution of heat. The large supporting posts were so set in plan as to form a double tier of alcoves on four sides of this room. Flood these side-alcoves with light from above: get a sense of a happy cloudless day into the room. And with this feeling for light the center ceiling between the four great posts became skylight, daylight sifting through between the intersections of concrete beams filtering through amber glass ceiling lights, thus the light would, rain or shine, have the warmth of sunlight. Artificial lighting took place there at night as well. This scheme of lighting was integral, gave diffusion and kept the room space clear.

The spacious wardrobes between the depressed foyers either side of the room and under the auditorium itself, were intended to give opportunity to the worshippers to leave their wraps before entering the worshipful room. And this wardrobe would work as well for the entertainments in the long room to the rear because it was just off the main entrance lobby.

The secular hall—Unity House—itself, was tall enough to have galleries at each side of the central space—convertible into class-room space.

A long kitchen connected to each end of the secular space was added to the rear of Unity House for the Temple "feasts."

The pastor's offices and study came of themselves over the

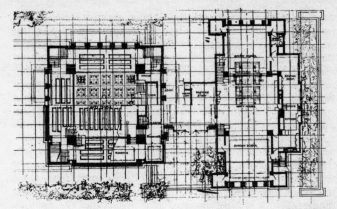

entrance lobby the connection between the two buildings. The study thus looked down through swinging windows into the secular hall—while it was just a step behind the pulpit.

All this seemed in proper order. Seemed natural enough.

Now for proportion—for the "concrete" expression of concrete in this natural arrangement—the ideal of an organic whole well in mind.

For observe, so far, what has actually taken place is only reasoned *arrangement*. The "plan" with an eye to an exterior in the realm of ideas but "felt" in imagination.

First came the philosophy of the thing in the little story repeated to the trustees. All artistic creation has its own. The first condition of creation. However, some would smile and say, "the result of it."

Second there was the general purpose of the whole to consider in each part: a matter of reasoned arrangement. This arrangement must be made with a sense of the yet-unborn-whole in the mind, to be blocked out as appropriate to concrete masses cast in wooden boxes. Holding all this diversity together in a preconceived direction is really no light matter but is the condition of creation. Imagination conceives here the PLAN suitable to the material and the purpose—seeing the probable —possible form.

Imagination reigns supreme, when now the *form* the whole will naturally take, must be seen.

And we have arrived at the question of *style*.

But if all this preliminary planning has been well conceived that question in the main is settled. The matter may be intensified, made eloquent or modified and quieted. It cannot much change. Organic is this matter of style now. The concrete

79

forms of Unity Temple will take the character of all we have so far done, if all we have so far done is harmonious with the principle we are waking to work. The structure will not put forth its forms as the tree puts forth branches and foliage—if we do not stultify it, do not betray it in some way.

We do not choose the style. Style is what this is now and what we *are*. A thrilling moment this in any architect's experience. He is about to see the countenance of something he is invoking. Out of this sense of order and his love of the beauty of life—something is to be born maybe to live long as a message of hope and joy or a curse to his kind. *His* message he feels. None the less is it "theirs," and rather more. And it is out of love and understanding such as this on the part of an architect that a building is born to bless or curse those it is built to serve.

Bless them if they will see and understand. Curse them and be cursed by them if either they or the architect should fail to understand. . . . This is the faith and the fear in the architect as he makes ready—to draw his design.

In all artists it is the same.

Now comes to brood—to suffer doubt and burn with eagerness. To test bearings—and prove assumed ground by putting all together to definite scale on paper. Preferably small scale at first. Then larger. Finally still larger scale studies of parts.

This pure white sheet of paper! Ready for the logic of the plan.

T-square, triangle, scale—seductive invitation lying upon the spotless surface.

Temptation!

"Boy! Go tell Black Kelly to make a blaze there in the workroom fire-place! Ask Brown-Sadie if it's too late to have baked Bermudas for supper! Then go ask your mother—I shall hear her in here—to play something—Bach preferred, or Beethoven if she prefers."

An aid to creative effort, the open fire. What a friend to the laboring artist, the poetic-baked-onion. Real encouragement to him is great music.

Yes, and what a poor creature, after all, creation comes singing through. About like catgut and horsehair in the hands of Sarasate.

Night labor at the draughting board is best for intense creation. It may continue uninterrupted.

Meantime reflections are passing in the mind—"design is abstraction of nature-elements in purely geometric terms"—that is what we ought to call pure design? . . . But—nature-pattern and nature-texture in materials themselves often approach conventionalization, or the abstract, to such a degree as to be superlative means ready to the designer's hand to qualify, stimulate and enrich his own efforts. . . . What texture this concrete mass? Why not its own gravel? How to bring the gravel clean on the surface?

Here was reality. Yes, the "fine thing" is reality. Always reality?

Realism, the subgeometric, is however the abuse of this fine thing.

Keep the straight lines clean and significant, the flat plane expressive and clean cut. But let texture of material come into them.

Reality is spirit . . . essence brooding just behind aspect!

Seize it! And . . . after all, reality *is* supergeometric, casting a spell or a "charm" over any geometry, as such, in itself.

Yes, it seems to me, that is what it means to be an artist . . . to seize this essence brooding just behind aspect. These questionings arising each with its train of thought by the way, as at work.

It is morning! To bed for a while!

Well, there is Unity Temple at last. Health and soundness in it, though still far to go.

But here we have penciled on the sheet of paper, in the main, the plan, section and elevation as in the drawings illustrated here, all except the exterior of "Unity House," as the room for secular recreation came to be called.

To establish harmony between these buildings of separate function proved difficult, utterly exasperating.

Another series of concentrations—lasting hours at a time for several days. How to keep the noble scale of the temple in the design of the subordinate mass of the secular hall and not falsify the function of that noble mass? The ideal of an organic architecture is severe discipline for the imagination. I came to know that full well. And, always, some minor concordance takes more time, taxes concentration more than all besides. To vex the architect, this minor element now becomes a major problem. How many schemes I have thrown away because some one minor feature would not come true to form!

Thirty-four studies were necessary to arrive at this as it is now seen. Unfortunately they are lost with thousands of others of other buildings. The fruit of similar struggles to coordinate and perfect them all as organic entities—I wish I had kept.

Unity House looks easy enough now, for it is right enough.

But this *"harmony of the whole"* where diverse functions cause diverse masses to occur is no light affair for the architect—nor ever will be if he keeps his ideal high.

Now observe the plans and the elevations, then the model or photograph of the building. See, now, how all that has taken place is showing itself *as it is* for what it is.

A new industrial method for the use of a new material is improved and revealed. Roof slabs—attic walls—screen walls—posts and glass screens enclose, as architecture, a great room.

The sense of the room is not only preserved—*it may be seen as the soul of the design.* Instead of being built into the heart of a block of sculptured building material, out of sight, sacrosanct space is merely screened in . . . it comes through as the living "motif" of the architecture.

The grammar of such style as is seen here is simply and logically determined by the concrete mass and flat layer formation of the slab and box construction of the square room, proportioned according to concrete-nature—or the nature of the concrete. All is assembled about the coveted space, now visibly cherished.

Such architectural forms as there are, each to each as all in all, are cubical in form, to be cast solid in wooden boxes. But *one* motif may be seen, the "inside" becoming "outside." The groups of monoliths in their changing phases, square in character, do not depart from that single IDEA. Here we have something of the organic integrity in structure out of which issues character as an aura. The consequence is style. A stylish development of the square becoming the cube.

Understanding Unity Temple one may respect it. It serves its purpose well. It was easy to build. Its harmonies are bold and striking, but genuine in melody. The "square," too positive in statement for current *"taste,"* the straight line and the flat plane uncompromising, yes. But here is an entity again to prove that architecture may, if need be, live again as the nature-of-the-thing in terms of building material. Here is one building rooted in such modern conditions of work, materials and thought, as prevailed at the time it was built. Single-minded in motif. Faithful in form.

Out of this concentration in labor will come many subsequent studies in refinement—correction of correlation, scale tests for integration. Overcoming difficulties in detail, in the effort to keep all clean and simple as a whole, is continued during the whole process of planning and building.

Many studies in detail yet remain to be made, to determine what further may be left out to protect the design. These studies seem never to end, and in this sense, no organic building may ever be "finished." The complete goal of the ideal of organic architecture is never reached. Nor need be. What worth while ideal is ever reached?

But, we have enough now on paper to make a perspective drawing to go with the plan for the committee of "good men and true" to see. Usually a committee has only the sketch to consider. But it is impossible to present a "sketch" when working in this method. The building as a whole must be all in order before the "sketch" not after it.

Unity Temple is a complete building on paper, already. There is no "sketch" and there never has been one.

from AN AUTOBIOGRAPHY, *1932*

Discovery

I remember Kuno Francke, German exchange-professor of aesthetics at Harvard (one of Theodore Roosevelt's exchange-professors), came from Harvard to Oak Park (1909) with his charming wife. Herr Professor came to see the work I had done of which he had heard at Harvard. Astonished and pleased by what he saw already accomplished when he came: the Coonley, Robie, Winslow and Cheney houses; Unity Temple; designs for other buildings; he urged me to come to Germany. Said Kuno Francke, "My people are groping, only superficially, for what I see you doing organically: your people are not ready for you. Your life here will be wasted. But my people are ready for you. They will reward you. Fifty years, at least, will pass before your people will be ready for you."

I did not want to go to Germany. I could not speak German. Fascinated by what I was already doing, I declined this invitation. Professor Francke soon returned to Germany. Several months later came the proposition from Wasmuth (well-known publisher in Berlin of art works) proposing to publish the work Kuno Francke had seen (all of it) if I would come to Germany to supervise preparation. A few months later, cancelling obligations of every nature in the field of architecture and at home, I went; risking the worm's-eye view of society I felt must follow. There in Germany and Italy I lived and worked for a year. In the little Villino Belvedere of Fiesole, massive door of the villino opening directly upon the steep, narrow little Via Verdi of the ancient old Roman town on the hill above Florence—I found sanctuary. Just below the little villino spread downward to ancient Firenze the slope where so many distinguished refugees from foreign lands had found sanctuary and were still finding harbor. Most of that year—1910—I worked preparing the forthcoming publication in German, *Ausgefuehrte Bauten und Entwuerfe.* Accordingly published in Berlin 1910–11. German edition promptly absorbed. Unfortunately the part of the edition bought for American distribution by two of my good clients, Francis W. Little and Darwin D. Martin, was temporarily stored below ground-level at Taliesin, previous to arrangements for distribution. The entire portion of the edition meant for America was consumed in the fire destroying the first Taliesin—1912. (First of three destructive fires at Taliesin.) Smoke rose from the smouldering mass below grade for several days. So America saw little of this original publication in German unless imported. But one whole copy only and about one-half of another now stays at Taliesin with me. The entire work was more cheaply reprinted (smaller in size) in Germany later —also reprinted, in still smaller format, by Japan. *Cahiers d'Art,* France, published a resume in 1911. These publications have all but disappeared.

from A TESTAMENT, *1957*

The Sovereignty of the Individual

Preface to AUSGEFÜHRTE BAUTEN UND ENTWÜRFE *published by Wasmuth Berlin, 1910. Reprinted as introduction to exhibition Palazzo Strozzi, Florence, Italy, 1951.*

Since a previous article• written in endeavor to state the nature of the faith and practices fashioning this work of mine I have had the privilege of studying here in Italy the work of that splendid group of Florentine sculptors, painters and architects; and the sculptor-painters and painter-sculptors who were also architects: Giotto, Masaccio, Mantegna, Pisano, Brunelleschi, Sansovino, Bramante, Angelo, and Leonardo.

No hard and fast line was drawn between the arts in their epoch. Some of the sculpture is good painting; much of the painting is good sculpture and craftsmanship was everywhere

• "The Art and Craft of the Machine"—1901, Hull House, Chicago.

excellent. In all lie patterns of Architecture. Where interfusion of the arts is not confusion and importunate it is amazing. To attempt to classify work severely as pure painting, pure sculpture, or pure architecture would be quite impossible even if desirable for educational purposes. Be this as it may, what these noble men of Florence absorbed from their Greek, Byzantine, and Roman forebears, they bequeathed to Europe as kernel of the great Renaissance. This bequest, if we deduct Gothic influence of the Middle Ages, has constituted the soul of Academic fine-art upon that Continent (and in England) to this very day.

From the flaming souls of these brilliant Italians were lighted myriads of French, German, Spanish, English, and many other lesser flames. They flourished, flickered feebly for a time to soon smoulder in sensuality and the extravagance of later periods until extinguished in banal architecture like the Rococo, or nondescript structures such as the Louvre of the Louis and the Paris Beaux Arts.

This applies to buildings more or less, shall we say, "professional" embodiments of cultured striving for the Beautiful: I mean those buildings which were "good school" performances; buildings seeking consciously to be beautiful, regardless. Here as elsewhere, nevertheless, the true basis for any serious study of the art of Architecture still lies in those indigenous structures; more humble buildings everywhere being to architecture what folk-lore is to literature or folk-song to music and with which Academic architects were seldom concerned. In the aggregate of these simple buildings lie traits which make them characteristically Italian, French, Dutch, German, Spanish, or English as the case may be. It is the traits of these many folk-structures that are of the soil. Natural. Though often slight, their virtue is intimately related to environment and to the heart-life of the people. Functions are usually truthfully conceived and rendered invariably with natural feeling. Results are often beautiful and always instructive. So, underlying the ambitious academic, more self-conscious blossoms of the human soul: these continuing expressions of "Maryolatry," adoration of divinity or cringing to temporal power, there is love of life quietly but inevitably finding the right way for the right people in the right places. Lovely in color, gracious in line and harmonious arrangement, they impart joy-in-living untroubled by any philosophical burden,—as little concerned with Fine Art or Literature or indebted to either as the flower by the wayside that turns its petals upward to the sun is concerned with the farmer who passes in the road or is indebted to him for the geometry of its petals.

Of this innate joy in living, so it seems to me, there is greater proof in Italy than elsewhere unless in "Dai Nippon"—in old Japan. Buildings, pictures and sculpture seem to be born, here as there, like the flowers by the roadside—to bloom or sing themselves into being. Approached in the spirit of conception, they inspire us with the very music of life.

As music still speaks Italian, so Architecture still points to antique Italy.

No really Italian building seems ill at ease in Italy. All are happily content with what ornament and color they carry naturally. The native rocks and trees and garden slopes are at one with them. Wherever the cypress rises, there, like the touch of a magician's wand, all resolves into composition harmonious and complete.

The secret of this ineffable charm would be sought in vain in the rarefied air of scholasticism or in the ateliers of any pedantic Fine Art. It all lies closer to Earth. Like a handful of moist, sweet earth itself. So simple that to modern minds trained in the intellectual gymnastics of "cultivated" taste it would seem unrelated to important purposes. So close to the heart it is that almost universally it is overlooked especially by the scholar.

As we pass along the wayside some blossom with unusually glowing color or prettiness of form attracts us. Held by it we gratefully accept its perfect loveliness. But, seeking the secret of its ineffable charm, we find the blossom whose more obvious claim first arrested our attention as nature intended, intimately related to the texture and shape of the foliage beneath it. We discover peculiar sympathy between the form of this flower and the system upon which leaves are arranged about the stalk. From this we are led on to observe a characteristic habit of growth and discover a resultant pattern of structure having first direction toward form deep down in roots hidden in the warm earth, kept moist there by a conservative covering of leaf-mould. Structure—as now we may observe—proceeds from generals to particulars arriving at the blossom, to attract us, proclaiming in its lines and form the Nature of the structure that bore it. We have here a thing organic. Law and order are the basis of a finished grace and beauty. "Beauty" is the expression of fundamental conditions in line, form and color true to those conditions and seeming to exist to fulfill them according to some thoughtful original design.

Though our intelligence may in no wise prove Beauty the result of these harmonious internal conditions, that which through the ages appeals to our instinct as beautiful, we may realize, does not ignore these basic elements of law and order. Nor does it take long to establish in our minds the fact that no lasting beauty ever does ignore them. They are ever present elements or are the actual conditions of the existence of Beauty. From the study of the forms, or styles which mankind has considered beautiful we see those living longest do in greatest measure fulfill these basic conditions. That anything grows is no concern of ours because the quality we call Life itself is beyond us. We are not necessarily concerned with that initial gift of Life, and Beauty its essence, is for us as mysterious as Life. All attempts to say what Life is are foolish, like cutting out the head of our drum to find whence comes the sound. But we may study with profit these manifest truths of form and structure; facts of form as related to function; material traits of line determining character. We may deduce laws of procedure inherent in all natural growths, to use as basic Principle for good building. We are ourselves a product of such natural law. These manifestations of Principle are harmonious with the essence of our own being and so perceived by us to be good. We feel "the good, true and beautiful" to be essentially one with our own souls in any last analysis. Within us all there is at work a divine principle of growth to some good end. Accordingly we select as "good" whatever is in harmony with innate law.

We thus reach for the light, spiritually in some innate spirit-pattern as the plant does physically. If we are sound of heart and not sophisticated by our education far beyond our capacity, we call that objective the Beautiful.

In other words, if and when we perceive anything to be beautiful we do instinctively recognize the "rightness" of that thing. This means that a glimpse of something essentially of the fibre of our own inner nature is revealed to us. Through his own deeper insight the Artist shares with us this revelation. His power to visualize his conceptions or visions, being greater than our own, a flash of truth from him stimulates us. We have a vision of innate harmony not fully understood today, though perhaps to be so appreciated tomorrow.

———

This experience being so easy to acquire in Nature, whence

came the corrupt styles like later phases of the Renaissance? From confusion of the curious with the beautiful: confounding the sensations awakened by the beautiful with those evoked by things merely curious: a growing tendency increasing as our civilization moves away from appreciation of the philosophy of Nature and founds conventions in ignorance or defiance of innate laws of harmonious structure. It would seem that appreciations of fundamental beauty on the part of primitive peoples is coming home to us today in another Renaissance to open our eyes so we may cut away dead wood and brush aside the accumulated rubbish-heaps of centuries of false adoration. This Renaissance-of-the-Primitive may mean eventual return to more simple conventions more in harmony with Nature. Primarily we all need simplifying, though we must avoid a nature-ism. Then, too, we should learn the more spiritual lessons the East has power to teach the West so that we may build upon these basic principles the more highly developed forms our more highly developed life will need if the Machine is to be a safe tool in our hands.

Nature, if sought in this interior sense alone can save us from the hopeless confusion of ideas resulting in the view that Beauty, a matter of caprice, being merely a freak of the imagination to the one man divine, to another hideous is to still another quite meaningless. To find inorganic things of no truth of relation beautiful is but to demonstrate the lack of beauty in oneself and one's unfitness for any office in administering the Beautiful. That degradation always provides another example of the stultification that comes from confusing the curious with the beautiful. The facility afforded by machinery only raises that affair to obscure heights. Our modern Education therefore seems to leave modern man less and less able than the savage to draw the fundamental line between these spirit properties or qualities. Science itself has no ability to draw this line in the right place.

So we may say that knowledge-of-cause-and-effect in terms of line, color and form as found in organic nature will furnish us with certain guide-lines within which any artist may sift materials, test motives and direct aims, thus roughly blocking out, at least a rational basis to nourish his ideas and ideals of work. Great artists usually do this by instinct. The thing felt is divined by inspiration perhaps, as synthetic analysis of their works will show. Poetry (it is always prophecy) is—in itself— no matter to be thus demonstrated. But what is of great value to every artist in his research is knowledge of those facts of relation; those inherent qualities of line, form and color which are in themselves a language of Truth as well as of sentiment and that characterizes the pine-tree as a pine as distinguished from those determining the willow as a willow; characteristic traits the Japanese can seize graphically and unerringly reduce to simple geometry. This graphic soul of the thing is seen in geometrical analyses by Hokusai. Korin was conscious master of this essential geometry in whatever he would portray. So it will be found with all great architecture and music: no less so with the paintings of Velasquez, Rembrandt and the great Italians. Organic character persists in and pervades them all with the quality of ineffable repose.

Only by patient study to acquire knowledge of Nature in this interior sense are guiding principles ever to be established by the Architect. Ideals gained by comprehension of these organic limitations are never lost. An artist having these may then defy his "education." If he is really for Nature in this inward sense he may be a rebel against his time and its laws but never lawless in his work nor as himself.

Debased periods of the world's art and craft are far removed from any conception of these simple, innate principles. Degenerate Renaissance, Baroque, Rococo, the styles of the Louis: none were developed from within. There is little or nothing organic in their nature. Freedom from the yoke of exterior authority which the Renaissance gave to men was seemingly a great gain. But it eventually served only to bind them senselessly to tradition, and to now mar the more genuine art of the Middle Ages past repair. One cannot go into the beautiful medieval edifices either made or marred in this later period without hatred of the word Renaissance growing in his soul. "Rebirth" proves itself most wantonly destructive of Birth: a hideous perversity. In every land where Gothic, Byzantine (or the Romanesque that was close to Byzantine) once grew it is now a soulless blight. What lovely things remain are left to us in spite of itself or when it was least itself. The Renaissance then was no development. No, it became scholastic eclecticism regardless of Principle.

This is why folk-buildings growing in response to actual needs, fitted into environment by people who knew no better than to fit them to it with native feeling,—buildings that grew as folk-lore and folk-song grew,—are today for us better worth study than all the highly self-conscious academic attempts at the beautiful throughout all Europe: these attempts which nations seem to possess in common as learned from Italy, after

89

acknowledging her own source of inspiration. Italian gifts which have been universally betrayed by all the cultures of the world before they were finally betrayed by our own new free country and later betrayed by the Italians themselves.

———

All Architecture, worthy the name will, henceforward, more and more be organic. Architecture will be native growth in accord with natural feeling and industrial means to serve with art —actual needs. Organic Architecture cannot be put on anywhere from the outside. There is little sympathy with the spirit creating it and the understanding of the ideals that shaped it that can be utilized by other peoples in other times and conditions. Attempts to use forms borrowed from other cultures and conditions other than one's own must end as the Renaissance ends,—with total loss of inherent relation of Art and Architecture to the soul-life of the People.

In the hands of professors, Fine Art can give us only an extraneous thing meaning little more than a mask for untoward circumstances or some mark of temporal power to those whose lives are eventually burdened, not expressed by it. The result is a terrible loss to life, world-wide, for which no Literature nor Science can compensate. The buildings we have a right to call Architecture will always remain the most valuable asset in a people's environment or Art: the asset most capable of joygiving, cultural reaction. Until our people find joy again in such Architecture as belongs to them, seen by them as the living art one sees recorded in buildings of all truly cultural periods of civilization, just so long will Architecture remain a dead thing. Architecture cannot live again until we break away entirely from adherence to the eclecticisms that were the effulgent glory of the Renaissance.

———

In America, we—a "new" country (even if composite) are more betrayed by ever-present parasitic conditions than people of the old-world. We have no traditional forms except those accumulated of all peoples at all times in all places and that do not, without great sacrifice of the appropriate, fit new conditions. In consequence among us there is no true reverence for Tradition except as a means to borrow respectability not our own. As some sort of architecture was quick necessity, so American-architects took their pick from the world's stock. "Readymade" architecture directly transplanted was too successful. Transplanting form for form, line for line, enlarging details by means of lantern slides from photographs of the originals, as were most of the buildings in New York and Washington, was accepted as the best possible practice.

Modern comforts were smuggled in, cleverly sometimes, as we must admit. But is this debased practice of the imitator the practice of Architecture? Is it thus that great Style was molded? In this polyglot tangle of borrowed forms, is there no Spirit able to bring order out of chaos: vitality, unity and greatness out of emptiness and discord? The record answers no. All may read that answer now not in the stars but in the city streets.

So, American-Renaissance of the various forms of Renaissance of the great Italian-Renaissance was the rebirth of a rebirth, by abortion, of an architecture thought to be "artistic," but before all else—inorganic: a nightmare.

Any reasonable conception of what now constitutes Organic-architecture will lead us to better things when once planted in the hearts and minds of men whose resource, skill, and real power, are unquestioned. True individuals. Were they not obsessed by expedients and forms now meaningless the nature and origin of which they have not studied in relation to what produced them they might, already, have done great things. This Nature of true Form is evaded, not honestly sought nor can be taught in any of the schools of any nation in which architects are now trained.

I suggest that a revival, not of the Gothic style but of the Gothic spirit, is needed in the Art and Architecture of the modern life of the world. We all now need interpretation of the best traditions in the world but made to match the great Tradition and our own individual methods. We must repulse every stupid attempt to imitate and fasten ancient forms, however scientific—upon a life that must outgrow them however great they seem. Reviving the Gothic-spirit would necessarily not mean using the forms of Gothic architecture as handed down to us from "Les Moyen Age." It necessarily would mean something quite different. Conditions and Ideals fixing the forms of the twelfth—say—are not those conditions and ideals that can truthfully (or profitably) fix forms of the amazing mechanization of the Twentieth Century. The Spirit that fixed those forms will be the Spirit that will fix the new forms. Classicist and schools will, of course, proceed to deny the new forms and finding no "Gothic" in them scorn and repulse them. It will not much matter. The new forms—if

actual—will be living, doing their work quietly and effectively
until all these borrowed garments now being cut over to fit
by Academies are cast off, having served only to hide the
pitiful nakedness of a moment when Art became detached,
alien to the lives of people: academic. An affair for museums,
of institutes and standardized universities—weaknesses only
exaggerated by the facilities afforded by modern machinery.

America—a democratic republic—more than any nation
poses this new architectural problem. In democratic spirit at
least, her institutions are (professedly) conceived. This should
mean that our country places a life-premium upon Individuality as the highest possible development of the individual
consistent with a harmonious life of the whole: believing that
any "whole" benefited by sacrifice of that quality in the individual rightly considered his "individuality" is at least unde-
veloped, if not gone wrong. Believing, too, that the whole to
be worthy as complete must consist of individual units, great
and strong in themselves, not units yoked from outside in
bondage but united by spirit from inside with the right to
freely move, resist aggression or invasion, but only each in its
own sphere. Yet, all preserving this right to the highest possible degree for all. This alone can mean greater individual
life and more privacy in life—concerns peculiarly one's own.
This is the only guarantee for human lives lived in greater
independence and seclusion with all toward which an English
nobleman once aspired. But, with absolute unwillingness to
pay the price in paternalism and patronage asked of him for
his privilege. I am sure that this dream of freedom was voiced
by our Declaration of Independence and was dear to the
heart of every man who caught the spirit of American institutions. Therefore it still is now the more or less conscious
Ideal of every man truly "American" in feeling and spirit in
whatever Nation he may be born or live. Individuality then is
a great, strong national Ideal. Where this Ideal degenerates
to petty individualism, nationalism or personal license it is
but a manifestation of weakness in the human nature involved.
Such degeneracy is not a fatal flaw in the Democratic Ideal.
Privileges accorded those who have not earned them either
from the top down or from the bottom up, cannot exist without damage to all concerned. The lower down abuse of privilege goes the greater the damage done the individual and
more likely the insult to Life itself.
    In America each man, then, does have this peculiar, inalien-

able right to live his life in his own house in his own way. He is pioneer, there at least—in the right sense of that word. So his home-environment may now face forward and portray his own character by way of his own "tastes" and preferably his ideas (if he has any). Every man has some somewhere about him?

————

Now this is a dangerous condition of society at which Englishmen and all Europeans, facing backward toward traditional forms which they feel in duty bound to preserve, may well stand aghast. But an American is in duty bound to establish new traditions in harmony with his new ideals of Freedom and Individuality. He wishes them to harmonize his still unspoiled sites with his new industrial opportunities. Industrially the American Nation is more completely committed to the Machine than any living. So the Machine has already given the citizen things which mean mastery over a dead past in a prolific but yet uncultured land,—where comfort and resources are easily his and, unfortunately, a taste for domination now where he—as a democratic citizen—has no business to be.

Therefore this great lever, the Machine, is the tool in the use of which his present opportunity lies. The Machine can only murder the traditional forms of other peoples and earlier times. All of them. To be true to himself in this new opportunity the architect must find new forms, new industrial methods or stultify the life of his greatest opportunity to live nobly as himself. Underneath all forms whatever in all ages whatsoever, certain conditions existed which determined the grammar of architectural forms naturally. In them all was a human-spirit in accord with which form came to be, or died. Wherever these forms became true to form they will be found to approach organic forms: to be an outgrowth of conditions of life and work they alone rose to express or could express. These are beautiful and humanly significant forms only if studied in this living-relation. They are dead to us if borrowed as they stand.

I have called this modern feeling for the Organic-character of form and treatment "the Gothic spirit" because it was more nearly realized in forms of that period, perhaps, than in any other period. At least the infinitely varied forms of Gothic architecture are often more literally organic. The Spirit in which they were conceived and wrought was usually one of integrity of means to ends. In this Spirit America—other nations no less—will find forms best suited to her opportunities, aims and her Life.

All great styles, approached from within, are spiritual treasure houses. Transplanted as mere styles, they are only the tombs of a life already lived and past. The grave of Style.

Reaction to this attempted transplantation by culture was inevitable.

It is of this reaction to the Old which we call the New that I feel qualified to speak because the work here illustrated, with the exception of the work of Louis Sullivan, is the first consistent affirmative protest in stone, timber, bricks and mortar against this pitiful waste of good life. Here then in this work is the one early, although belated, serious attempt to formulate new industrial and aesthetic ideals based upon the best of the old ones: an attempt that in quiet, rational ways would help make a lovely thing of the home environment of modern man produced by him with his own tools without abuse: dedicated in spirit and letter to Life as lived by him today.

Ideals of Ruskin and Morris and teaching of the Beaux Arts of Paris especially, have so far prevailed in America as to steadily confuse and demoralize, as well as in some respects unconsciously to reveal to us, our wasted opportunities. The more "cultured" American, too, (of some little old-world culture I mean), disgusted by this state of imitation, and having the beautiful harmony in mind, say of the architecture of an old English village or the better European rural-community, not the dormitory towns, or—sad to say—of the grandiloquent planning of Paris in view, has too easily persuaded himself that the best thing we as a people could do was to adopt some style of planning least foreign to us, stick to that style, plant it and re-plant it continually. A parasitic proceeding at best and in any case—as indigenous Culture—perfectly futile. New York is a tribute to the Beaux Arts in this respect so far as surface-effects go while underneath a tribute to steel in the hands of the American engineer.

Other overgrown (or overgrowing) cities in America have followed New York more or less.

Our better-class residences are chiefly dubious tributes to English architecture. They are "manors" cut open and embellished inside to suit the ignorant "taste." Porches and "conveniences" were added as a matter of course. The result in all cases was and still is a more or less pitiful mongrel. Painfully conscious of their lack of traditions, our powerful get-rich-quick citizens attempt to buy Tradition ready made and are dragged forward facing backwards in attitudes most absurd to contemplate by those whom they would emulate: our most characteristic example of "conspicuous waste." Read Thorstein Veblen.

Well, the point in all this cultural debauchery is the fact that any honest practice of the ideals of an Organic-architecture will have to contend with this rapidly increasing sweep of imported folly, translated to international terms. Even the American with some little culture (going contrary to his usual course in other matters) is becoming painfully aware of his inferiority in matters of dress, Art and Architecture. Egged on by Museums, he is still going "abroad" to import those things to be sure they are correct. Thus assured by our provincial aesthetes he is then no longer concerned. He promptly forgets both. But that ignoble parasitism is more characteristic of the Eastern citizen on the cinder-strip than the Western citizen of the great prairies. The real American spirit, capable of judging an issue for itself upon its own merits lies West and Middle West where breadth of view, independent thought and a tendency to take common-sense into the realm of Art, as in life, are more characteristic. It is alone in an atmosphere of this nature that the Gothic-spirit can be revived in building. In this atmosphere, among clients of this type, I have lived and worked.

Even now, "taking common-sense into this holy realm of Art" is shocking and, so, most unpopular. Really dangerous to all academic circles. The affair as conceived, by them, is a species of vulgarity. Some of these now compromising questions in aesthetics have become so vexed or perplexed and so encrusted by the savants and academies with layer upon layer of "good school" that their very nature is falsified or hidden. Approached with common-sense, they become childishly simple. Perhaps all too simple for those educated so far beyond their capacity as the "Technic first" seem to be.

Nevertheless (rather the more) I believe every matter of artistic import which concerns good building may be put to the common-sense of an American business-man on the right side every time and, thus given a chance to choose, he rarely gives wrong decisions. The difficulty found with this man by the Renaissance however, when the Renaissance tries to get him inside or get inside him (that is, if he is to do more than merely give the order to "go ahead")—arises from the fact that the Renaissance has no organic basis to give him. Beyond "taste" educated or uneducated there is no good reason for doing anything any particular way rather than another way which can be grasped by him as organic. Or, by anybody else. All is "a matter of taste." Taste always is a matter of ignorance. In any organic scheme there are excellent and solemn, even splendid reasons why every solvent is as it is; what the thing is therefore and where and why the whole is going. If not, it ought not to go. As a general thing it doesn't go.

The people themselves are part and parcel helpful in producing the organic thing. They can comprehend and make it theirs.

Organic Architecture is thus the only form of art-expression to be considered for the human faith that is Democracy. I will go so far as to say, the truest of all forms at all times, everywhere, from now forward.

———

So I submit that the buildings illustrated here have, for the greatest part, been conceived and worked to conclusion in the Gothic-spirit both in respect to the tools that produced them, the method of work behind them, and, finally, in their organic-nature when, and if, considered in themselves. These are all most unattractive limitations at present but there is no project in Fine Art that is not at first a problem and that does not carry right there within itself its own solution.

With this idea as basis (and thesis) comes altogether another conception of what constitutes a good building.

The question now arises—what, really, is Style? That problem no longer remains a matter of working in some prescribed style proscribed with what variation it may bear without absurdity if the owner happens to be a restless individualist. Whether individualist or not most owners are restless and fearful of change. So this question of Style is not so easily answered.

"There is nothing so timid as a million dollars. Unless it is ten million." I quote myself.

———

What is Style? Every flower has it; every animal too; every individual worthy the name, has style in some degree no matter how much sandpaper (the University) may have done for him. Style is a free product but, still, a by-product: the result of the organic working in, and out of, a project entirely in character, altogether and in one state of feeling.

An harmonious entity of whatever sort in its entirety cannot fail of style in the best sense. Entity alone lives.

So in all matters of Fine Art the individual feeling of the

creative artist can give but the color of his own likes and dislikes—his own soul—to anything he shapes. His individuality (above personality) he gives—truly—but this will not prevent the building he designs from being characteristic of those it was built to serve. Because what he gives is necessarily a solution of conditions those for whom it was built, themselves make. The opus is made to serve their ends in their own way but with a skill far greater than their own. In so far as these client-conditions are peculiar in themselves, or real sympathy exists between them and their architect—as it should—the building will be their building no less than their architect's: theirs more truly than though in ignorant selfhood they had stupidly sought to use means they had never conquered to an end imperfectly foreseen. The Architect, then, is their technique and interpreter. Their building is interpretation if the client is true to his architect and the architect is true to the client in Gothic sense. If an architect is chiefly concerned with some marvelous result that shall stand as architecture in good form to his own credit, client be damned? Why that is misfortune which may be said to be only another species of the unwisdom of his client. Of course this kind of architect is a dangerous man and there are many of his kind outside (and some temptations to him inside) the ranks of the Gothic spirit. But that man who loves the beautiful with ideals of organic Nature (if he is artist) is too keenly sensible of the nature of his client as a fundamental condition in his problem to cast him off although he may give him something to grow to; some finer thing in which he may be a little ill at ease at the outset.

In all this—as a matter of course—lie temptation to abuses. Where ignorance of the nature of anything exists or where there exists a particular character or preference it is to a certain extent the duty of an architect to give his client something to grow toward—something dated ahead. Because he is entrusted with his client's interests in matters of which, more frequently than not, his client is wholly ignorant. Therefore a "commission" becomes a trust to the architect. Any architect is bound to educate his client to the extent of his true skill and capacity in what he as a true advisor believes fundamentally right in the circumstances. But even in this matter there is plenty of leeway for abuse of the client; temptations to sacrifice him in the interest of personal idiosyncrasies or to work along lines instinctively the architect's own preference and therefore easier to him. But in any trust there is some chance of failure? This educational relationship between Client and Architect is no exception. This is more or less to be expected and of value artistically, too, for the reason that while the architect is educating the client his client is educating him. The client himself is a certain determining factor in this quality of style so this matter of style grows partly out of this relation of architect and client to the work in hand, as well as to the more definite elements of construction. So Style, as a quality, is a subtle thing and should remain so. Style is not to be defined in itself as much as it is to be regarded as the net result of artistic integrity on the part of the creative Architect.

"Style," then, if conditions are consistently and artistically cared for little by little will, out of itself, take care of itself. As for any working in a prenominated "style" beyond the natural predilection for certain forms, it is unthinkable by the author of any true building fit to be called creative architecture.

Given similar conditions, similar tools, similar people, similar language, I believe architects will, with proper regard for the organic nature of the thing produced arrive at greatly varied results; buildings sufficiently harmonious with each other and more and more so with great individuality. One might sweep all the Gothic architecture of the world together into a single nation, mingle it with buildings treated horizontally just as they were once treated vertically or treated diagonally; buildings and towers with flat roofs, long low buildings with square openings mingled with tall buildings with pointed ones in all the bewildering variety of that marvelous architectural manifestation and harmony in the general ensemble be inevitably the result. The common chord in all individual building being sufficient to bring building in general, unconsciously into harmonious relation throughout.

It is this ideal of a true organic working-out of a building problem to a consistent end with normal means at hand that is real salvation for any client if his "organic" architect is entrusted with true liberty. This architect is really more severely disciplined by his interior ideal than his brothers of "the styles" ever were. He is less likely to falsify his issue.

Therefore to professors looking askance at the mixed "youth material" entrusted to their charge, thinking to save the nation a terrible infliction of the wayward dreams of mere idiosyncrasy by teaching "the safe course of a good copy," we owe thanks for the usual conservative attitude—to be sure. But sharp censure for failure to give to growing material so profoundly needed by our nation today constructive ideals that would from within discipline the architect sufficiently, at the same time leaving him a chance to work out a real building in touch with the new Reality that is now the new Romance with such soul as he might have. In other words Education, world-wide, is to be blamed for not inculcating in students the conception of Architecture as an organic expression of the Nature of an actual building-problem in place and time; teaching them not to look to this actual Nature for the elements of its development in accord with principles easily found in Nature and seen in nature-organisms. Any profound study of the great architectures of the world solely in regard to the Spirit that—once upon a time—found expression in the forms, should go along with this deeper study. But before all should come study of the nature of materials, the nature of the tools and processes at command and the Nature—with capital N—of the thing they are to be called upon to do. By Nature with capital N I mean the word used in interior sense: the nature of an idea—a hand—a thought—a personality, etc., etc.

———

Training of this sort was instinctively accorded the great artists of Japan. Although that training may not have been intellectually self-conscious, I have no doubt that apprenticeship of "Les Moyen Age" wrought for like results.

Some few German and Austrian art-schools now seem to be on the way back to these ideas. But until the student is taught to approach the Beautiful from the within moving to the outward there will be no great, living buildings which in themselves, or in the aggregate, show the Spirit of a true modern Architecture.

———

An Architect, then, in this revived Gothic sense, is a man disciplined from within by a conception of the organic Nature of his task: knowing well his tools, his opportunity and—most important—himself. An Individual working out his problems with what sense of Beauty the gods gave to him.

He, because disciplined by himself from within himself by the very nature of his undertaking is the only safe man for society to employ to build buildings for Today or the Yesterday which is also tomorrow.

To work with this architect is to find master of means to a certain end. By experience, in action, he acquires his own technique in the uses of his tools and materials. His "mastery" may be as complete and in every sense as remarkable as the great composer's mastery of the resources of the instruments for which he composes. In no other spirit is the architect's hold upon true culture to be acquired in any vital sense. Without it? Well . . . a good copy is the safest thing.

If one cannot live an independent life of one's own, one may at least become a modest parasite and, instead of honest arrogance practice hypocritical humility.

———

It is with the courage given by conviction of the truths—though not the expediency—of this point of view that has given you now, A.D. 1910, the solutions of the problems in architecture I have myself attempted. In the spirit I have described they have all been worked out: with what degree of failure or success no one can know better than I. To be of value to sympathetic contemporaries they must be approached from within, and not viewed from the standpoint of the stand-patter looking largely at our foreground from the hinterland of any Renaissance. In so far as the buildings shown here are grasped as organic solutions of conditions which they came to exist but to serve with proper respect to the limitations imposed by our modern industrial conditions, and inasmuch as they have within themselves a harmony of idea in form and treatment that makes something fairly beautiful of them in relation to the life they serve—they will be found helpful—even admirable. Approached from the point of view of one seeking characteristic beauty of form and feature familiar as that of the Greeks, say, or the Japanese, they may be disappointing. I can only add, it may be a little too soon yet to look for the perfect attainment of such familiar recognition. But the quality of Style, in the indefinable sense possessed by the organic thing—that they have. Repose and quiet attitudes they have. Unity of idea, resourceful adaptation of means to ends will not be found wanting nor that simplicity of rendering which the Machine—as a tool not as a fetish—makes not imperative but opportune. Although many of the structures are not so complete or highly developed in detail as I might wish all pay homage to the thought here expressed in this brochure.

Self-imposed limitations are in part responsible for lack of more intricate enrichment. Partly the imperfectly developed resources of our industrial system are responsible. I believe that much ornament in the old sense of "applique" is not for us, because we have lost its significance. I cannot believe in adding enrichment merely for its own sake. Unless "enrichment" by detail adds clearness to the enunciation of the architectural theme, it is always undesirable. Ornament is very little understood by people today. Especially not by Architects.

I wish to say, also, more to the point, that if a structure is conceived in organic sense all ornamentation is conceived as of the very ground plan and is therefore of the very constitution of the structure itself. What ornamentation may be found added purely as such in these structures is thus a makeshift or a confession of weakness or failure, as it actually is and also was in the early days of "grandomania," wherein human scale was belittled by useless exaggeration.

Where the warp and woof of any building-fabric yields insufficient incident or variety, these are seldom patched on for effect. Tenderness in modern building has often to be sacrificed to integrity but human sympathy is not sacrificed.

————

So it is fair to explain the point which seems to be missed in studies of this work of mine—that in the conception of these structures they are regarded by myself as severe conventions whose chief office is good background or a sympathic frame for the life going on within them and around about them. Modern life itself should and does look well in them. Consider them, too, as companions for the foliage and bloom they are arranged to carry as well as that to which they stand as a distinct chord or sometimes merely a contrast. In their severely conventionalized nature they yet do sympathize with the profusion of trees and foliage in which their sites abound and with which they are designed to associate. Surrounding trees flock to them although the buildings are organic abstractions in themselves.

The forms, superdivisions and refinements of form, especially the basic unit-system of the planning are all, perhaps, more elemental in character and more highly developed expressions of structure than has hitherto been the case in Architecture. Ornamental forms of one's environment to be lived with should be designed to wear well which means all must have absolute repose and should make no disturbing claim upon attention by inflexible composition or arrangement; but be removed as far from realistic tendencies only as a sense of the new Reality will take them. Good "alive" color, soft textures, textural materials, beauty of all materials and methods revealed and utilized in the building scheme itself—these are all means of "decoration," so called, although not considered, as such by myself.

———

In Organic Architecture then, it is quite impossible to consider the building as one thing, its furnishings another and its setting and environment still another. The Spirit in which these buildings are conceived sees all these together at work as one thing. All are to be studiously foreseen and provided for in the nature of the structure. All these should become mere details of the character and completeness of the structure. Incorporated (or excluded) are lighting, heating and ventilation. The very chairs and tables, cabinets and even musical instruments, where practicable, are of the building itself, never fixtures upon it. No appliances or fixtures are admitted as such where circumstances permit the full development of the organic character of the building-scheme.

Floor coverings and hangings are at least as much a part of the house as the plaster on the walls or the tiles on the roof. This feature of development called "the furnishings"—has given most trouble so far and is least satisfactory to myself because of difficulties inherent in the completeness of conception and execution necessary within the usual building-budget and total lack of suitable materials in the market. Suitable fabrics, hardware, furniture and all else has yet to be especially made. All available is senselessly ornate. To make these necessary appurtenances elements, themselves sufficiently light, graceful and flexible features of the informal use of an abode, requires much more time and thought on my part as well as more money to spend than is usually forthcoming in our country at this time. But in time this will be accomplished by improvements in all stock articles. This is still in a comparatively primitive stage of development. Yet, stoves and radiators have disappeared, lighting fixtures are becoming incorporated, floor coverings and hangings are becoming textured instead of patterned and many things are even now easily made-over to conform. But chairs as informal movable articles of common use are still at large in most cases. Although I have designed them in feeling with the building I am not satisfied with the comfort they provide.

———

However, there are no "decorations" as such nor is there any place for their application. The easel picture—for instance —has no place on the walls. It is regarded as music might be,

suited to a mood and provided for in a recess of the wall
if desired, where a door like the cover of a portfolio might be
dropped and the particular thing desired revealed and studied
for a time; left exposed for several days perhaps, to give place
to another. Or, be entirely put away by simply closing the
wooden portfolio. Easel pictures might then be possible. Great
pictures should have their gallery. Oratorio is not performed in
a drawing room. The piano or organ wherever possible may and
should disappear in the structure, the key-board or whatever
openwork or tracery is necessary for sound to emerge its only
visible feature. Dining table and chairs are easily managed
with the architecture of the building. Only so far as this has
development progressed.

In our vast country alternate violent extremes of heat and
cold, of sun and storm have to be considered. In the North frost
goes four feet into the ground in winter while in summer the
sun beats fiercely on the roofs with almost tropical heat. Um-
brageous architecture is therefore desirable—almost a necessity
both to shade the building from the sun and protect the walls
from alternate freezing and thawing. Changes of temperature
are more rapidly destructive to buildings than almost all other
natural causes. Overhanging eaves, however, leave the house
in winter without necessary sun, and this is overcome by the
way in which the window groups in certain rooms and exposure
are pushed out to the gutter line and the eaves perforated to
allow sunlight to penetrate. Gently sloping roofs on most of
these houses are grateful to the prairie on which they stand
as well as to the hills and valleys. They also leave insulating
air spaces above the rooms. The chimney has grown and is
still growing in dimensions and importance. The kitchen also.
In hot weather both features ventilate the whole edifice at
these high parts. Circulating air-spaces beneath the roofs are
also included, fresh air entering beneath the eaves through
openings easily closed in winter.

Conductor pipes, disfiguring down-spouts, particularly
where eaves overhang, freeze in this climate, become useless
in winter or burst with disastrous results. So concrete rain-
basins are built on the ground-level beneath the outer corners
of the eaves. Roof-water drops down through open spouts in
the eaves into their concave surfaces to be conducted to the
cistern by underground drain-tiles.

Another modern opportunity is afforded by our effective
system of hot water heating. By this means the forms of
buildings may be more completely articulated: light, air and

view had on several sides. By keeping ceilings generally low in cold climates the walls may be opened with series of windows to the outer air and the surrounding flowers and trees, to the general prospects, so one may live with a greater sense of space as comfortably as formerly but much less shut in. Many of these structures carry this principle of space and articulation of various parts to the point where each room has its own individuality and its use completely recognized in floor-plan. Dining-room, kitchen and sleeping rooms thus may become small buildings in themselves. All rooms are grouped together as a whole, as in the Coonley house. It is also possible to spread the buildings which once upon a time in our climate of extremes were a compact box cut into compartments, and expand them into a more spacious expression of organic space—making a house in a garden or in the country the delightful thing in relation to either or both that fresh imagination would have it.

The horizontal line is the line of domesticity.

The virtue of horizontal lines is respectfully invoked in almost all of these buildings. Inches in height gain tremendously in force compared with any spread practicable upon the ground.

To Europeans these buildings may, on paper, seem uninhabitable; but they derive air and dignity by quite other means than excess height and all respect one ancient tradition at least—the only one here worthy of respect—the good ground itself.

In considering the various forms and types of these structures, the fact that nearly all were buildings for our vast Western-prairie should be borne in mind; the gently rolling or level prairies of our great Middle west; the great rolling prairies where every detail of elevation becomes exaggerated; every tree towers above the great calm plains of flowered surfaces as the plain lies serene beneath a wonderful unlimited sweep of sky. The natural tendency of every ill-considered thing on the prairie is to detach itself and stick out like a sore thumb in surroundings, by nature perfectly quiet. All unnecessary heights have for that reason and the human scale (for other reasons, economic) been eliminated. More intimate relation with outdoor environment and far-reaching vista is sought to compensate desirable loss of height.

The differentiation of a single, certain simple form charac-

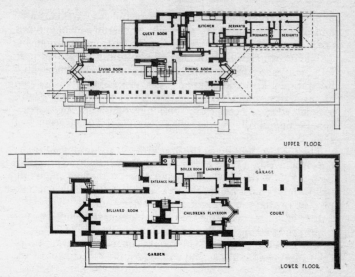

UPPER FLOOR

LOWER FLOOR

1909 Frederick C. Robie house, *Chicago, Ill.* Plans of upper and lower floors.

terizes the expression of any one building. Quite a different one may serve for another. But, from one basic idea all form or formal elements of design are in each case derived and held firmly together in human-scale and appropriate character. The form chosen may flare outward opening flower-like to the sky as in the Thomas house; another, droop to accentuate artistically the weight of the masses; another be non-committal or abruptly emphatic. Or, grammar may be deduced from some plant form that has appealed to me, as certain properties in line and form of the sumac were used in the Lawrence house at Springfield. But in every case the motif is adhered to throughout the building.

The buildings themselves, in the sense of the whole, lack neither richness nor incident. But these qualities are secured not by applied decoration. They are found in the fashioning of the whole in which color, too, plays as significant a part as it does in an old Japanese wood block print.

These ideals when put into practice take buildings out of school and marry them to the ground; make them all intimate expressions (or revelations) of interiors and individualize them regardless of preconceived notions of Style. I have tried to make their grammar perfect in its way and to give their forms and proportions integrity that will bear study although few of them can be intelligently studied apart from environment.

The drawings will show that the buildings presented here fall readily into three groups having a family resemblance; the low-pitched hip roofs heaped together in pyramidal fashion or presenting quiet unbroken sky lines; the low roofs with simple pediments countering on long ridges; and those structures economically topped with a simple flat projecting roof slab.

The Larkin Building is the first great protestant against the outrageous elaboration of the period. An affirmative negation, however. It is the simple, dignified direct utterance of a plain, utilitarian type, with sheer brick walls and the indispensable protective stone-copings this climate demands.

It is of course desirable that suitable mural-decoration and appropriate sculpture should again take place in these structures as architectural developments conceived to conform to their fabric and purpose and to modern life.

To thus make of a human dwelling-place a complete work of art, in itself expressive and beautiful, intimately related to modern life and fit to live in, lending itself more freely and suitably to the individual needs of the dwellers as itself an harmonious entity, fitting in color, pattern and nature the utilities and be really an expression of them in character,—this is the tall modern American opportunity in Architecture. True basis of a true Culture. An exalted view to take of the "property instinct" of our times? But once founded and on view I believe this Ideal will become a new Tradition: a vast step in advance of the prescribed fashion in a day when a dwelling was a composite of cells arranged as separate rooms: chambers to contain however good aggregations of furniture, utility comforts not present: a property-interest chiefly. An organic-entity, this modern building, as contrasted with that former insensate aggregation of parts. Surely we have here the higher ideal of unity as a more intimate working out of the expression of one's life in one's environment. One great thing instead of a quarreling collection of so many little things.

1908 Avery Coonley house, *Riverside, Ill.* Detail.

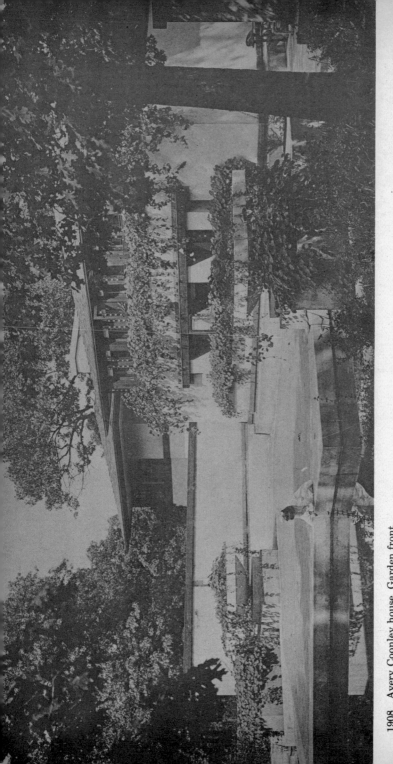

1908 Avery Coonley house. Garden front.

1909   Frederick C. Robie house, *Chicago, Ill.*

1904   Larkin Company administration building, *Buffalo, N.Y.*
(Demolished 1950.) Interior.

1904   Larkin Company administration building.

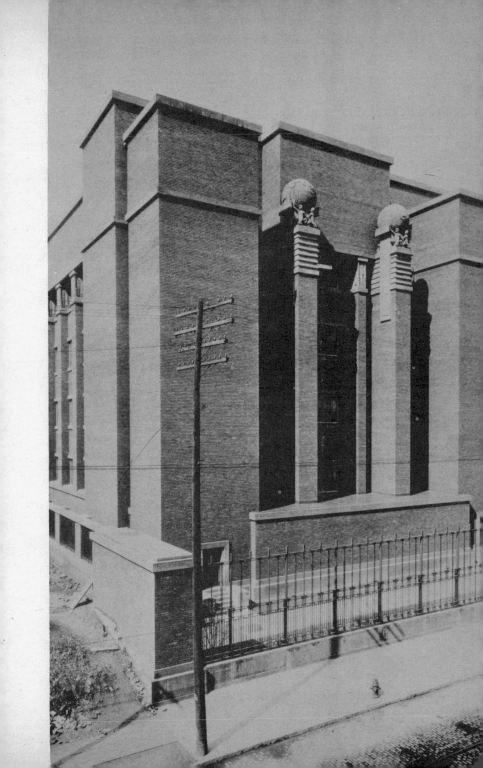

1904   Steel office furniture for
the Larkin Company building.

1895   Frank Lloyd Wright studio, *Oak Park, Ill.*

1915   American System Ready-Cut prefabricated flats, project. Perspective.

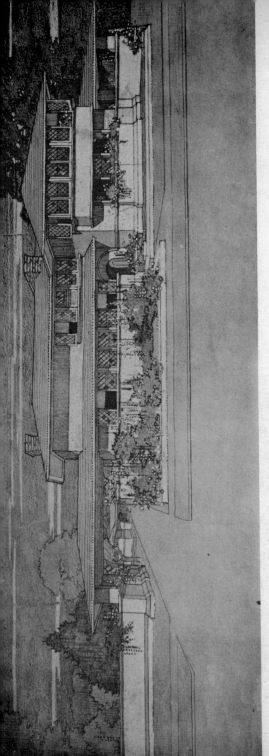

1900 "Home in a Prairie Town" for the *Ladies' Home Journal.* Perspective.

1906 Unity Church and Parish House, *Oak Park, Ill.*

1911   Taliesin, Frank Lloyd Wright's home, remodeled through 1959, *Spring Green, Wis.* Courtyard.

1911   Taliesin. Terrace.

1911   Taliesin. Balcony.

1911   Taliesin. Detail.

1914   Midway Gardens, restaurants and concert garden,
Chicago, Ill. (Demolished 1923.) Detail.

1914 Midway Gardens.

1911 Sherman N. Booth house, project, *Glencoe, Ill.* Perspective.

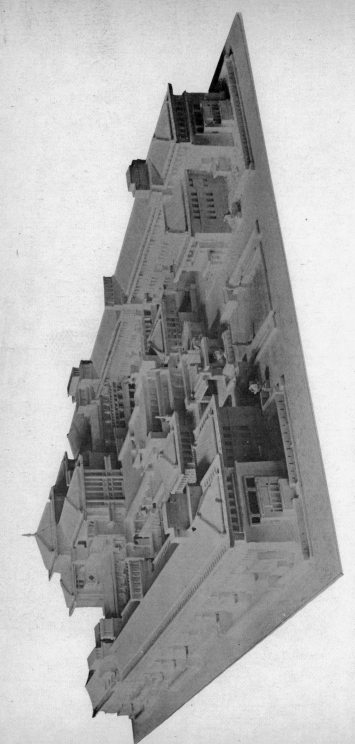

1916 Imperial Hotel, *Tokyo, Japan*. (Completed 1922.) Model.

1916   Imperial Hotel. Courtyard.

1916 Imperial Hotel. Garden.

1920 Hollyhock House, Olive Hill, Hollywood, Los Angeles, Cal.

126

1923   La Miniatura, *Pasadena, Cal.*
Concrete Block construction.

1923   La Miniatura. Entrance.

1923   Dr. John Storer house, *Los Angeles, Cal.* Concrete block construction.

1924   Charles Ennis house, *Los Angeles, Cal.* Concrete block construction. Detail.

128

1922   Cabin for resort project, *Lake Tahoe, Cal.*

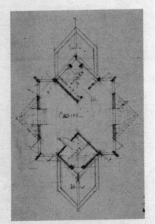

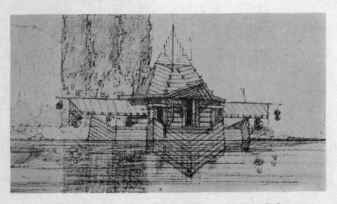

1922   Barge for resort project (with plan), *Lake Tahoe, Cal.*

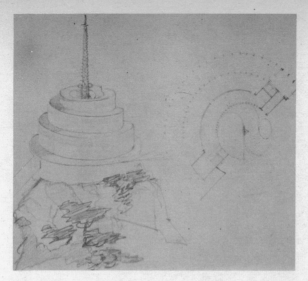

1925 Planetarium, project for *Sugar Loaf Mountain, Md.*
Sketch.

1929 Rosenwald Foundation, school project, *La Jolla, Cal.* Perspective.

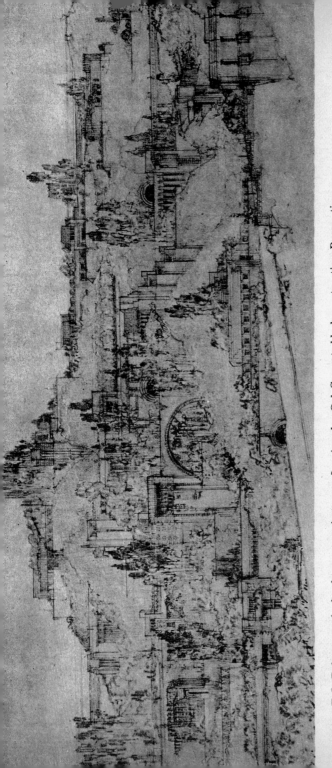

130

1921 E. L. Doheny ranch, development project, near *Los Angeles, Cal.* Concrete block construction. Perspective.

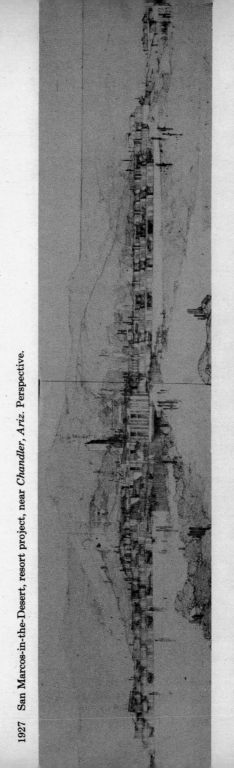

1927   San Marcos-in-the-Desert, resort project, near *Chandler, Ariz.* Perspective.

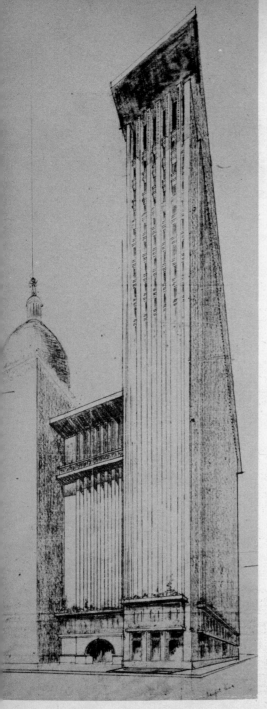

1920 Press Building project, *San Francisco, Cal.* Perspective.

1953   H. C. Price Company, tower with offices and apartments,
Bartlesville, Okla. (Completed 1956; based on project of 1929.)

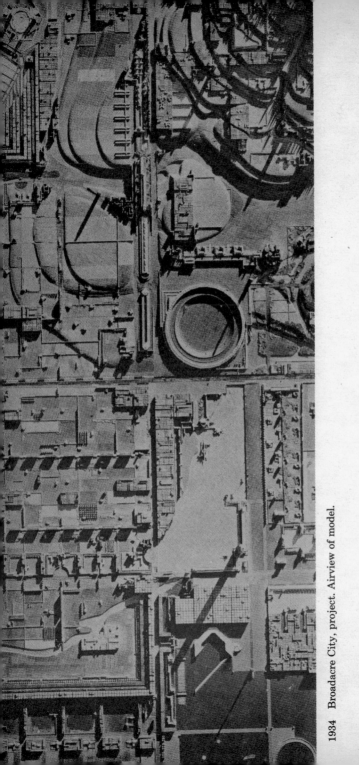

1934 Broadacre City, project. Airview of model.

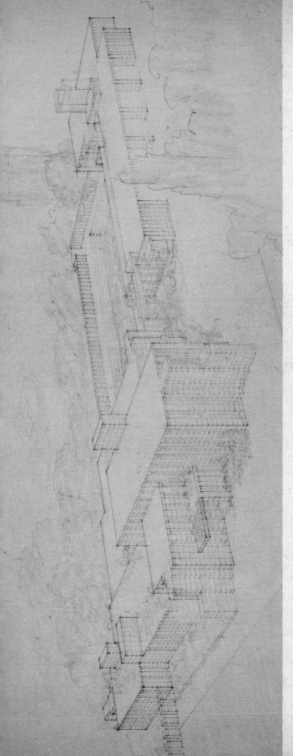

1929   Richard Lloyd Jones house, *Tulsa, Okla.* Concrete block construction. Perspective.

1939 Fallingwater, on *Bear Run, Pa.* Terrace.

1936 Fallingwater.

1944   S. C. Johnson and Son, Laboratory Tower. (Completed 1950.) Night view.

1936   S. C. Johnson and Son, administration center. (Completed 1950.) Airview.

1936   S. C. Johnson and Son, main administration building. (Completed 1939.) Lobby.

141

1936   S. C. Johnson and Son, main administration building, *Racine, Wis.*
(Completed 1939.) Main office.

142

1939   Winkler-Goetsch house, *Okemos, Mich.*

1949   Lowell Walter house, *Quasqueton, Iowa.*

1941 C. D. Wall house, *Plymouth, Mich.*

145

1940 Lloyd Lewis house, *Libertyville, Ill.* Living room.

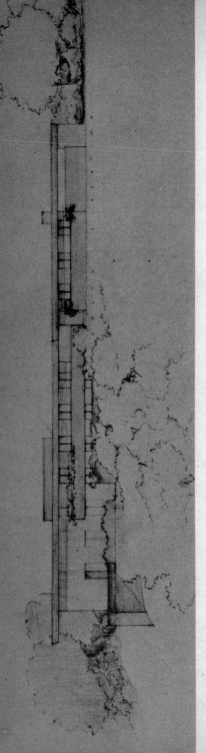

1945   Douglas Grant house, near *Des Moines, Iowa.* (Completed 1951.) Perspective.

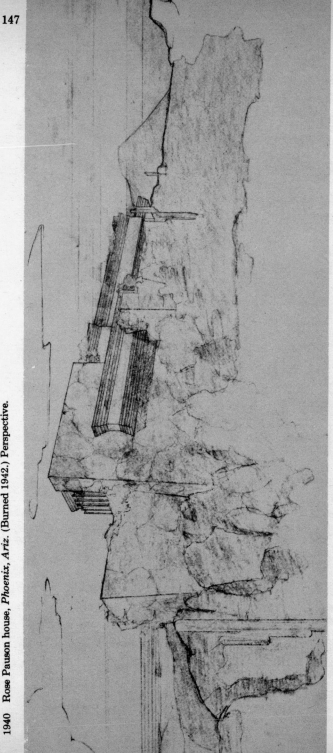

147

1940 Rose Pauson house, *Phoenix, Ariz.* (Burned 1942.) Perspective.

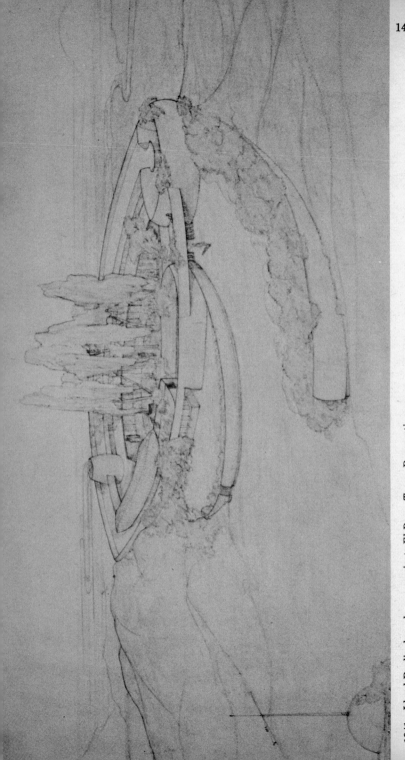

1941 Lloyd Burlingham house, project, *El Paso, Texas.* Perspective.

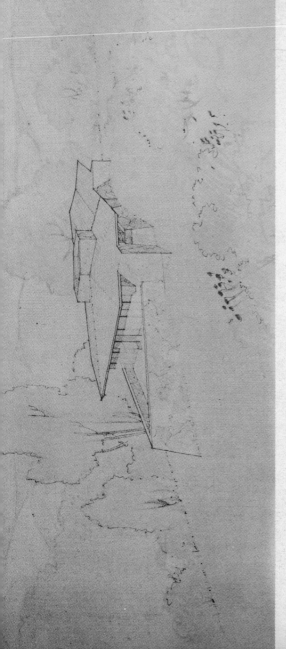

149

1951   Robert Berger house, *San Anselmo, Cal.* (1952–) Perspective.

1938 Florida Southern College, *Lakeland, Fla.*
(Continued through 1959.) Library.

1940 Florida Southern College. Ann Pfeiffer Chapel.

151

1938   Florida Southern College. Administration building.

1938   Taliesin West, Frank Lloyd Wright's winter home, near *Scottsdale, Ariz.* (Remodeled through 1959.) General view.

1938 Taliesin West. Pool near terrace.

1938   Taliesin West. Fireplace.

1938   Taliesin West. Interior of loggia.

1938   Taliesin West. Terrace.

1958   Taliesin West. Bridge and pool.

1943   Solomon R. Guggenheim Museum, *New York, N.Y.* (Completed 1959.) Interior.

1943   Solomon R. Guggenheim Museum. Perspective.

1943   Solomon R. Guggenheim Museum. Interior.

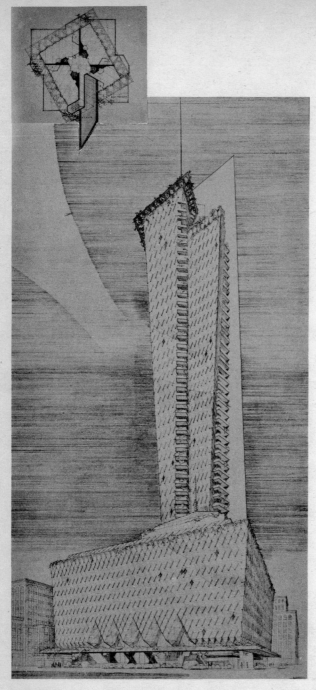

1946   Rogers Lacy Hotel, project, *Dallas, Texas.*
Perspective and plan.

1957   State Capitol, project, near *Phoenix, Ariz.* Perspective.

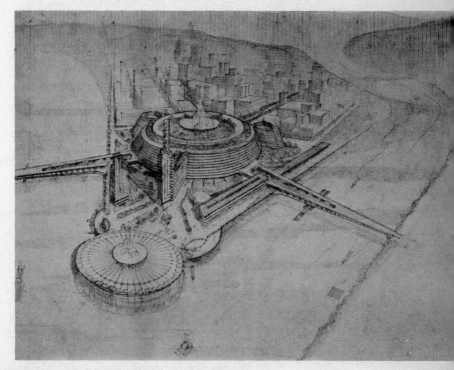

1947   Point Park, project, *Pittsburgh, Pa.* Perspective.

1945   V. C. Morris house, project, *San Francisco, Cal.* Perspective.

161

1947 Huntington Hartford Country Club, project, *Hollywood, Los Angeles, Cal.* Cottage center.

1949   Kenneth Laurent house, *Rockford, Ill.*
(Completed 1951; enlarged 1959.) Perspective.

1950   David Wright house, *Phoenix, Ariz.*
(Completed 1952.) Perspective.

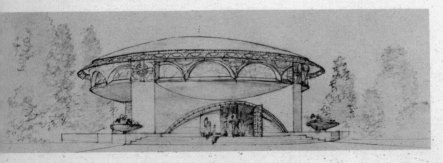

1956   Greek Orthodox Church, *Wauwatosa, Wis.*
(In construction.) Perspective.

1947   V. C. Morris gift shop, *San Francisco, Cal.* Interior.

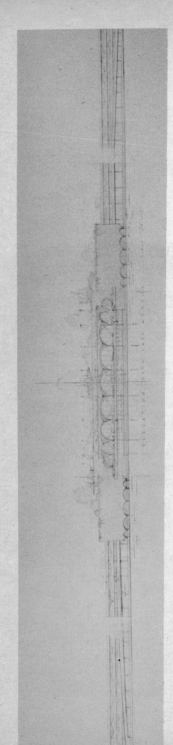

1955 Monona Terrace, civic center project, *Madison, Wis.* Perspective.

1955   H. C. Price house, *Phoenix, Ariz.*

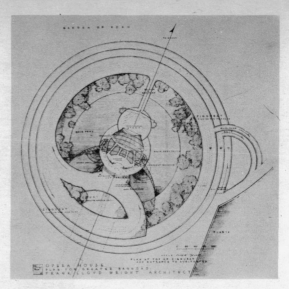

1957   Opera House, project for *Baghdad, Iraq*. Plan.

1957   Opera House. Perspective.

1958 Marin County Government Buildings, near *San Francisco, Cal.* (Under construction 1960.) Perspective.

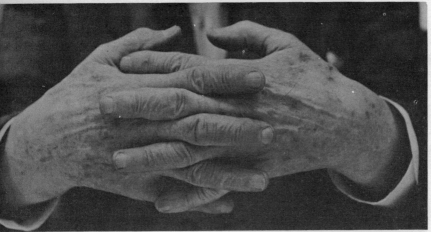

1953 Frank Lloyd Wright demonstrates structure with his hands: (top) "the expression of reverence and aspiration without recourse to the steeple" (in the Unitarian Church, Madison, Wis.); (center) the tensile strength of organic architecture as against "the old post and beam construction" (bottom).

1959 Mrs. D. J. Donahoe, project of three connected houses, near *Scottsdale, Ariz.* Perspective.

169

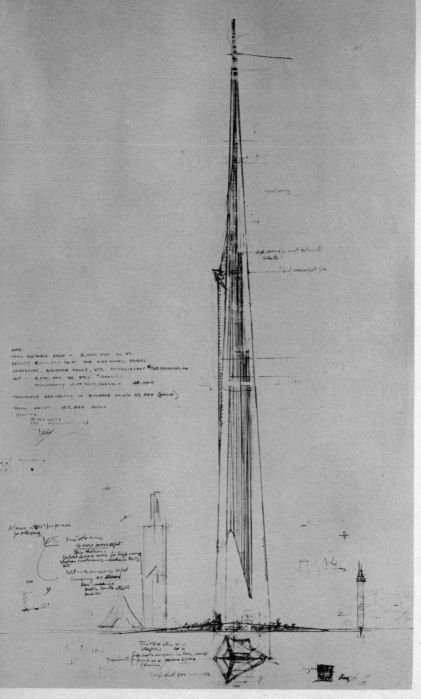

1956   The Mile-High Illinois, skyscraper project, 528 floors,
Chicago, Ill. Perspective.

1911-1916

Frank Lloyd Wright returned from Europe, after his works were published in 1910, to live on the Wisconsin farmland where he had worked summers as a lad. More of his effort now was spent planning real-estate developments and pre-fabricated structural systems than homes. The first slab skyscraper (a form adapted to vertical transportation shafts) was designed for San Francisco by Wright at this time in a relatively untried material, concrete; it was never built, but the form has become standard. Another exceptional commission of these years was Midway Gardens, a large popular restaurant and concert hall for Chicago. Though destined for demolition in the unprofitable Prohibition years, the Gardens were Wright's most accomplished experiment in total design. He was responsible for a complex, extended building framed in concrete, complete with planting, lighting, decorations both mural and sculptural, and a variety of furnishings, not all carried out. The artistic success was undeniable; the artistic daring equalled it. In these same years arose the first Taliesin, Wright's country home that was to be twice destroyed by fire (see An AUTOBIOGRAPHY). As Midway Gardens neared completion, the first and worst fire occurred. Wright determined to rebuild his home in spite of all. A new, more handsome structure arose on the beautiful Wisconsin hillside. Europe, which accepted Wright as his own country did not, was closed by war; but Japan, where Wright had visited ten years earlier as an amateur of prints, now sent emissaries of its Emperor to invite Wright to design a new hotel for Tokyo. Selected after a world-wide search for the best talent, Wright could hardly refuse an opportunity so flattering and challenging, to work in a culture that he admired, with almost every physical factor unlike those he was used to. His preliminary ideas were accepted, and he sailed for Japan.

Taliesin

Taliesin was the name of a Welsh Poet. A druid-bard or singer of songs who sang to Wales the glories of Fine Art. Literally the Welsh word means "shining brow." Many legends cling to the name in Wales.

And Richard Hovey's charming masque "Taliesin" had made me acquainted with his image of the historic bard. Since all my relatives had Welsh names for their places, why not for mine? . . .

This hill on which Taliesin now stands as "brow" was one of my favorite places when I was a boy, for pasque flowers grew there in March sun while snow still streaked the hillsides.

When you are on its crown you are out in mid-air as though swinging in a plane, as the Valley and two others drop away leaving the tree-tops all about you. "Romeo and Juliet" stands in plain view to the southeast, the Hillside Home School just over the ridge.

As "the boy" I had learned the ground-plan of the region in every line and feature.

Its "elevation" for me now is the modelling of the hills, the weaving and the fabric that clings to them, the look of it all in tender green or covered with snow or in full glow of summer that bursts into the glorious blaze of autumn.

I still feel myself as much a part of it as the trees and birds and bees, and red barns, or as the animals are, for that matter.

So, when family-life in Oak Park in that spring of 1909, con-spired against the freedom to which I had come to feel every soul entitled and I had no choice would I keep my self-respect, but go out, a voluntary exile, into the uncharted and unknown deprived of legal protection to get my back against the wall and live, if I could, an unconventional life—then I turned to the hill in the Valley as my Grandfather before me had turned to America—as a hope and haven—forgetful for the time being of grandfathers' "Isaiah." Smiting and punishment.

Architecture, by now, was mine. It had come by actual experience to mean to me something out of the ground of what we call "America," something in league with the stones of the field, in sympathy with "the flower that fadeth, the grass that withereth," something of the prayerful consideration for the lilies of the field that was my gentle grandmother's. Something natural to the change that was "America" herself.

And it was unthinkable that any house should be put *on* that beloved hill.

I knew well by now that no house should ever be *on* any hill or *on* anything. It should be *of* the hill, belonging to it, so hill and house could live together each the happier for the other. That was the way everything found round about it was natu-rally managed, except when man did something. When he added his mite he became imitative and ugly. Why? Was there no natural house? I had proved, I felt, that there was, and now

1925 Taliesin, Frank Lloyd Wright's home, *Spring Green, Wis.* Plan. This version expanded from the 1911 plan. (Photographs on pages 116–118.)

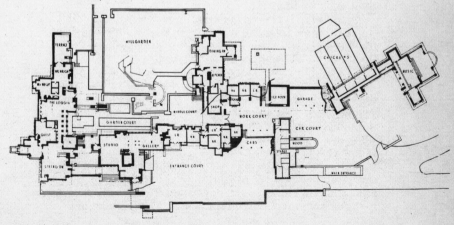

I, too, wanted a *natural* house to live in myself. I scanned the hills of the region where the rock came cropping out in strata to suggest buildings. How quiet and strong the rock-ledge masses looked with the dark red cedars and white birches, there, above the green slopes. They were all part of the countenance of southern Wisconsin.

I wished to be part of my beloved southern Wisconsin and not put my small part of it out of countenance. Architecture, after all, I have learned, or before all, I should say, is no less a weaving and a fabric than the trees. And as anyone might see, a beech tree is a beech tree. It isn't trying to be an oak. Nor is a pine trying to be a birch although each makes the other more beautiful when seen together.

The world has had appropriate buildings before—why not more appropriate buildings now than ever before? There must be some kind of house that would belong to that hill, as trees and the ledges of rock did; as Grandfather and Mother had belonged to it, in their sense of it all.

Yes, there must be a natural house, not natural as caves and log-cabins were natural but native in spirit and making, with all that architecture had meant whenever it was alive in times past. Nothing at all that I had ever seen would do. This country had changed all that into something else. Grandfather and Grandmother were something splendid in themselves that I couldn't imagine in any period houses I had ever seen. But there was a house that hill might marry and live happily with ever after. I fully intended to find it. I even saw, for myself, what it might be like and began to build it as the "brow" of the hill.

It was still a very young faith that undertook to build it. But it was the same faith that plants twigs for orchards, vineslips for vineyards, and small whips that become beneficent shade trees. And it did plant them, too, all about!

I saw the hill crown back of the house, itself a mass of apple trees in bloom, the perfume drifting down the valley, later, the boughs bending to the ground with the red and white and yellow spheres that make the apple tree no less beautiful than the orange tree. I saw the plum trees, fragrant drifts of snow-white in the spring, in August loaded with blue and red and yellow plums, scattering over the ground at a shake of the hand. I saw the rows on rows of berry bushes, necklaces of pink and green gooseberries hanging to the under side of green branches. Saw thickly pendent clusters of rubies like tassels in the dark leaves of the currant bushes. The rich odor of the

black currant, I remembered and looked forward to in quantity.
Black cherries. White cherries.

The strawberry beds, white, scarlet and green over the covering of clean wheat-straw.

I saw abundant asparagus in rows and a stretch of sumptuous rhubarb that would always be enough. I saw the vineyard on the south slope of the hill, opulent vines loaded with purple, green and yellow grapes, boys and girls coming in with baskets filled to overflowing to set about the rooms, like flowers. Melons lying thick in the trailing green on the hill slope. Bees humming over all storing up honey in the white rows of hives beside the chicken yard.

And the herd that I would have! The gentle Holsteins and a monarch of a bull—a glittering decoration of the fields and meadows as they moved. The sheep grazing the meadows and hills, the bleat of the little white lambs in the spring.

The grunting sows to turn the waste to solid gold.

I saw the spirited—well-schooled horses, black horses and white mares with glossy coats and splendid strides, being saddled and led to the mounting-block for rides about the place and along the country lanes I loved—the best of companionship alongside. The sturdy teams ploughing in the fields. The changing colors of the slopes, from seeding time to harvest. I saw the scarlet comb of the rooster and his hundreds of hens—their white eggs. The ducks upon the pond. The geese—and swans floating in the shadow of the trees upon the water.

I saw the peacocks Javanese and white on the walls of the courts. And from the vegetable gardens I walked into a deep cavern in the hill—the rootcellar of my grandfather—and saw its wide sand floor planted with celery, piled with squash and turnips, potatoes, carrots, onions, parsnips, cabbages wrapped and hanging from the roof. Apples, pears and grapes stored in wooden crates walled the cellar from floor to roof. And cream! All the cream the boy had been denied. Thick—so lifting it in a spoon it would float like an egg on the fragrant morning cup of coffee or ride on the scarlet strawberries.

Yes, Taliesin should be a garden and a farm behind a workshop and a home.

I saw it all, and planted it all and laid the foundation of the herd, flocks, stable and fowls as I laid the foundation of the house.

All these items of livelihood came back—improved—from boyhood.

And so began a "shining brow" for the hill, the hill rising

unbroken above to crown the exuberance of life in all these rural riches.

There was a stone quarry on another hill a mile away, where the yellow sand-limestone, when uncovered, lay in strata like the outcropping ledges in the façades of the hills.

The look of it was what I wanted for such masses as would rise from the slopes. The teams of neighboring farmers soon began hauling it over to the hill, doubling the teams to get it to the top. Long cords of this native stone, five hundred or more from first to last, got up there, ready to hand, as Father Larson, the old Norse stone mason working in the quarry beyond blasted and quarried it out in great flakes. The stone went down for pavements of terraces and courts. Stone was sent along the slopes into great walls. Stone stepped up like ledges on to the hill, and flung long arms in any direction that brought the house to the ground. The ground! My Grandfather's ground: It was lovingly felt as part of all this.

Finally it was not so easy to tell where pavements and walls left off and ground began. Especially on the hill-crown which became a low-walled garden above the surrounding courts, reached by stone steps walled into the slopes. A clump of fine oaks that grew on the hill top stood untouched on one side above the court. A great curved stone-walled seat enclosed the space just beneath them and stone pavement stepped down to a spring or fountain that welled up into a pool at the center of the circle. Each court had its fountain and the winding stream below had a great dam. A thick stone wall thrown across it, to make a pond at the very foot of the hill, and raise the water in the valley to within sight from Taliesin. The water below the falls thus made, was sent, by hydraulic ram, up to a big stone reservoir built into the higher hill, just behind and above the hill top garden, to come down again into the fountains and go on down to the vegetable gardens on the slopes below the house.

Taliesin, of course, was to be architect's workshop, a dwelling as well for young workers who came to assist. And it was a farm cottage for the farm help. Around a rear court were to be farm buildings, for Taliesin was to be a complete living unit, genuine in point of comfort and beauty, from pig to proprietor.

The place was to be self-sustaining if not self-sufficient and with its domain of two hundred acres, shelter, food, clothes and even entertainment within itself. It had to be its own light-plant, fuelyard, transportation and water system.

Taliesin was to be recreation ground for my children and

their children perhaps for many generations more. This modest human programme in terms of rural Wisconsin arranged itself around the hilltop in a series of four varied courts leading one into the other, courts together forming a sort of drive along the hillside flanked by low buildings on one side and by flower gardens against the stone walls that retained the hill crown on the other.

The strata of fundamental stone-work reached around and on into the four courts, and made them. Then stone, stratified, went into the lower house walls and on up into the chimneys from the ground itself. This native stone prepared the way for the lighter plastered construction of the upper-wood-walls. Taliesin was to be a combination of stone and wood as they met in the aspect of the hills around about. The lines of the hills were the lines of the roofs. The slopes of the hills their slopes, the plastered surfaces of the light wood-walls, set back into shade beneath broad eaves, were like the flat stretches of sand in the river below and the same in color, for that is where the material that covered them came from.

The finished wood outside was the color of gray tree-trunks, in violet light.

The shingles of the roof surfaces were left to weather, silver-gray like the tree branches spreading below them.

The chimneys of the great stone fireplaces rose heavily through all, wherever there was a gathering place within, and there were many such places. They showed great rock-faces over deep openings inside. Outside they were strong, quiet, rectangular rock-masses bespeaking strength and comfort, within.

Country masons laid all the stone with the quarry for a pattern and the architect for teacher. They learned to lay the walls in the long, thin, flat ledges natural to it, natural edges out. As often as they laid a stone they would stand back to judge the effect. They were soon as interested as sculptors fashioning a statue. One might imagine they were, as they stepped back, head cocked one side, to get the effect. Having arrived at some conclusion, they would step forward and shove the stone more to their liking, seeming never to tire of this discrimination. They were artistic for the first time, many of them, and liked it. There were many masons from first to last, all good, perhaps Dad Signola, in his youth a Czech, the best of them until Philip Volk came. He worked away five years at the place as it grew from year to year, for it will never be finished. And with no inharmonious discrepancy, one may see each mason's individuality in his work at Taliesin to this day. I frequently recall the man as I see his work.

At that time, to get this mass of material to the hill-top meant organizing man and horsepower. Trucks came along years later. Main strength and awkwardness directed by commanding intelligence got the better of the law of gravitation by the ton, as sand, stone, gravel and timber went up into appointed places. Ben Davis was commander of these forces at this time. Ben was a creative cusser. He had to be. To listen to Ben back of all this movement was to take off your hat to a virtuoso. Men have cussed between every word, but Ben split the words, artistically worked an oath in between every syllable. One day Ben with five of his men was moving a big rock that suddenly got away from its edge and fell over flat, catching Ben's big toe. I shuddered for that rock, as, hobbling slowly back and forth around it, Ben hissed and glared at it, threatening, eyeing and cussing it. He rose to such heights, plunged to such depths of vengeance, as I had never suspected, even in Ben. No Marseillaise or any damnation in the mouth of Mosaic prophet ever exceeded Ben at this high spot in his career as cusser. William Blake says exuberance is beauty. It would be profane, perhaps, to say that Ben at this moment was sublime. But he was.

And in "Spring Green"—the names in the region are mostly simple like "Black Earth," "Blue Mounds," "Lone Rock," "Silver Creek," etc.—I found a carpenter.

William Weston was a natural carpenter. He was a carpenter such as architects like to stand and watch work. I never saw him make a false or unnecessary movement. His hammer, extra-light, with a handle fashioned by himself, flashed to the right spot every time, like the rapier of an expert swordsman. He with his nimble intelligence and swift sure hand, was a gift to any architect.

That William stayed with Taliesin through trials and tribulations the better part of fourteen years. America turns up a good mechanic around in country places every so often. Billy was one of them.

Winter came. A bitter one. The roof was on, plastering done, windows in, the men working inside. Evenings, the men grouped around the open fire-places, throwing cord-wood into them to keep themselves warm as the wind came up through the floor boards. All came to work from surrounding towns and had to be fed and bedded on the place during the week. Saturday nights they went home with money for the week's

work in pocket, or its equivalent in groceries and fixings from
the village. Their reactions were picturesque. There was
Johnnie Vaughn, who was, I guess, a genius. I got him because
he had gone into some kind of concrete business with another
Irishman for partner, and failed. Johnnie said, "We didn't fail
sooner because we didn't have more business." I overheard this
lank genius, he was looking after the carpenters nagging little
Billy Little, who had been foreman of several jobs in the city
for me. Said Johnnie, "I built this place here off a shingle."
"Huh," said Billy, "that ain't nothin'. I built them places in
Oak Park right off'd the air." No one ever got even, a little,
over the rat-like perspicacity of that little Billy Little.

Workmen never have enough drawings or explanations no
matter how many they get—but this is the sort of slander an
architect needs to hear occasionally.

The workmen took the work as a sort of adventure. It was
adventure. In every realm. Especially in the financial realm. I
kept working all the while to make the money come. It did.
And we kept on inside with plenty of clean soft wood that could
be left alone, pretty much, in plain surfaces. The stone, too,
strong and protective inside, spoke for itself in certain piers,
and walls.

Inside floors, like the outside floors, were stone-paved or if
not were laid with wide, dark-streaked cypress boards. The
plaster in the walls was mixed with raw sienna in the box, went
on to the walls "natural," drying out tawny gold. Outside, the
plastered walls were the same but grayer with cement. But in
the *constitution* of the whole, in the way the walls rose from the
plan and the spaces were roofed over, was the chief interest of
the whole house. The whole was all supremely natural. The
rooms went up into the roof, tent-like, and were ribanded
overhead with marking-strips of waxed, soft wood. The house
was set so sun came through the openings into every room
sometime during the day. Walls opened everywhere to views
as the windows swung out above the tree-tops, the tops of red,
white and black oaks and wild cherry trees festooned with wild
grape-vines. In spring, the perfume of the blossoms came full
through the windows, the birds singing there, the while, from
sunrise to sunset—all but the several white months of winter.

I wanted a home where icicles by invitation might beautify
the eaves. So there were no gutters. And when the snow piled
deep on the roofs and lay drifted in the courts, icicles came to
hang staccato from the eaves. Prismatic crystal in pendants
sometimes six feet long, glittered, between the landscape and

the eyes inside. Taliesin in winter was a frosted palace roofed and walled with snow, hung with iridescent fringes, the plate-glass of the windows delicately fantastic with frosted arabesques. A thing of winter beauty. But the windows shone bright and warm through it all as the light of the huge fire-places lit them from the firesides within and streams of wood-smoke from a dozen such places went straight up toward the stars.

The furnishings inside were simple and temperate. Thin tan-colored flax rugs covered the floors, later abandoned for the severer simplicity of the stone pavements and wide boards. Doors and windows were hung with modest, brown checkered fabrics. The furniture was "home-made" of the same wood as the trim and mostly fitted into the trim. I got a compliment on this from old Dan Davis, a rich and "savin'" Welsh neighbor, who saw we had made it ourselves. "Gosh-dang it Frank," he said, "Ye're savin' too, ain't ye?" Although Mother Williams, another neighbor, who came to work for me, said, "Savin'? He's nothin' of the sort. He could 'ave got it most as cheap ready-made from that Sears and Roebuck. . . . I know."

A house of the North. The whole was low, wide and snug, a broad shelter seeking fellowship with its surroundings. A house that could open to the breezes of summer and become like an open camp if need be. With Spring came music on the roofs for there were few dead roof-spaces overhead, and the broad eaves so sheltered the windows that they were safely left open to the sweeping, soft air of the rain. Taliesin was grateful for care. Took what grooming it got with gratitude and repaid it all with interest.

Taliesin's order was such that when all was clean and in place its countenance beamed, wore a happy smile of well-being and welcome for all.

It was intensely human, I believe.

Although, thanks to "bigger and better publicity," among those who besieged it Saturdays and Sundays from near and far came several characteristic ladies whose unusual enterprise got them as far as the upper half of the Dutch door, standing open to the living room. They couldn't see me. I was lying on a long walled-seat just inside. They poked in their heads and looked about with oh's and ah's. A pause. In the nasal twang of the more aggressive one "I wonder" . . . "I wonder, now, if I'd like living in a place like this as much as I would living in a regular home?"

The studio, lit by a bank of tall windows to the north,

really was a group of four studies, one large, three small. And in their midst stood a stone fire-proof vault for treasures. The plans, private papers, and such money as there was, took chances anywhere outside it. But the Taliesin library of Genroku embroidery and antique colored wood-block prints, all stayed safely inside. But, as work and sojourn overseas continued, Chinese pottery and sculpture and Momoyama screens overflowed into the rooms where, in a few years, every single object used for decorative accent became an "antique" of rare quality.

If the eye rested on some ornament it could be sure of worthy entertainment. Hovering over these messengers to Taliesin from other civilizations and thousands of years ago, must have been spirits of peace and good-will? Their figures seemed to shed fraternal sense of kinship from their places in the stone or from the broad ledges, where they rested.

For the story of Taliesin, after all, is old: old as the human spirit. These ancient figures were traces of that spirit, left behind in the human procession as Time went on, and they now came forward to find rest and feel at home. So it seemed as you looked at them. But they were only the story within the story: ancient comment on the New.

The New lived for itself for their sake as, long ago, they had lived, for its sake.

from AN AUTOBIOGRAPHY, *1932*

In the Cause of Architecture

"Nature has made creatures only; art has made men." Nevertheless, or perhaps for that very reason, every struggle for truth in the arts and for the freedom that should go with the truth has always had its own peculiar load of disciples, neophytes, and quacks. The young work in architecture here in the Middle West, owing to a measure of premature success, has for some time past been daily rediscovered, heralded and drowned in noise by this new characteristic feature of its struggle. The so-called "movement" threatens to explode soon in foolish exploitation of unripe performances or topple over in pretentious attempts to "speak the language." The broker, too, has made his appearance to deal in its slender stock in trade, not a wholly new form of artistic activity certainly, but one serving to indicate how profitable this intensive rush for a place in the "new school" has become.

Just at this time it may be well to remember that "every form of artistic activity is not art." Obviously this stage of development was to be expected and has its humorous side. It has also unexpected and dangerous effects, astonishingly in line with certain prophetic letters written by honest "conservatives" upon the publication of the former paper of 1908.

Although an utterance from me of a critical nature is painful, because it must be a personal matter, perhaps a seeming retraction on my part, still all that ever really happens is "personal matter" and the time has come when forbearance ceases to be either virtue or convenience. A promising garden seems to be rapidly overgrown with weeds, notwithstanding the fact that "all may raise the flowers now, for all have got the seed." But the seed has not been planted; transplanting is preferred, but no amount of transplanting can raise the needed flowers.

To stultify or corrupt our architectural possibilities is to corrupt our aesthetic life at the fountain head. Her architecture is the most precious of the susceptibilities of a young, constructive country in this constructive stage of development; and maintaining its integrity in this respect, therefore, distinctly a cause.

When, 21 years ago, I took my stand, alone in my field, the cause was unprofitable, seemingly impossible, almost unknown, or, if known, was, as a rule, unhonored and ridiculed; Montgomery Schuyler was the one notable exception to the rule. So swiftly do things "come on" in this vigorous and invigorating age that although the cause itself has had little or no recognition, the work has more than its share of attention and has attracted to itself abuses seldom described (never openly attacked) but which a perspective of the past 6 years will enable me to describe, as I feel they must render the finer values in this work abortive for the time being, if they do not wholly defeat its aim. Many a similar work in the past has gone prematurely to ruin owing to similar abuses; to rise again, it is true; but retarded generations in time.

I still believe that the ideal of an organic architecture forms the origin and source, the strength and, fundamentally, the significance of everything ever worthy the name of architecture.

And I know that the sense of an organic architecture, once

grasped, carries with it in its very nature the discipline of an ideal at whatever cost to self-interest or the established order.

It is itself a standard and an ideal and I maintain that only earnest artist integrity, both of instinct and of intelligence, can make any forward movement of this nature in architecture of lasting value.

The ideal of an organic architecture for America is no mere license for doing the thing that you please to do as you please to do it in order to hold up the strange thing when done with the "see what I have made" of childish pride. Nor is it achieved by speaking the fancied language of "form and function"; cant terms learned by rote; or prating foolishly of "progress before precedent"; that unthinking, unthinkable thing! In fact, it is precisely the total absence of any conception of this ideal standard that is made conspicuous by this folly and the practices that go with it. To reiterate the statement made in 1908: this ideal of an organic architecture for America was touched by Richardson and Root, and perhaps other men; but was developing consciously 28 years ago in the practice of Adler and Sullivan when I went to work in their office. This ideal combination of Adler and Sullivan was then working to produce what no other combination of architects nor any individual architect at that time dared even preach: a sentient, rational building that would owe its "style" to the integrity with which it was individually fashioned to serve its particular purpose; a "thinking" as well as "feeling" process, requiring the independent work of true artist imagination; an ideal that is dynamite, cap and fuse, in selfish, insensible hands; personal ambition, the lighted match.

At the expiration of a 6-year apprenticeship, during which time Louis Sullivan was my master and inspiration, 21 years ago I entered a field he had not, in any new spirit, touched, the field of domestic architecture, and began to break ground and make the forms I needed, alone, absolutely alone.

These forms were the result of a conscientious study of materials and of the machine which is the real tool, whether we like it or not, that we must use to give shape to our ideals; a tool which at that time had received no such artistic consideration from artist or architect. And that my work now has individuality, the strength to stand by itself, honors Mr. Sullivan the more. The principles, however, underlying the fundamental ideal of an organic architecture, common to his work and to mine, are common to all work that ever rang true in the architecture of the world, and free as air to any pair of honest young lungs that will breathe deeply enough. But I have occasion to refer only to that element in this so-called "new movement" which I have characterized by my own work and which should and, in a more advanced stage of culture, would be responsible to me for use or abuse of the forms and privileges of that work. Specifically, I speak only to that element within this element, now beyond private reach or control, ruthlessly characterizing and publicly exploiting the cause it does not comprehend or else that it cannot serve.

Someone for the sake of that cause must have some conscience in the matter and tell the truth. Since disciples, neophytes, and brokers will not, critics do not, and the public cannot, I will. I will be suspected of the unbecoming motives usually ascribed to any man who comes to the front in behalf of an ideal, or his own; nevertheless, somehow, this incipient movement, which it has been my life work to help outfit and launch, must be protected or directed in its course. An enlightened public opinion would take care of this, but there is no such opinion. In time there will be; meantime good work is being wasted, opportunities destroyed or, worse, architectural mortgages on future generations forged wholesale; and in architecture they must be paid with usurious interest.

The sins of the architect are permanent sins.

To promote good work it is necessary to characterize bad work as bad.

Half-baked, imitative designs (fictitious semblances) pretentiously put forward in the name of a movement or a cause, particularly while novelty is the chief popular standard, endanger the cause, weaken the efficiency of genuine work, for the time being at least; lower the standard of artistic integrity permanently; demoralize all values artistically; until utter prostitution results. This prostitution has resulted in the new work partly, I have now to confess, as a byproduct of an intimate, personal touch with the work, hitherto untried in the office of an American architect; and partly, too, perhaps, as one result of an ideal of individuality in architecture, administered in doses too strong, too soon, for architectural babes and sucklings; but chiefly, I believe, owing to almost total lack of any standard of artist integrity among architects, as a class, in this region at least. Of ethics we hear something occasionally; but only in regard to the relation of architects to each other when a client is in question; never in relation to sources of inspiration, the finer material the architect uses in shaping the thing he gives to his client. Ethics that promote integrity in this respect are as yet unformed and the young man in architecture is adrift in the most vitally important of his experiences; he cannot know where he stands in the absence of any well-defined principles on the part of his confreres or his elders. Such principles must now be established.

If I had a right to project myself in the direction of an organic architecture 21 years ago, it entailed the right to my work and, so far as I am able, a right to defend my aim. Also, yet not so clearly, I am bound to do what I can to save the public from untoward effects that follow in the wake of my own break with traditions. I deliberately chose to break with traditions in order to be more true to tradition than current conventions and ideals in architecture would permit. The more vital course is usually the rougher one and lies through conventions oftentimes settled into laws that must be broken, with consequent liberation of other forces that cannot stand freedom. So a break of this nature is a thing dangerous, nevertheless indispensable, to society. Society recognizes the danger and makes the break usually fatal to the man who makes it. It should not be made without reckoning the danger and sacrifice, without ability to stand severe punishment, nor without sincere faith that the end will justify the means; nor do I believe it can be effectively made without all these. But who can reckon with the folly bred by temporal success in a country that has as yet no artistic standards, no other god so potent as that same success? For every thousand men nature enables to stand adversity, she, perhaps, makes one man capable of surviving success. An unenlightened public is at its mercy always; the "success" of the one thousand as well as of the one in a thousand; were it not for the resistance of honest enmity, society, nature herself even would soon cycle madly to disaster. So reaction is essential to progress, and enemies as valuable an asset in any forward movement as friends, provided only they be honest; if intelligent as well as honest, they are invaluable. Some time ago this work reached the stage where it sorely needed honest enemies if it were to survive. It has had some honest enemies whose honest fears were expressed in the prophetic letters I have mentioned.

But the enemies of this work, with an exception or two, have not served it well. They have been either unintelligent or careless of the gist of the whole matter. In fact, its avowed enemies have generally been of the same superficial, time-serving spirit as many of its present load of disciples and neophytes. Nowhere even now; save in Europe, with some few notable exceptions in this country; has the organic character of the work been fairly recognized and valued; the character that is perhaps the only feature of lasting vital consequence.

As for its peculiarities; if my own share in this work has a distinguished trait, it has individuality undefiled. It has gone forward unswerving from the beginning, unchanging, yet developing, in this quality of individuality, and stands, as it has stood for 19 years at least, an individual entity, clearly defined. Such as it is, its "individuality" is as irrevocably mine as the work of any painter, sculptor, or poet who ever lived was irrevocably his. The form of a work that has this quality of individuality is never the product of a composite. An artist knows this; but the general public, near artist and perhaps "critic," too, may have to be reminded or informed. To grant a work this quality is to absolve it without further argument from anything like composite origin, and to fix its limitations.

There are enough types and forms in my work to characterize the work of an architect, but certainly not enough to characterize an architecture. Nothing to my mind could be worse imposition than to have some individual, even temporarily, deliberately fix the outward forms of his concept of beauty upon the future of a free people or even of a growing city. A tentative, advantageous forecast of probable future utilitarian development goes far enough in this direction. Any

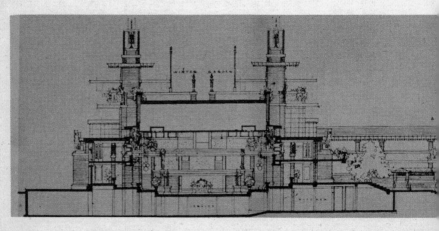

individual willing to undertake more would thereby only prove his unfitness for the task, assuming the task possible or desirable. A socialist might shut out the sunlight from a free and developing people with his own shadow, in this way. An artist is too true an individualist to suffer such an imposition, much less perpetrate it; his problems are quite other. The manner of any work (and all work of any quality has its manner) may be for the time being a strength, but finally it is a weakness; and as the returns come in, it seems as though not only the manner of this work or its "clothes," but also its strength in this very quality of individuality, which is a matter of its soul as well as of its forms, would soon prove its undoing, to be worn to shreds and tatters by foolish, conscienceless imitation. As for the vital principle of the work (the quality of an organic architecture) that has been lost to sight, even by pupils. But I still believe as firmly as ever that without artist integrity and this consequent individuality manifesting itself in multifarious forms, there can be no great architecture, no great artists, no great civilization, no worthy life. Is, then, the very strength of such a work as this is its weakness? Is it so because of a false democratic system naturally inimical to art? Or is it so because the commercialism of art leaves no noble standards? Is it because architects have less personal honor than sculptors, painters, or poets? Or is it because fine buildings are less important now than fine pictures and good books?

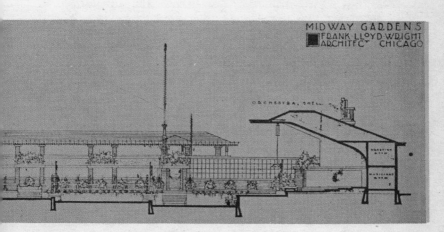

In any case, judging from what is exploited as such, most of what is beginning to be called the "New School of the Middle West" is not only far from the ideal of an organic architecture, but getting farther away from it everyday.

A study of similar situations in the past will show that any departure from beaten paths must stand and grow in organic character or soon fall, leaving permanent waste and desolation in final ruin; it dare not trade long on mere forms, no matter how inevitable they seem. Trading in the letter has cursed art for centuries past, but in architecture it has usually been rather an impersonal letter of those decently cold in their graves for sometime.

One may submit to the flattery of imitation or to caricature personally; everyone who marches or strays from beaten paths must submit to one or to both, but never will one submit tamely to caricature of that which one loves. Personally, I too am heartily sick of being commercialized and traded in and upon; but most of all I dread to see the types I have worked with so long and patiently drifting toward speculative builders, cheapened or befooled by senseless changes, robbed of quality and distinction, dead forms or grinning originalities for the sake of originality, an endless string of hacked carcasses, to encumber democratic front yards for five decades or more. This, however, is only the personal side of the matter and to be endured in silence were there any profit in it to come to the future architecture of the "melting pot."

The more serious side and the occasion for this second paper is the fact that emboldened or befooled by its measure of "success," the new work has been showing weaknesses instead of the character it might have shown some years hence were it more enlightened and discreet, more sincere and modest, prepared to wait, to wait to prepare.

The average American man or woman who wants to build a house wants something different, "something different" is what they say they want, and most of them want it in a hurry. That this is the fertile soil upon which an undisciplined "language-speaking" neophyte may grow his crop to the top of his ambition is deplorable in one sense but none the less hopeful in another and more vital sense. The average man of business in America has truer intuition, and so a more nearly just estimate of artistic values, when he has a chance to judge between good and bad, than a man of similar class in any other country. But he is prone to take that "something different" anyhow; if not good then bad. He is rapidly outgrowing the provincialism that needs a foreign-made label upon "art," and so, at the present moment, not only is he in danger of being swindled, but likely to find something peculiarly his own, in time, and valuable to him, if he can last. I hope and believe he can last. At any rate, there is no way of preventing him from getting either swindled or something merely "different"; nor do I believe it would be desirable if he could be, until the inorganic thing he usually gets in the form of this "something different" is put forward and publicly advertised as of that character of the young work for which I must feel myself responsible.

I do not admit that my disciples or pupils, be they artists, neophytes, or brokers, are responsible for worse buildings than nine-tenths of the work done by average architects who are "good school"; in fact, I think the worst of them do better; although they sometimes justify themselves in equivocal positions by reference to this fact. Were no more to come of my work than is evident at present, the architecture of the country would have received an impetus that will finally resolve itself into good. But to me the exasperating fact is that it might aid vitally the great things we all desire, if it were treated on its merits, used and not abused. Selling even good versions of an original at second hand is in the circumstances not good enough. It is cheap and bad, demoralizing in every sense. But, unhappily, I have to confess that the situation seems worse where originality, as such, has thus far been attempted, because it seems to have been attempted chiefly *for its own sake,* and the results bear about the same resemblance to an organic architecture as might be shown were one to take a classic column and, breaking it, let the upper half lie carelessly at the foot of the lower, then setting the capital picturesquely askew against the half thus prostrate, one were to settle the whole arrangement as some structural feature of street or garden.

For worker or broker to exhibit such "designs" as efforts of creative architects, before the ink is yet dry on either work or worker, is easily done under present standards with "success," but the exploit finally reflects a poor sort of credit upon the exploited architect and the cause. As for the cause, any growth that comes to it in a "spread" of this kind is unwholesome. I insist that this sort of thing is not "new school," nor this the way to develop one. This is piracy, lunacy, plunder, imitation, adulation, or what you will; it is not a developing architecture when worked in this fashion, nor will it ever become one until purged of this spirit; least of all is it an organic architecture. Its practices belie any such character.

"Disciples" aside, some 15 young people, all entirely inexperienced and unformed—but few had even college educations —attracted by the character of my work, sought me as their employer. I am no teacher; I am a worker; but I gave to all, impartially, the freedom of my workroom, my work, and myself, to imbue them with the spirit of the performances for their own sakes; and with the letter for my sake; so that they might become useful to me; because the nature of my endeavor was such that I had to train my own help and pay current wages while I trained them.

The nature of the profession these young people were to make when they assumed to practice architecture entails much more careful preparation than that of the "good school" architect; theirs is a far more difficult thing to do technically and artistically, if they would do something of their own. To my chagrin, too many are content to take it "ready-made," and with no further preparation hasten to compete for clients of their own. Now 15 good, bad, and indifferent are practicing architecture in the Middle West, South, and Far West and with considerable "success." In common with the work of numerous disciples (judging from such work as has been put forward publicly), there is a restless jockeying with members, one left off here, another added there, with varying intent; in some a vain endeavor to reindividualize the old types; in others an attempt to conceal their origin, but always—ad nauseam—the inevitable reiteration of the features that gave the original work its style and individuality. To find fault with this were unfair. It is not unexpected nor unpromising except in those unbearable cases where badly modified *inorganic* results seem to satisfy their authors' conception of originality; and banalities of form and proportion are accordingly advertised in haste as work of creative architects of a "new school." That some uniformity in performance should have obtained for some years is natural; it could not be otherwise, unless unaware I had harbored marked geniuses. But when the genius arrives nobody will take his work for mine; least of all will he mistake my work for his own creation.

"The letter killeth." In this young work at this time, still it is the letter that killeth, and emulation of the "letter" that gives the illusion or delusion of "movement." There is no doubt, however, but that the sentiment is awakened which will mean progressive movement in time. And there are many working quietly who, I am sure, will give a good account of themselves.

Meanwhile, the spirit in which this use of the letter has its rise is important to any noble future still left to the cause. If the practices that disgrace and demoralize the soul of the young man in architecture could be made plain to him; if he could be shown that inevitably equivocation dwarfs and eventually destroys what creative faculty he may possess; that designing lies, in design to deceive himself or others, shuts him out absolutely from realizing upon his own gifts; no matter how flattering his opportunities may be; if he could realize that the artist heart is one uncompromising core of truth in seeking, in giving, or in taking; a precious service could be rendered him. The young architect who is artist enough to know where he stands and man enough to use honestly his parent forms as such, conservatively, until he feels his own strength within him, is only exercising an artistic birthright in the interest of a good cause; he has the character at least from which great things may come. But the boy who steals his forms; "steals" them because he sells them as his own for the moment of superficial distinction he gains by trading on the results; is no artist, has not the sense of the first principles of the ideal that he poses and the forms that he abuses. He denies his birthright, an act characteristic and unimportant; but for a mess of pottage, he endangers the chances of a genuine forward movement, insults both cause and precedent with an astounding insolence quite peculiar to these matters in the United States, ruthlessly sucks what blood may be left in the tortured and abused forms he caricatures and exploits, like the parasite he is.

Another condition as far removed from creative work is the state of mind of those who, having in the course of their day's labor put some stitches into the "clothes" of the work, assume, therefore, that style and pattern are rightfully theirs and wear them defiantly unregenerate. The gist of the whole matter artistically has entirely eluded them. This may be the so-called "democratic" point of view; at any rate it is the immemorial error of the rabble. No great artist nor work of art ever proceeded from that conception, nor ever will.

Then there is the soiled and soiling fringe of all creative effort, a type common to all work everywhere that meets with any degree of success, although it may be more virulent here because of low standards; those who benefit by the use of another's work and to justify themselves depreciate both the work and worker they took it from; the type that will declare, "In the first place, I never had your shovel; in the second place, I never broke your shovel; and in the third place, it was broken when I got it, anyway;" the type that with more crafty intelligence develops into the "coffin worm." One of Whistler's "coffin worms" has just wriggled in and out.

But underneath all, I am constrained to believe, lies the feverish ambition to get fame or fortune "quick," characteristic of the rush of commercial standards that rule in place of artist standards, and consequent unwillingness to wait to prepare thoroughly.

"Art to one is high as a heavenly goddess; to another only the thrifty cow that gives him his butter," said Schiller; and who will deny that our profession is prostitute to the cow, meager in ideals, cheap in performance, commercial in spirit: demoralized by ignoble ambition? A foolish optimism regarding this only serves to perpetuate it. Foolish optimism and the vanity of fear of ridicule or "failure" are both friends of ignorance.

In no country in the world do disciples, neophytes, or brokers pass artist counterfeit so easily as in these United States. Art is commercialized here rather more than anything else, although the arts should be as free from this taint as religion. But has religion escaped?

So the standard of criticism is not only low; it is often dishonest or faked somewhere between the two, largely manufactured to order for profit or bias. Criticism is worked as an advertising game, traders' instincts subject to the prevailing commercial taint. Therein lies a radically evil imposition that harms the public; that also further distorts, confuses and injures values and promotes bad work; that tends to render the integrity of artist and commerce alike a stale and unprofitable joke, and to make honest enemies even harder to find than honest friends. The spirit of fair play, the endeavor to preserve the integrity of values, intelligently, on a high plane in order to help in raising the level of the standard of achievement in the country, and to refrain from throwing the senseless weight of the mediocre and bad upon it; all this is unhappily too rare among editors. The average editor has a "constituency," not a standard. This constituency is largely the average architect who has bought the "artistic" in his architecture as one of its dubious and minor aspects, or the sophisticated neophyte, the broker, and the quack, to whom printers' ink is ego-balm and fortune.

So until the standard is raised any plea for artist integrity is like a cry for water in the Painted Desert. As for competent criticism, the honest work of illuminating insight, where is it? Nothing is more precious or essential to progress. Where is the editor or critic not narrow or provincial? Or loose and ignorant? Or cleverly or superficially or cowardly. commercial? Let him raise this standard! Friend or foe, there is still a demand for him even here; but if he did, he would fail, gloriously fail, of "success."

Is architecture, then, no longer to be practiced as an art? Has its practice permanently descended to a form of mere "artistic activity"?

The art of architecture has fallen from a high estate, lower steadily since the men of Florence patched together fragments of the art of Greece and Rome and in vain endeavor to reestablish its eminence manufactured the Renaissance. It has fallen from the heavenly "Goddess of Antiquity" and the Middle Ages to the thrifty cow of the present day. To touch upon these matters in this country is doubly unkind, for it is to touch upon the question of "bread and butter" chiefly. Aside from the conscienceless ambition of the near artist (more sordid than any greed of gold) and beneath this thin pretense of the ideal that veneers the curious compound of broker and neophyte there lurks, I know, for any young architect an ever present dread of the kind of "failure" that is the obverse of the kind of "success" that commercialized standards demand of him if he is to survive. Whosoever would worship his heavenly goddess has small choice; he must keep his eye on the thrifty cow or give up his dream of "success"; and the power of discrimination possessed by the cow promises ill for the future integrity of an organic architecture. The net result of present standards is likely to be a poor wretch, a coward who aspires pretentiously or theoretically, advertises cleverly and milks surreptitiously. There is no real connection between aspiration and practice except a tissue of lies and deceit; there never can be. The young architect before he ventures to practice architecture with an ideal, today, should first be sure of his goddess and then, somehow, be connected with a base of supplies from which he cannot be cut off, or else fall in with the rank and file of the "good school" of the hour. Anyone who has tried it knows this; that is, if he is honest and is going to use his own material as soon as he is able. So the ever present economic question underlies this question of artist integrity, at this stage of our development, like quicksand beneath the footing of a needed foundation, and the structure itself seems doomed to shreds and cracks and shores and patches, the deadening compromises and pitiful make-shifts of the struggle to "succeed"! Even the cry for this integrity will bind the legion together, as one man, against the crier and the cry.

This is art, then, in a sentimental democracy, which seems to be only another form of self-same hypocrisy? Show me a man who prates of such "democracy" as a basis for artist endeavor, and I will show you an inordinately foolish egotist or a quack. The "democracy" of the man in the American street is no more than the gospel of mediocrity. When it is understood that a great democracy is the highest form of aristocracy conceivable, not of birth or place or wealth, but of those qualities that give distinction to the man as a man, and that as a social state it must be characterized by the honesty and responsibility of the absolute individualist as the unit of its structure, then only can we have an art worthy the name. The rule of mankind by mankind is one thing; but false "democracy," the hypocritical sentimentality politically practiced and preached here, usually the sheep's clothing of the proverbial wolf, or the egotistic dream of self-constituted patron saints is quite another thing. "The letter killeth," yes; but more deadly still is the undertow of false democracy that poses the man as a creative artist and starves him to death unless he fakes his goddess or persuades himself, with "language," that the cow is really she. Is the lack of an artist conscience, then, simply the helpless surrender of the would-be artist to this wherewithal democracy with which a nation soothes itself into subjection? Is the integrity for which I plead here no part of this time and place? And is no young aspirant or hardened sinner to blame for lacking it? It may be so. If it is, we can at least be honest about that, too. But what aspiring artist could knowingly face such a condition? He would choose to dig in the ditch and trace his dreams by lamplight, on scrap paper, for the good of his own soul; a sweet and honorable, if commercially futile, occupation.

It has been my hope to have inspired among my pupils a personality or two to contribute to this work, some day, forms of their own devising, with an artistic integrity that will help to establish upon a firmer basis the efforts that have gone before them and enable them in more propitious times to carry on their practice with a personal gentleness, wisdom, and reverence denied to the pioneers who broke rough ground for them, with a wistful eye to better conditions for their future.

And I believe that, cleared of the superficial pose and push that is the inevitable abuse of its opportunity and its nature, and against which I ungraciously urge myself here, there will be found good work in a cause that deserves honest friends and honest enemies among the better architects of the country. Let us have done with "language" and unfair use of borrowed forms; understand that such practices or products are not of the character of this young work. This work is a sincere endeavor to establish the ideal of an organic architecture in a new country; a type of endeavor that alone can give lasting value to any architecture and that is in line with the spirit of every great and noble precedent in the world of forms that has come to us as the heritage of the great life that has been lived, and in the spirit of which all great life to be will still be lived.

And this thing that eludes the disciple, remains in hiding from the neophyte, and in the name of which the broker seduces his client, What is it? This mystery requiring the catch phrases of a new language to abate the agonies of the convert and in the name of which ubiquitous atrocities have been and will continue to be committed, with the deadly enthusiasm of the ego-mania that is its plague. First, a study of the nature of materials you elect to use and the tools you must use with them, searching to find the characteristic qualities in both that are suited to your purpose. Second, with an ideal of organic nature as a guide, so to unite these qualities to serve that purpose, that the fashion of what you do has integrity or is *natively fit,* regardless of preconceived notions of style. *Style* is a byproduct of the process and comes of the man or the mind in the process. The style of the thing, therefore, will be the man; it is his. *Let his forms alone.*

To adopt a "style" as a motive is to put the cart before the horse and get nowhere beyond the "styles"; never to reach *style.*

It is obvious that this is neither ideal nor work for fakers or tyros; for unless this process is finally so imbued, informed, with a feeling for the beautiful that grace and proportion are inevitable, the result cannot get beyond good engineering.

A light matter this, altogether? And yet an organic architecture must take this course and belie nothing, shirk nothing. Discipline! The architect who undertakes his work seriously on these lines is emancipated and imprisoned at the same time. His work may be severe; it cannot be foolish. It may

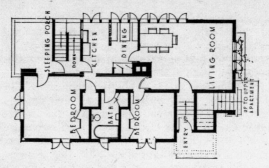

1915   American System Ready-Cut prefabricated flats, project. Plan.
(Perspective on page 113.)

lack grace; it cannot lack fitness altogether. It may seem ugly;
it will not be false. No wonder, however, that the practice of
architecture in this sense is the height of ambition and the
depth of poverty!

Nothing is more difficult to achieve than the integral simplicity of organic nature, amid the tangled confusions of the
innumerable relics of form that encumber life for us. To
achieve it in any degree means a serious devotion to the "underneath" in an attempt to grasp the *nature* of building a
beautiful building beautifully, as organically true in itself, to
itself and to its purpose, as any tree or flower.

That is the need, and the need is demoralized, not served,
by the same superficial emulation of the letter in the new
work that has heretofore characterized the performances of
those who start out to practice architecture by selecting and
electing to work in a ready-made "style."

from THE ARCHITECTURAL RECORD, *May, 1914*

Japan

1916-1922

For six years, Frank Lloyd Wright lived in Tokyo, with regular visits home. The huge job of making the drawings, organizing the crew and building the phenomenal Imperial Hotel occupied most of his time. Small-scaled and richly decorated, the hotel just outside the Emperor's palace moat was intended for certain more Westernized state functions and for luxury-loving tourists. Hardly had it been completed when the great earthquake of 1923 and the fires that followed wreaked great havoc in Tokyo and all Japan. The Imperial Hotel, flexibly constructed in sections of concrete for such dangers, stood undamaged—a haven of safety—unlike other modern buildings nearby, built with conventional Western rigid frames. Wright's long adventure into unknown conditions, and his client's confidence in him despite unexpectedly high construction costs, were brilliantly justified. An official commission sent by the American Institute of Architects to study the effects of the earthquake nevertheless failed to mention Wright's accomplishment, and this confirmed an established prejudice. Although thirty years later a younger generation gave Wright the A.I.A. Gold Medal, he never would accept membership in

197

*what he considered more a protective than a professional as-
sociation. Today Wright's Imperial Hotel, sadly neglected, is
still in use. In Japan Wright built a school and four houses,
and sketched other projects. In the United States some lesser
works, often unsupervised, arose, and a beautiful home for
the Henry Allens in Wichita. Throughout the whole period
was woven the elaborate story of Hollyhock House on Olive
Hill in Hollywood, a small palatial estate planned with many
buildings, some of which were executed and some not. The
main house, today the Municipal Art Center of Los Angeles,
was built as a superbly romantic setting for an unconventional
heiress who loved the world of theatre and music. Massive
concrete forms recall the stone ruins of Yucatan that Wright
admired, much as Dvorak's* NEW WORLD SYMPHONY *suggests
American folk tunes. Wright's architecture reflects several
such echoes, but never fails to maintain its own character, as
this masterwork clearly shows.*

The Imperial Hotel

A social clearing house, call it a hotel, became necessary to
official Japan as a consequence of new foreign interest in the
Japanese. A new hotel becomes necessary, because no for-
eigner, no matter how cultivated, could live on the floor, as
the Japanese do, with any grace or comfort. It was also necessary for another reason: a Japanese gentleman does not entertain strangers, no matter how gentle, within his family circle.
So the building will be more a place for entertainment with
private supper rooms, banquet hall, theater and cabaret than
it will be a hotel.

No foreign architect yet invited to work in Japan ever took
off his hat to the Japanese and respected either Japanese conditions or traditions. And yet those aesthetic traditions are at
the top among the noblest in the world. When I accepted the
commission to design and build their building it was my instinct and definite intention not to insult them. Were they
not a feature of my first condition, the ground? They were.
The Japanese were more their own ground than any people I
knew.

198

So while making their building "modern" in the best sense, I meant to leave it a sympathetic consort to Japanese buildings. I wanted to show the Japanese how their own conservation of space and the soul of their own religious shinto, which is "be clean," might, in the use of all materials, take place as effectively for them indoors in sound masonry construction when on their feet as it had taken place for them when they were down upon their knees in their own inspired carpentry.

I meant to show them how to use our new civilizing-agents —call them plumbing, electrification, and heating—without such outrage to the art of building as we ourselves were practicing and they were then copying. I intended to make all these appurtenance systems a practical and aesthetic part of the building itself. It was to be given a new simplicity by making it a complete whole within itself.

Mechanical systems should be an asset to life and so an asset to architecture. They should be no detriment to either. Why shouldn't the Japanese nation make the same coordination of furnishing and building when they came to be at home on their feet that they had so wonderfully made for themselves at home on their knees?

And I believed I could show them how to build an earthquake-proof masonry building.

In short, I desired to help Japan make the transition from wood to masonry, and from her knees to her feet, without too great loss of her own great accomplishments in culture. And I wished to enable her to overcome some of the inherent weaknesses of her building system where the temblor was a constant threat to her happiness and to her very life.

There was this natural enemy to all building whatsoever: the temblor. And, as I well knew, the seismograph in Japan is never still. The presence of the temblor, an affair of the ground, never left me while I planned and for four years or more worked upon the plans and structure of the new hotel. Earthquakes I found to be due to wave movement of the ground. Because of wave movement, foundations like long piles oscillate and rock the structure. Heavy masses of masonry inevitably would be wrecked. The heavier the masonry the greater the wreck.

The feature of the ground that was the site itself was a flat 500- by 300-foot plot of ground composed of sixty feet of liquid mud overlaid by eight feet of filled soil. The filling was about the consistency of hard cheese. The perpetual water level stood within fifteen inches of the level of the ground. In short, the building was to stand up on an ancient marsh, an arm of the bay that had been filled in when Tokyo became the capital of the empire.

But the mud beneath the filling seemed to me a good cushion to relieve earthquake shocks. A building might float upon the mud somewhat as a battleship floats on salt water. Float the building upon the mud? Why not? And since it must float, why not extreme lightness combined with the tenuity and flexibility that are a property of steel instead of the great weight necessary to the usually excessive rigidity which, no matter how rigid, could never be rigid enough? Probably the answer was a building made flexible as the two hands thrust together, fingers interlocked, yielding to movement yet resilient to return to position when force exerted upon its members and membranes ceased. Why fight the force of the quake on its own terms? Why not go with it and come back unharmed? Outwit the quake?

That was how the nature of the site, the ground, entered into the conception of the building. Now, to carry out in detail these initial perceptions.

I took a preliminary year in which to acquire necessary data, making tests for the new type of foundation. Finally flexible foundations, economical too, were provided by driving tapered wooden piles, only eight feet long, into the strata of filled soil, pulling them out and throwing in concrete immediately, to form the thousands of small piers or concrete pins two feet apart on centers upon which the jointed footing courses were laid. Nine pile drivers dotted the ground, each with its band of singing women pulling on the ropes lifting and dropping the drive-head—twelve ropes, one for each pair of hands.

The good sense of careful calculation so far: now what about the superstructure?

The building was going native, so intensive hand methods would have to be used and native materials too. The nature of the design therefore should be something hand methods could do better than machinery. It was impossible to say how far we could go in any direction with machines, probably not very far.

Evidently the straight line and flat plane to which I had already been committed by machines in America should be modified in point of style if I would respect the traditions of the people to whom the building would belong. The Japanese, centuries ago, had come nearer the ideal of an organic architecture in their dwellings than any civilized race on earth. The ideals we have been calling organic are even now best exemplified in their wood and paper dwellings where they lived on their knees. As I have already said, I wanted to help the Japanese get to their feet indoors and learn to live in fireproof masonry buildings, without loss of their native aesthetic prestige where the art of architecture was a factor. Trained by the disasters of centuries to build lightly on the ground, the wood and paper homes natural to them are kindled by any spark. When fire starts it seldom stops short of several hundred homes, sometimes destroys thousands, and ends in complete destruction of a city. After the irresistible wave movements have gone shuddering and jolting through the earth, changing all overnight in immense areas, islands disappearing, new ones appearing, mountains laid low and valleys lifted up taking awful toll of human life, then come the flames! Conflagration always at the end.

The cost of metal frames and sash at that time was prohibitive, but the plans were made for an otherwise completely fireproof building and the designs were so made that all architectural features were practical necessities.

The flexible light foundations had saved one hundred thousand dollars over the customary massive foundations. Now how could the building be made as light and flexible? I divided the building into sections about sixty feet long. This is the safe limit for temperature cracks in reinforced concrete in that climate. Wherever part met part I provided through joints.

To insure stability I carried the floor and roof loads as a waiter carries his tray on his upraised arm and fingers. At the center all supports were centered under the loaded floor-slabs; balancing the load instead of gripping the load at the edges with the walls, as in the accepted manner. In any movement a load so carried would be safe. The waiter's tray balanced on his hand at the center is the cantilever in principle.

This was done. This meant that the working principle of the cantilevers would help determine the style of the structure. So the cantilever became the principal feature of the structure and a great factor in shaping its forms throughout as the floor-slabs came through the walls and extended into various balconies and overhangs.

Tokyo buildings were top heavy. The exaggerated native roofs were covered deep with clay, and the heavy roof tiles laid on over the clay would come loose and slide down with deadly effect into the narrow streets crowded with terrified humanity.

So the outer walls, spread thick and heavy at the base and tapering towards the top, were crowned there by a light roof covered with hand-worked sheet copper tiles. The light roof framing rested upon a concrete ceiling slab extended outward over the walls into an overhang, perforated to let sunlight into the windows of the rooms beneath.

Now as to materials. What would be desirable and available? Again we go to the ground.

A stone I had seen under foot and in common use in Tokyo building was a light, workable lava, called oya, weighing about as much as green oak and resembling travertine. It was quarried at Nikko and was floated down on rafts by sea to Tokyo and then by canal to the site. I liked this material for its character but soon found that the building committee, made up of the financial autocracy of the empire, considered it sacrilege to use a material so cheap and common for so dignified a purpose. But finally the building committee gave in and we bought our own quarries at Nikko. We used oya (the lava) throughout the work, combining it with concrete walls cast in layers within thin wall shells of slender bricks.

Large or small, the pieces of lava could be easily hollowed out at the back and set up with the hollow side inside, as one side of the slab-forms for casting the concrete. In this way the three materials were cast solidly together as a structural unit when the concrete was poured into them.

Copper, too, was a prominent feature in our list of available handworked materials.

Thus the "Teikoku" (Imperial Hotel) after these measures were taken became a jointed steel-reinforced monolith with a thin integral facing of lava and thin brick, the whole sheltered overhead by light copper tiles. The mass of the structure rests upon a kind of pincushion. The pins were set close enough together to support, by friction, the weight calculated to be placed upon them. To the lengthwise and crosswise work in this particular structure all piping and wiring were made to conform. Both were designed to be laid in shafts and trenches free of construction. The pipes were of lead, sweeping with easy bend from trenches to shafts and curving again from shafts to fixtures. Thus any earthquake might rattle and flex the pipes as they hung but could break no connections. Last, but by no means least, an immense pool of water as an architectural feature of the extensive entrance court to the hotel was connected to its own private water system. This was to play its part in conflagration following in the wake of earthquake.

During the execution of these ideas I found the language a barrier. Men and methods were strange. But the "foreign" architect with twenty Japanese students from Tokyo and Kyoto University courses in architecture, some of whom were taken to Taliesin during the preliminary plan making, and one excellent American builder, Paul Mueller, made up the band that built the Imperial Hotel. Hayashi San, the general manager of the Imperial Hotel, was in direct charge of everything. The principal owner, the Imperial Household, was represented by Baron Okura. And there was a board of directors composed of five captains of Japanese big business—ships, tobacco, cement, and banking.

The original plans which I had worked out at Taliesin for the construction I threw aside as educational experience for the architect only and worked out the details on the ground as we went along. Plans served only as a preliminary study for final construction.

Those Japanese workmen! How clever they were. What skill and industry they displayed! So instead of trying to execute preconceived methods of execution, thereby wasting this precious human asset in vainly trying to make the workmen come our way, we learned from them and willingly went with them, their way. I modified many original intentions to make the most of what I now saw to be naturally theirs. But, of course, curious mistakes were common. I had occasion to learn that the characteristic Japanese approach to any subject is, by instinct, spiral. The Oriental instinct for attack in any direction is oblique or volute and becomes wearisome to a direct Occidental, whose instinct is frontal and whose approach is rectilinear.

But, then, they made up for this seeming indirection by gentleness, loyalty, and skill. Soon we began to educate the "foreigners" as they did us, and all went along together pretty well.

As the countenance of their building began to emerge from seeming confusion the workmen grew more and more interested in it. It was a common sight to see groups of them intelligently admiring and criticizing some finished feature as it would emerge to view. There was warmth of interest and depth of appreciation, unknown to me in the building circles of our country in our own day, to prove the sincerity of their pleasure and interest in their work.

Finally, out of this exercise of free will and common sense, with this unusual Western feeling of respect for the East and for Japanese life and traditions in view as discipline and inspiration, what would emerge?

A great building is to be born; one not looking out of place where it is to stand across the park from the Imperial Palace. The noble surrounding walls of the Palace rose above the ancient moat. The gateways to the Palace grounds, guarded by blue-tiled, white-walled buildings nesting on the massive stone walls, were visible above the moat across the way. It was architecture perfect of its kind and as Japanese as the countenance of the race. I conceived the form of this new associate—the Imperial—as something squat and strong, as harmonious with this precedent as the pines in the park. It should be a form seen to be bracing itself against storm and expected temblor. Appeal has already been made to imagination in a realm scientific; but pure reason and science must now wait there at the doorstep.

Wait there while something came to Japanese ground—something not Japanese, certainly, but sympathetic, embodying modern scientific building ideas by old methods not strange to Japan. No single form was really Japanese but the whole was informed by unity. The growing proportions were suitable to the best Japanese tradition. We have here in the individuality of the architect a sincere lover of old Japan, his hat in hand, seeking to contribute his share in the transition of a great old culture to a new and inevitably foreign one. Probably the new one was unsuitable. Certainly it was as yet but imperfectly understood by those who were blindly, even fatuously, accepting it as superior to their own. A great tragedy, it may be.

Looking on then as now, it seemed to me as though tragedy it must be. The Far East had so little to learn from our great West, so much to lose where culture is concerned.

I might ameliorate their loss by helping to make much that was spiritually sound and beautiful in their own life, as they had known it so well, over into a pattern of the unknown new life they were so rashly entering. To realize this ambition in concrete form, apparent in a structure that acknowledged and consciously embodied this appropriate pattern, was what I intended to do in this masonry building 500 feet long by 300 feet wide. It was a world complete within itself. It now may be seen. It is known far and wide as it stands on the beaten path around the world. Said Baron Takahashi to a conscientious objector from America, "You may not like our Imperial Hotel but we Japanese like it. We understand it."

Two years later—1923—in Los Angeles: news was shouted in the streets of awful disaster. Tokyo and nearby Yokohama were wiped out by the most terrific temblor in history. Appalling details came in day after day after the first silence when no details could be had. As the news began to add up it seemed that nothing human could have withstood the cataclysm.

Too anxious to get any sleep I kept trying to get news of the fate of the New Imperial and of my friends, Shugio, Hayashi, Endo San, my boys and the Baron, hosts of friends I had left over there. Finally the third or fourth day after the first outcry, about two o'clock in the morning, the telephone bell. Mr. Hearst's *Examiner* wished to inform me that the Imperial Hotel was completely destroyed. My heart sank as I laughed at them. "Read your dispatch," I said. The *Examiner* read a long list of "Imperial" this and "Imperial" that.

"You see how easy it is to get the Imperial Hotel mixed with other Imperials. If you print the destruction of the new Imperial Hotel as news you will have to retract. If anything is above ground in Tokyo it is that building," I said, and hoped.

Their turn to laugh while they spread the news of destruction with a photograph across the head of the front page in the morning. Then followed a week or more of anxiety. Conflicting reports came continually because during that time direct communication was cut off.

Then—a cablegram.

"FRANK LLOYD WRIGHT, OLIVE HILL RESIDENCE, HOLLYWOOD, CALIFORNIA.
FOLLOWING WIRELESS RECEIVED TODAY FROM TOKYO, HOTEL STANDS UNDAMAGED AS MONUMENT TO YOUR GENIUS HUNDREDS OF HOMELESS PROVIDED BY PERFECTLY MAINTAINED SERVICE. CONGRATULATIONS.

OKURA."

For once in a lifetime good news was newspaper news and the Baron's cablegram flashed around the world to herald what? To herald the triumph of good sense in the head of an architect tough enough to stick to it through thick and thin. Yes, that. But it was really a new approach to building, the ideal of an organic architecture at work, that really saved the Imperial Hotel.

Both Tokyo houses of the Baron were gone. The splendid museum he gave to Tokyo was gone. The building by an American architect, whose hand he took to see him through, was what he had left in Tokyo standing intact, nor could love or money buy a share in it, now.

When letters finally came through, friends were found to be safe. And it appeared that not one pane of glass was broken in the building—no one harmed. Neither was the plumbing or the heating system damaged at all. But something else was especially gratifying to me. After the first great quake was over, the dead lying in heaps, the Japanese came in droves, dragging their children into the courses and up onto the terraces of the building, praying for protection by the God that had protected the Teikoku. Then, as the wall of fire that follows every great quake came sweeping across the city toward the long front of the Imperial, driving a continuous wail of human misery before it, the Hotel boys formed a bucket line to the big pool of the central entrance court (the city mains were disrupted by the quake) and found there a reserve of water to keep the wood window frames and sash wet to meet the flames. The last thought for the safety of the Imperial had taken effect.

Early in the twentieth century, a world in itself, true enough to its purpose and created spontaneously as any ever fashioned by the will of any creator of antiquity, had been completed within a sector of the lifetime of its one architect. Such work in ancient times generally proceeded from generation to generation and from architect to architect. Strange! Here expert handicraft had come at the beck and call of one who had, up to that time, devoted most of his effort to getting buildings true to modern machine processes built by machine.

Here in the Far East a significant transition building was born. Are really good buildings all transition buildings? But for the quality of thought that built it, the ideal of an organic

1917   Odawara Hotel, project. *Nagoya, Japan.*

architecture, it would surely have been just "another one of those things" and have been swept away.

While the New Imperial only partially realized the ideal of an organic architecture, the pursuit of that ideal made the building what it really was, and enabled it to do what it did do. The fact that were I to build it again it would be entirely different, although employing the same methods and means, does not vitiate my thesis here. It greatly strengthens it.

Now let us glance at what followed this natural approach to the nature of a problem as a natural consequence. Opposition, of course, followed until finally Baron Okura took full responsibility and saw the building through. There was the unfriendly attitude of Americans and Englishmen. Though none too friendly to each other, they opposed this approach. They had owned Tokyo up to now because, where foreign culture was being so freely and thoughtlessly bought, they were best sellers. The Germans were there, strong too, but they were almost out of the running by now. My sympathetic attitude, Japan for the Japanese, was regarded as treason to American interests. I encouraged and sometimes taught the Japanese how to do the work on their building themselves. The American construction companies were building ten-story steel buildings with such architecture as they had hung to the steel, setting the steel frames on long piles which they floated across the Pacific from Oregon and drove down to hard pan. I suppose they were built in this fashion so the steel might rattle the architecture off into the streets in any severe quake? These companies were especially virulent where I was concerned.

The Western Society of American Engineers gratuitously warned me that my "scheme for foundations was unsound." The A.I.A.—American Institute of Architects—passing through Tokyo when the building was nearly finished, took notice and published articles in Tokyo papers declaring the work an insult to American architecture, notifying my clients, and the world generally, that the whole thing would be down in the first quake with horrible loss of life.

Finally, when the building was about two-thirds completed, it came directly to the diréctors from such sources that their American architect was mad. Now every director except one (my sponsor, the Baron), so worked upon continually for several years, became a spy. The walls had ears. Propaganda increased. General Manager Hayashi was "on the spot." My freedom was going fast and I worked on under difficulties greater than ever. Hayashi San, the powerful Okura, and my little band of Japanese student apprentices were loyal and we got ahead until the final storm broke in a dark scene in a directors' meeting. Then the Baron took over the reins himself to see me through with my work, and the building of the New Imperial went forward more smoothly to conclusion.

I have learned that wherever reason shows its countenance and change is to take place, the reaction in any established order, itself not organic, is similar. Therefore organic architecture has this barrier to throw down or cross over or go around.

As for government, I should say here that no permit to build the Imperial Hotel was ever issued by the government. I explained to the proper Imperial Department our intention, registered the drawings. The result was visitation by Japanese authorities, more explanations, head shakings. But the attitude was entirely friendly and sympathetic in contrast to the attitude that might be expected in our own country. Finally we were told no permit was needed, to go ahead, they would watch proceedings and hoped to learn something from the experiment. They could not say that most of the ideas did not seem right but, having no precedent, they could not officially act. They could wink, however, and "wink" the government did.

This "wink" is the utmost official sanction organic architecture or any thought-built action of the sort in any medium may expect from a social order itself inorganic and in such danger of disturbance if radical examination is permitted that even an approach in that direction is cause for hysteria. Institutions such as ours are safe, in fact remain "institutions" only upon some status quo, some supreme court, which inevitably becomes invalid as life goes on.

from ARCHITECTURE AND MODERN LIFE,
copyright 1937, Harper & Brothers

Great Projects and Small Houses

1920-1929

After Olive Hill, Frank Lloyd Wright settled in California and began to build differently from the extended, horizontal houses of his Prairie Architecture. Now in a hot, dry climate he erected closed, cubic forms that had appeared in his work only occasionally before. Concrete, a humble, usually ugly, material had long preoccupied him; like Edison he was experimenting with it for prefabricated, fireproof houses as early as 1906. Now he developed a system of small blocks, often modelled or pierced decoratively, set up with steel reinforcing rods in the joints, both vertical and horizontal. A flexible, inexpensive structure resulted, durable and delightful. The grandeur of Olive Hill became the hospitable grace of La Miniatura. A series of individual homes in the same technique followed, among the most livable and attractive of Wright's works.

These works were paralleled by several ambitious projects, prophetic of what was to come in Wright's architecture and in modern architecture generally. A cantilevered concrete skyscraper frame, sheathed entirely in metal and glass, was a notable advance over the San Francisco project of 1912; both its forms and its light skin were eventually adopted and are

209

now conventional. Concrete was the main material in a project for E. H. Doheny, the oil man, where hills and ravines were encircled by a continuous structure that was roadway, viaducts and luxury residences, all interconnected, of reinforced blocks; a vision of the future that also harked back to the hill towns of the Mediterranean, where masonry of road and shelter imperceptibly blend. For Lake Tahoe he designed a magical recreation center, half afloat, and for Wisconsin a country club with daring angles; for both, the tepee of the American Indian is echoed in steep, triangular roofs. None of these was built; and in 1925 his home, Taliesin, once again had to be reconstructed after a disastrous fire. In 1925 also the Dutch periodical, WENDINGEN, *published a monograph on Frank Lloyd Wright with many large illustrations and essays by eminent American and European architects. No similar tribute was published in the United States, but* THE ARCHITECTURAL RECORD *printed a long series of articles by Wright.*

Wright now drew up a vast steel cathedral for all faiths, a shimmering pyramid of light; and a spiral ramp for a planetarium in the Maryland mountains; both forms recurred in the latest and most challenging buildings of Frank Lloyd Wright's career. But the 1920s had several adventures in store for him yet. In Arizona Wright designed a splendid and luxurious resort, San-Marcos-in-the-Desert, a large hotel with several nearby homes, that showed for the first time the freely developed use of triangular units in the plans, evolving naturally from triangular concrete building blocks. Wright's cantilevered, mast-like frame for high buildings was used in an apartment tower, carefully worked out for St. Mark's-in-the-Bouwerie, New York. The evangelist's patronage in both cases failed to survive the 1929 stock market crash. A lone,

1917–1920 Hollyhock House, *Olive Hill, Hollywood, Los Angeles, Cal.* Architect's original sketch, 1917. Construction three years later. (Photograph on page 125.)

large commission was carried out in the late 1920s, a house in Tulsa for Wright's cousin, Richard Lloyd Jones, newspaper editor. In concrete block this house achieves an ultimate statement of such amazing directness that even after thirty years it daunts the appreciation of most observers; yet it is an undeniable landmark of Frank Lloyd Wright's architectural development.

La Miniatura

La Miniatura happened as the cactus grows, in a region that still shows what folk from the Middle-Western prairies did when, inclined to quit, the prosperous came loose and rolled down into that far corner to bask in eternal sunshine.

Near by that arid, sunlit strand is still unspoiled—to show what a poetic thing it was before this homely invasion. Curious tan-gold foothills rise from the tatooed sand-stretches to join slopes spotted as the leopard-skin, with grease-bush.

This foreground spreads to distances so vast—human scale is utterly lost as all features recede, turn blue, recede and become bluer still to merge their blue mountain shapes, snow capped, with the azure of the skies.

The one harmonious note man has introduced into these vast perspectives, aside from the long, low plastered wall, is the eucalyptus tree. Tall, tattered ladies, these trees stand with careless feminine grace in the charming abandon appropriate to perpetual sunshine, adding beauty to the olive-green and ivory-white of an exotic symphony in silvered gold and rose-purple.

Water comes, but comes as a deluge once a year to surprise the roofs, sweep the sands into ripples and roll the boulders along in the gashes combed by sudden streams in the sands of the desert—then—all dry as before.

No, not all, for man has caught and held the fugitive flood behind great concrete walls in the hills while he allows it to trickle down by meter to vineyards, orchards and groves. And —yes—to neat, shaven lawns two by twice. Little "lots" just like those "back home" in the Middle West. Those funny and fixed little features—the homes—stand above the lawns wear-

211

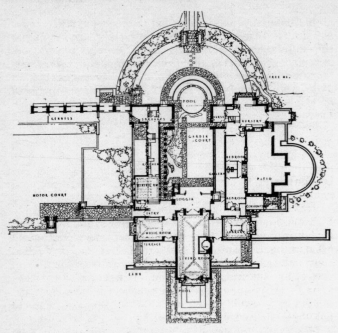

1917–1920   Hollyhock House.

ing as many curiously unvaried expressions of the same fixed face as there are people looking out of the windows at each other.

The newcomer from the fertile midwestern prairies came here to make sunshine his home. But at first his home did not know how to bask any more than he himself did. Shirt sleeves were his limit and his home had no shirt sleeves nor anything at all "easy" about it.

No indeed, that home of his was still as hard and self-assertive as the sticks he made it out of: as defiant as ever it was in the snows back there at home at zero. This Yankeefied house looked even more hard in perpetual sunshine where all need of its bristling defenses had disappeared.

Nor when the sunshiners turned to the planting of their places was the result much better. They could easily grow in that sunshine all kinds of strange plants and trees. They did so, as a neat, curious little "collection"—all nicely set out together on the clipped lawns of little town-lots.

212

And the Porch and the Parlor had come along with the pie and the ice-water, the rocking chair, and the chewing gum with the appropriate name.

But before long Fra Junipero and Father Latour would begin to have incidental influence, for it appeared that the Italo-Spanish buildings of the early missionaries' own "back home" had just happened to be more in keeping with California.

This Southern type of building had already given shelter from a sun that could blister the indiscreet in Spain or Mexico as it was able to do now in Southern California. So it came to pass that the old Catholic Missions as buildings lived long enough to transform and characterize the Middle-Westerner's home in California at this late day although the *actual* mission was rejected as being far from midwestern spiritual conviction.

So sunshiners fell to copying Fra Junipero's buildings, copying his furniture, copying his gardens and style. Fell to buying his antiques. But tho' invading Middle West had fallen it still clung in toto to its hard-straw hat, English coat, trousers and boots, and other customs in general.

As a concession to climate however, the middle westerner himself occasionally did put on a shirt with a soft collar and forgot his hat. But when he "dressed" not one iota would he budge. And he looked in his "Fra" surroundings as the Fra himself or a silken Spaniard would have looked in little midwestern parlors. Only for the Fra it would be plus—for the sunshiner it was minus.

By now Spain, by way of despised Mexico, had gradually moved up into the midst of this homely invasion. The plain, white-plastered walls—so far so good—of the little pictorial caverns gleam or stare through the foliage in oases kept green by great mountain reservoirs. A new glint of freshness, a plainness as refreshing foil for exotic foliage.

There are cool *patios,* too, for the Joneses and Smiths. Luxurious haciendas for the richer Robinsons. Arched loggias and vine-covered pergolas. Loose, rude Spanish-tiled roofs give back the sunshine stained pink. Adzed beams or rude beam-construction real or imitated, are covered by gay stretched awnings.

California has retraced the first steps of an earlier invasion by priests who came there from a climate more like California climate than that of the Middle West. But the Californians of today—née Iowan, Wisconsiniano, Ohioan—have yet nothing to say for themselves in all this except acquired taste for the

Spanish antique, to go with the missionaries' house. Nevertheless, the town-lot on the gridiron; the modern bathroom; the incorporation of the porch and the kitchenette with the cozy breakfast-nook: all these prize possessions of his own "backhome" are now "features" of the "mission" style. Such is progress. To have and to hold while seeming to *be.* But California—given to drink—smothers the whole in eucalyptus and mimosa arms as she gently kisses all with roses. Thus are buried the mistakes of the decorative picturizing architect, whose art and decoration have entirely taken the place of architecture, there.

Here then, at some length, is the pictorial background against which La Miniatura, the little studio-house, stands— the flourishing sentimentality into which it was born.

All true building in our land of the brave and home of the free is a soul-trying crusade just as Fra Junipero Serra's mission that failed was a crusade. But his building that succeeded was not high adventure because he just brought it with him from "back home" and just because, too, and solely—he had none other to bring.

No, that building of his was no high adventure, in this sense, for it, too, was the nearest he could get done, by primitive means, to what he, too, had "back home."

Not so La Miniatura. This little building scientifically and afresh began to search for what was missing in all this background. And what was missing? Nothing more or less than a distinctly genuine expression of California in terms of modern industry and American life—that was all.

Few out there seemed to miss anything of the sort, but La Miniatura desired to be justly considered *architecture.* Mrs. George Madison Millard from those same midwestern prairies near Chicago was the heroine of its story: Mrs. Millard, slender—energetic—fighting for the best of everything for everyone. Be it said she knew it when she saw it. Got it if she could.

The Millards had lived in a dwelling I had built for them fifteen years ago at Highland Park near Chicago. I was proud to have a client survive the first house and ask me to build a second. Out of one hundred and seventy-two buildings this made only the eleventh time it had happened to me. I was glad to add to these "laurels."

Gratefully I determined she should have the best in my portfolio. That meant, to begin with, something that belonged to the ground on which it stood. Her house should be a sensible

214

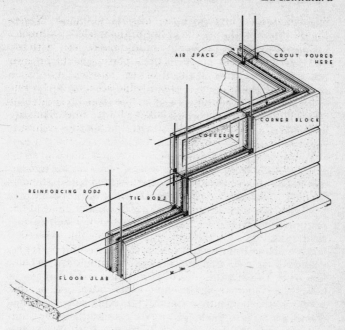

Concrete Block Construction.

matter entirely—an interpretation of her needs in book-collecting for book-collectors. Should she have one of those gun-nite Spanish blisters with a paper roof—decorator's supply company's Spanish-decorations pasted on it? She should not, nor anything of the scene-painting the San Diego Exposition had started and subsequent born-imitators sponsored. No, she should have a real home. Mrs. Millard, artistic herself, with her frank blue-eyed smile didn't fully know that she was to be lightly but inexorably grasped by the architectural fates and used for high exemplar, though she probably suspected it. I don't know why houses have so much grief concealed in them, if they try to *be* anything at all and try to live as themselves. But they do. Like people in this I suppose.

Gradually I unfolded the scheme of the textile block-slab house gradually forming in my mind since I got home from Japan. She wasn't frightened by the idea.

We would take that despised outcast of the building industry —the concrete block—out from underfoot or from the gutter— find a hitherto unsuspected soul in it—make it live as a thing of

215

beauty—textured like the trees. Yes, the building would be made of the "blocks" as a kind of tree itself standing at home among the other trees in its own native land.

All we would have to do would be to educate the concrete block, refine it and knit it together with steel in the joints and so construct the joints that they could be poured full of concrete after they were set up and a steel-strand laid in them. The walls would thus become thin but solid reinforced slabs and yield to any desire for form imaginable. And common labor could do it all.

We would make the walls double of course, one wall facing inside and the other wall facing outside, thus getting continuous hollow spaces between, so the house would be cool in summer, warm in winter and dry always. Inside, the textured blocks—or plain ones—would make a fine background for old pictures, fine books, and tapestries. Outside—well, in that clear sunshine, even the eucalyptus tree would respect the house and love it for what it was. Instead of a fire-trap for her precious book-collections and antiques she would have a house fire-proof. I talked this idea over with her, and the more she listened to it the more she liked it. I made some tentative plans.

I forgot to mention that Alice Millard had just ten thousand dollars to put into the house—might get two thousand more, probably not. Bankers were Yesterday, out there too, and hostile to ideas as everywhere. The greater the idea the greater banker-animosity. So the whole scheme must be excessively modest. For instance, Alice Millard wanted only an unusually large living-room with a great fireplace, a beautiful balcony over it from which her own sleeping-room might open. That bedroom should be roomy too, with dressing room, another balcony in that and a bath, of course. One for the balcony would be nice to have.

Then there must be a good sized guest-room that might be an office when not in use otherwise, and a bath. Two baths of course. And a dining room, not so small either—little parties —with pantry, kitchen, servants' bedroom, store-rooms and baths. Making three baths of course. My client's tastes were good. She did not want cheap woods. She did not want, of all things, cheap hardware. She abominated poor workmanship and knew it when she saw it. She never failed to see it. There was to be nothing shoddy about that house. And a garage was to be thrown in as integral feature of the whole just for good measure. She would be glad to have all this permanent, have it fire-proof, and have it beautiful for $10,000.00. (The first sum mentioned.)

One day after the plans were ready she came enthusiastically to say: "I've found just the man to build our 'thoroughbred' house. I've been talking with him and went with him to see a house he's just finished for a friend of mine. It cost her less than he said it would. He gave her lots of little extras and never charged for them. He was so good and efficient they scarcely needed an architect at all. Let's go and see the house."

Here the other leg of the "triangle" showed its foot once more—its toes at least and ingratiating smile. But I could not refuse to go—yet. And so—we went.

That house was not badly done, a lot for the money, almost as much as Alice Millard wanted. I talked with the contractor, and she even went so far as to say, by now, she wouldn't have anyone else build her house anyway. "I feel," said she, "we can trust him 'utterly.'"

Now, she had been just as uncompromising about her architect. I understood her regard for her contractor. But here was already familiar and pretty slippery ground.

"How do you like him?" said she, brightly, but as I could see, anxiously.

"Well," I said, "a woman's intuition is valuable even in these matters. He does seem intelligent. He has had a good deal of independent experience. He likes this block-slab idea and

1923   La Miniatura, *Pasadena, Cal.* Plans of mezzanine floor, main-floor, and lower-floor. (Photograph on page 126.)

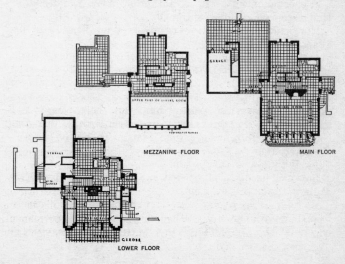

MEZZANINE FLOOR

MAIN FLOOR

LOWER FLOOR

volunteers to take the contract without any profit . . . for the sake of experience, as he says. Therefore he is a volunteer. Since you won't have anyone else build for you anyway, I am inclined to take him at face-value."

She sighed with relief.

She felt now quite safe. I had no good reason to oppose her ultimatum. But—I wish I had felt as safe as she. In honesty, I should add to this that I knew of no one else in that region, anyway, who could, or would, make such sacrifices for her, or for me.

Some material supply-men recommended him highly. I called them up. We got the god-father to the idea.

Here the familiar A.I.A. villain enters the piece in disguise, with Alice Millard's ultimatum for my flimsy excuse. But I knew just how staunch her faith could be and dreaded any attempt to change it. Had she not disregarded the warnings of her friends and consented to the loss of some life-long friendships that she might embark with me in this innocent challenge to their ways and what they approved?

He began well. They all do.

You see I explain this in detail to show how every idea even as the "Romanza" enters and encounters life, as does a new-born child, pretty much as things happen to be—to take all when and where it comes. The idea then begins to grow up, to work like yeast in these haphazard conditions and may survive and become important or dwindle and die as the child may. It is at every moment up to the author of its being to defend it. He has to save its life—continually.

Here's for confession: let's see how good for the soul—in this affair.

Let's call this builder-fellow god-father of our idea. I could add appropriate adjectives to the word god and to the word father. But you do it.

Alice Millard trusted the gift and felt she needed him, I am ashamed to say this. Trusted him. Out there where, as I learned, no one ever thinks of trusting anyone or anything. And because everything and everyone is too much "on the surface" or too recent or too something or other.

I didn't know this at the time.

But I've hardly ever trusted anyone since, nor has Alice Millard . . . scarcely even me.

As you may see by now, architect and client were by nature incorrigibly young. Firmly believing in Santa Claus. They were encouraged by Mrs. Millard's builder to believe they could accomplish their "mission," for eleven thousand some odd dollars. That was the contractor's estimate. Unhesitating, he signed a contract.

Why should he not sign a contract?

Or sign anything at all?

Meantime we had rejected the treeless lot originally purchased by Mrs. Millard as my eye had fallen on a ravine near by in which stood two beautiful eucalyptus trees. The ravine was reached from the rear by Circle Drive. Aristocratic Lester Avenue passed across the front.

No one would ever want to build down in a ravine out there I believed. They all got out on to the top of everything or anything to build and preferably in the middle of the top. It was a habit. I considered it a bad habit. But because of this idiotsyncracy of the region we could get this lot very cheap. We got it at half price—and it was better than the best at full price.

We would head the ravine at the rear on Circle Drive with the house ... thus retaining the ravine at the front toward Lester Avenue as a sunken garden. The house would rise tall out of the ravine gardens between the two eucalyptus trees. Balconies and terraces would lead down to the ravine from the front of the house. The neighbors on either side liked this idea as we left the entire front of the lot next their homes for a garden.

We began to build. Soon the builder grew in Mrs. Millard's estimation. Well over life-size. He settled full in the saddle. I could not fail to see this with some alarm and chagrin. It is not pleasant for an architect to see his client clinging to a contractor as safe insurance against what might prove to be too single-minded devotion to an idea on the part of her architect. Her friends had got that far with her? Or perhaps it was her nature. But she would not have admitted this, so I admit it for her here with wrinkles at the corners of my eyes. The architect has not infrequently in this region—for some peculiar reason, perhaps the climate—to endure this rivalry for the confidence and esteem of his client, I have learned from others. But what is this "something" about a contractor or builder that inspires confidence in the client—especially if the client be a woman? Of course, it is easy to believe that he is, before all, "practical." It is easy to believe that *he* is the man who really builds the building, in spite of the troublesome architect? He knows clapboards and shingles and so he must know concrete blocks, etc. etc. Always, to the woman client, the appeal of this "practical" man seems irresistible. Woman is far more objective than man—more susceptible to the obvious.

Still smiling, though I will say I resented this rivalry, I cheerfully did nothing about it. Let me admit, if less cheerfully, that I *could* have done nothing about it anyway, had I wanted to. So I helped along, every day on the ground myself, as best I might. I made more studies and details until finally we got the flasks and boxes made in which to make the blocks; got the right mixture of sand and gravel and cement, which we carefully chose; and so varied it that the blocks would not all be the same color. The "builder" had picked up some relations of his in Los Angeles to make them. We had no skilled labor, and the builder's relatives set the blocks, carrying them up ladders on their shoulders to their scheduled places in the walls. You see, this model house had to be clumsily home-made, as might be, for the price was very low. A good deal would have to be "put up with" on that account. Otherwise everything went along according to design—smoothly enough.

And, by now, that house represented about as much studious labor over a drawing board and attention to getting construction started as the Cathedral of St. John the Divine in New York City, certainly more trouble to me than any the architect had with the Woolworth Building.

Inventive effort was all "thrown in."

The house was by now, to me, far more than a mere house. Yes—Mrs. Millard's friends were right. Her architect had gone deep into his idea with concentration upon it amounting to passion. The blocks began to take the sun and creep up between the eucalypti. The "Weaver"—dreams regarding their effect. Came visions of a new Architecture for a new Life—the life of romantic, beautiful California—the reaction upon a hitherto unawakened people; other buildings sprang full-born into mind from that humble beginning in bewildering variety and beauty. Gradually all complications, and needless expense of the treacherous and wasteful building system of a whole country all went by the board. Any humble cottage might now live as architecture with the integrity known only in former ages. The machine should be no longer bar to beauty in our own. At last, here I grasp near end of great means to a finer "order." Standardization *was* the soul of the machine, and here the architect was taking it as a principle and "knitting" with it. Yes, crocheting with it a free masonry fabric capable of great variety in architectural beauty. And, I might as well admit it —I quite forgot this little building belonged to Alice Millard at all. Palladio! Bramante! Sansovino. Sculptors—all! Here was I the "Weaver." What might not now grow out of this little commonplace circumstance?

The "Weaver" concentrated on other studies and drawings to carry the idea further. Yes, argued the "Weaver,"—is any one smiling?—have not all great ideas in Art had an origin as humble? At last: a real building-method beginning in this little house; here was a "weaving" in building that could not go wrong for anyone: a prohibition by nature, of affectation, sham or senseless extravagance: integrity in architecture in the realm prostitute to the expedient. Mechanical means to infinite variety was no longer an impractical dream! Thus I—already far beyond little La Miniatura!

from AN AUTOBIOGRAPHY, *1932*

The Concept and the Plan

. . . Conceive the buildings in imagination, not first on paper but in the mind, thoroughly, before touching paper. Let the building, living in imagination, develop gradually, taking more and more definite form before committing it to the drafting board. When the thing sufficiently lives for you then start to plan it with instruments, not before. To draw during the conception or sketch, as we say, experimenting with practical adjustments to scale, is well enough if the concept is clear enough to be firmly held meantime. But it is best always thus to cultivate the imagination from within. Construct and complete the building so far as you can before going to work on it with T square and triangle. Working with triangle and T square should be only to modify or extend or intensify or test the conception; finally to correlate the parts in detail.

If original concept is lost as the drawing proceeds, throw away all and begin afresh. To throw away a concept entirely to make way for a fresh one, that is a faculty of the mind not easily cultivated. Few architects have that capacity. It is perhaps a gift, but may be attained by practice. What I am trying to express is the fact that the plan is the gist of all truly creative matter and must gradually mature as such.

. . . In the logic of the plan what we call standardization is seen to be fundamental groundwork in architecture. All things in nature exhibit this tendency to crystallize; to form mathe-

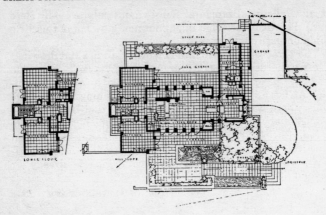

1923   Dr. John Storer house, *Los Angeles, Cal.* Plans of lower floor (left) and upper floor (right). (Photograph on page 127.)

matically and then to conform, as we may easily see. There is the fluid, elastic period of becoming, as in the plan, when possibilities are infinite. New effects may then originate from the idea or principle that conceives. Once form is achieved, however, that possibility is dead so far as it is a positive creative flux.

from THE ARCHITECTURAL RECORD, *January, February, 1928*

The Nature of Materials

The country between Madison and Janesville, near Taliesin my home and workshop, is the bed of an ancient glacier drift. Vast busy gravel pits abound there, exposing heaps of yellow aggregate once and still everywhere near, sleeping beneath the green fields. Great heaps, clean and golden, are always waiting there in the sun. And I never pass on my way to and from Chicago without an emotion, a vision of the long dust-whitened stretches of the cement mills grinding to impalpable fineness the magic powder that would "set" my vision all to shape; I wish both mill and gravel endlessly subject to my will.

Nor do I ever come to a lumber yard with its citylike, graduated masses of fresh shingles, boards and timbers, without taking a deep breath of its fragrance, seeing the forest laid low in it by processes that cut and shaped it to the architect's scale of feet and inches, coveting it all.

The rock ledges of a stone quarry are a story and a longing to me. There is a suggestion in the strata, and character in the formation. I like to sit and feel the stone as it is there. Often I have thought, were monumental great buildings ever given me to build I would go to the Grand Canyon of Arizona to ponder them.

When in early years I looked south from the massive stone tower in the Auditorium Building, a pencil in the hand of a master, the red glare of the Bessemer steel converters to the south of Chicago would thrill me as pages of the Arabian Nights used to do with a sense of terror and romance.

And the smothered incandescence of the kiln: in the fabulous heat, mineral and chemical treasure baking on mere clay, to issue in all the hues of the rainbow, all the shapes of imagination that never yield to time, subject only to the violence or carelessness of man. These great ovens would cast a spell upon me as I listened to the subdued roar deep within them.

The potter's thumb and finger deftly pressing the soft mass whirling on his wheel as it yielded to his touch, the bulbous glass at the end of the slender pipe as the breath of the glass blower and his deft turning decided its shape—its fate fascinated me. Something was being born.

Colors; in paste or crayon, pencil; always a thrill. To this day I love to hold a handful of many-colored pencils and open my hand to see them lying loose upon my palm, in the light.

Mere accidental colored chalk marks on the sunlit sidewalk, perhaps, will make me pause and something in me harks back to something half remembered, half felt, and as though an unseen door had opened and distant music had, for an instant, come trembling through to my senses.

In this sense of earth!—deep-buried treasure there without end. Mineral matter and metal stores folded away in veins of gleaming quartz. Gold and silver, lead and copper, tawny iron ore; all will yield themselves up to roaring furnaces and flow obedient to the hands of the architect; all become pawns to human will in the plan of the human mind.

And jewels, happy discoveries. The gleam of mineral colors and flashing facets of crystals. Gems to be sought and set; to forever play with light to man's delight, in never-ending beams of purest green, or red or blue or yellow, and all that lives between. Light! Living in the mathematics of form to match with the mathematics of sound.

Crystals are proof of nature's matchless architectural principle.

All this I see as the architect's garden, his palette. . . .

Materials! What a resource.

from THE ARCHITECTURAL RECORD, *October, 1928*

Wood

Wood is universally beautiful to man. It is the most humanly intimate of all materials. Man loves his association with it; likes to feel it under his hand, sympathetic to his touch and to his eye.

And yet, passing by the primitive uses of wood, getting to higher civilization, the Japanese understood it best. The Japanese have never outraged wood in their art or in their craft. Japan's primitive religion, Shinto, with its "be clean" ideal found in wood ideal material and gave it ideal use in that masterpiece of architecture, the Japanese dwelling, as well as in all that pertained to living in it.

In Japanese architecture may be seen what a sensitive material let alone for its own sake can do for human sensibilities, as beauty, for the human spirit.

Whether pole, beam, plank, board, slat, or rod, the Japanese architect got the forms and treatments of his architecture out of tree nature, wood wise, and heightened the natural beauty of the material by cunning peculiar to himself.

The possibilities of the properties of wood came out richly as he rubbed into it the natural oil of the palm of his hand, ground out the soft parts of the grain to leave the hard fiber standing, an "erosion" like that of the plain where flowing water washes away the sand from the ribs of the stone.

No Western people ever used wood with such understanding as the Japanese used it in their construction, where wood always came up and came out as nobly beautiful.

And when we see the bamboo rod in their hands, seeing a whole industrial world interpreting it into articles of use and art that ask only to be bamboo, we reverence the scientific art that makes wood theirs.

The simple Japanese dwelling with its fences and utensils is the revelation of wood.

from THE ARCHITECTURAL RECORD, *May, 1928*

Concrete

Aesthetically concrete has neither song nor any story. Nor is it easy to see in this conglomerate, in this mud pie, a high aesthetic property, because in itself it is amalgam, aggregate compound. And cement, the binding medium, is characterless.

... I finally had found simple mechanical means to produce a complete building that looks the way the machine made it, as much at least as any fabric need look. Tough, light, but not "thin"; imperishable; plastic; no unnecessary lie about it anywhere and yet machine-made, mechanically perfect. Standardization as the soul of the machine here for the first time may be seen in the hand of the architect, put squarely up to imagination, the limitations of imagination the only limitation of building.

Steel

In the steel and glass buildings I have designed, there are no walls, only wallscreens. The method of the cantilever in concrete and steel yields best to suspended screens or shells in place of outer walls; all may be shop-fabricated. The spider web is a good inspiration for steel construction. A slender mechanized fabric for all walls and partitions enters here to give the form and style that is architecture.

from THE ARCHITECTURAL RECORD,
January, August, 1928; July, 1929

Sheet Metal

What is left of the architectural framework of the modern world after concrete and steel have done with it will probably be in some form or other, sheet metal.

The machinery at work in the sheet metal trades easily crimps, folds, trims, and stamps sheets of metal as an ingenious child might his sheets of paper. The finished product may have the color brought up in surface treatment, or be enameled and colored with other durable substances, or as in galvanizing the finished work may be dipped and coated entire. But copper is the only sheet metal that has yet entered into architecture as beautiful permanent material. Its verdigris is always a great beauty in connection with stone or brick or wood, and copper

225

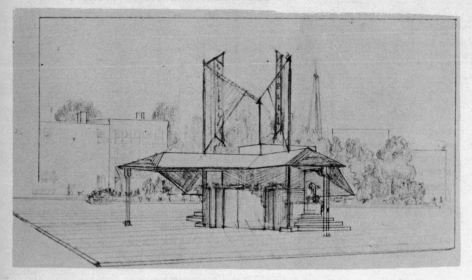

1928   Service Station for automobiles.

is more nearly permanent than anything we have at hand as an architect's medium.

from THE ARCHITECTURAL RECORD, *October, 1928*

Glass and Light

... As glass has become clearer and clearer and cheaper and cheaper from age to age, about all that has been done with it architecturally is to fill with a perfect visibility now the same building openings that opaque, ill-made but beautiful glass screened long ago.

... The machine gives prismatic opportunity in glass. The machine process can do any kind of glass: thick, thin, colored, textured to order; and cheap; and the machine in the architect's hand can now set it, protect it, and humanize its use completely.

... Lighting may be made a part of the building itself. No longer any appliance or even appurtenance is needed. But all this may be made, really, architecture.

... Imagine a city iridescent by day, luminous by night, imperishable! Buildings, shimmering fabrics, woven of rich glass; glass all clear or part opaque and part clear, patterned in color or stamped to harmonize with the metal tracery that is to hold all together, the metal tracery to be, in itself, a thing of delicate beauty consistent with slender steel construction, expressing the nature of that construction in the mathematics of structure, which are the mathematics of music as well. Such a city would clean itself in the rain, would know no fire alarms; no, nor any glooms.

To any extent the light could be reduced within the rooms by screens, blinds, or insertion of translucent or opaque glass. The heating problem would be no greater than with the rattling windows of the imitation masonry structure, because the fabric now would be mechanically perfect, the product of the machine shop instead of the makeshift of the topsy-turvy field. And the glass area would be increased only by about 10 percent over such buildings as they still continue to build of masonry.

I dream of such a city. I have worked enough on such a building to see definitely its desirability and its practicability.

from THE ARCHITECTURAL RECORD, *April, 1928*

Style

... Young critics, I believe, intrigued by the science and philosophy of the great art, love architecture as a mysterious essence. They see in the surface and mass abstractions by "great and gifted" Europeans, inspired by French painting, the truth. But I know these abstractions repudiate the third dimension, ignoring depth of matter to get surface effects characteristic of canvas and pigment, as painting, but not of architecture no matter howsoever stark or begot by gas pipe, thin slabs, and naked steel work. Materials may now be used as decorative clichés too, witness the concoctions of wire, lead pipe, plumbing fittings, brass keys, bits of glass and wood, of this school. Sophisticated, ingenious, cleverly curious, they smell of the dissecting room, affect me as cadavers. ...

These walls artificially thin, like cardboard bent and glued together. ...

Standardization is a mere but indispensable tool; a tool to be used only to a certain extent in all matters not purely technical or commercial or mere matters of method. Standardization is only a means to an end.

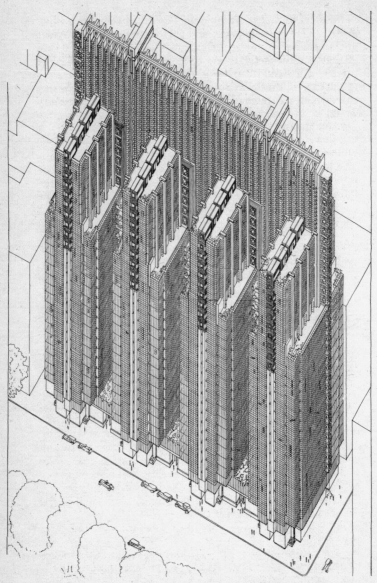

1920–1925   National Life Insurance Company, project, *Chicago, Ill.*

Used so that it leaves the spirit free to destroy the static element in the will; on suspicion maybe; used so only that it does not become a style, or inflexible rule, only to that extent is it desirable to the architect.

To the extent that it remains a servant of new forms or the new sense of inherent style, it is desirable.

Standardization should be put to work but never allowed to master the process that yields the original form.

Terminal masses are most important as to form. Nature will show this to you in her own fabrications. Take good care of the terminals and the rest will take care of itself.

from THE ARCHITECTURAL RECORD,
January, February, 1928; July, 1929

Fellowship

The depression years of the early 1930s brought more unexe-
cuted projects into Wright's oeuvre, but these were notably
realistic and unornamented compared to the rich fantasies of
the '20s. The House on the Mesa, 1931, was even more stark
than the Tulsa house of two years earlier; five years later the
house on Bear Run is similarly restrained. The Capital
Journal, a projected newspaper plant of 1931, introduced the
hollow-cored mushroom columns that were features of the
Johnson wax company's administrative center, designed 1936.
Wright projected great skyscraper schemes for the Chicago
Century of Progress exhibition, and also drew detailed plans
for metal prefabricated farm buildings. His ideas for a theatre,
originally stimulated by the client of Olive Hill, now were
clarified and presented in a scheme that waited a quarter of a
century more for its fulfilment in Dallas. The solid achieve-
ments of these years lay in a series of books: the Princeton lec-
tures, delivered 1930, were published in 1931; the next year saw
THE DISAPPEARING CITY (revised as WHEN DEMOCRACY
BUILDS, 1945, and THE LIVING CITY, 1958) and AN AUTOBI-
OGRAPHY, Wright's major writing. At the same time Wright

began to accept resident apprentices in The Taliesin Fellowship, a combined school, office and farm, which today continues as the Taliesin Associated Architects, successor to Wright's practice. The Fellowship buildings next to Taliesin were in large part remodelled and built to Wright's designs by the apprentices from 1932 on. The entire group moved to Arizona for the winters and there, in rented quarters, the great model of Broadacre City was built, Wright's vision of a community combining the best of rural living and urban amenities.

With 1936 the surge of returning economic vitality was felt in Frank Lloyd Wright's office, as it was generally. Two great structures were designed and built that placed Wright, at the age of 67, among the most daring and accomplished architects of the day. These were the house on Bear Run and the Johnson administrative offices.

These unusual opportunities were balanced by Wright's active interest in the design of modest homes for average families: he developed the "Usonian" houses—built usually of boards and roofing paper skilfully sandwiched, brick cores, and heated concrete floor-slabs. From the Jacobs house of 1937 to the Winkler-Goetsch house of 1939 and for some years thereafter, numbers of these very liveable, rectangular dwellings were designed. Prefabricated steel homes were also projected by Wright in these years; and the great Johnson house, Wingspread, arose north of the Racine administrative center. There followed Wright's own famous Taliesin West in Arizona, the settled winter home of the Fellowship, a wizardry in desert rock (placed in forms with concrete binding), roughsawn planks, and canvas roofing and shutters. A campus was planned for Florida Southern College that, as late as 1959, was adding new units accordingly. Both a church in Kansas City and an early version of a civic center for Madison, Wisconsin, failed to be carried out as planned.

In 1940 Wright designed the lyrical Lloyd Lewis house, a new kind of prairie home, and its perfect counterpart, the Pauson house in Phoenix. In the South Carolina swamps Wright built the dream-like plantation, Auldbrass; and in Madison, the down-to-earth but still poetic Pew residence. But war was making building difficult once more. The gently perfected Burlingham design remained a project, as did several others. The spiral ramp of the Guggenheim Museum—Wright's most significant exploration of unconventional space—designed in 1943, waited fourteen years for construction. In 1944 the Johnson laboratory tower, first executed and clearest of

Wright's cantilevered tall buildings, began to be built. A cliff-hung house was designed for V. C. Morris in San Francisco but not built, nor was a desert resort projected for Elizabeth Arden. The Douglas Grant house of 1945, however, was built by 1951, a unique and very beautiful home for Midwestern country living.

To the Young Man in Architecture

Today the young man I have in mind hears much, too much about new and old. Sporadic critics of the "new" take their little camera-minds about—(snapshot emulation by the half-baked architect)—and wail, or hail the dawn. If by chance the novice builds a building the cackling, if not the crowing, out-does the egg. Propagandists, pro and con, classify old as new and new as old. Historians tabulate their own oblique infer-ences as fact. The "ites" of transient "ists" and "isms" pro-claim the modern as new. And yet architecture was never old and will ever be new. From architecture the main current, little streams detach themselves, run a muddy course to be regathered and clarified by the great waters as though the little rills and rivulets had never been. All art in our time is like that and we witness only the prodigal waste Nature sponsors when she flings away a million seeds to get a single plant,—seeming in the meantime to enjoy her extravagance. Nature's real issue, no doubt, in the life of the mind is no less wasteful, and she may enjoy her extravagance in the million fancies for one idea: millions of cerebrations for one thought: a million buildings for even one small piece of genuine architecture. Yes, she gives gladly a million for one now, because the species has declined five hundred years to the level of a commercially expedient *appliance.* The species itself, you see, is in danger. So be glad to see as evidence of life the babel of personal books, the derelic-tion of aesthetic movements,—especially be glad to see the halfbaked buildings by the novitiate.

But confusion of ideas is unnatural waste of purpose. Such confusion as we see means a scattering of aim nature herself would never tolerate. The confusion arises because there is doubt in some minds and fear in some minds and hope in other minds that architecture is shifting its circumference. As the hod of mortar and some bricks give way to sheet-metal, the lockseam, and the breaker,—as the workman gives way to the automatic machine,—so the architect seems to be giving way either to the engineer, the salesman or the propagandist.

I am here to assure you that the circumference of architecture *is* changing with astonishing rapidity, but that its *center* remains unchanged. Or am I here only to reassure you that architecture eternally returns upon itself to produce new forms that it may live on forever? In the light of the new and with pain of loss, only now does America waken to see why and how "art" conceived as a commercial expedient, or degraded to the level of a sentimental appliance, has betrayed American life. Yes, that is one reason why the circumference of art, as a whole, is rapidly shifting. The circumference is shifting because hunger for reality is not yet dead and because human vision widens with science as human nature deepens with inner experience.

The center of architecture remains unchanged because,— though all unconfessed or ill-concealed,—beauty is no less the true purpose of rational modern architectural endeavor than ever, just as beauty remains the essential characteristic of architecture itself. But today because of scientific attainment the modern more clearly perceives beauty as integral order; order divined as an image by human sensibility; order apprehended by reason, executed by science. Yes, by means of a greater science, a more integral order may now be executed than any existing. With integral order once established you may perceive the rhythm of consequent harmony. To be harmonious is to be beautiful in a rudimentary sense: a good platform from which to spring toward the moving infinity that is the present. It is in architecture in this sense that "God meets with nature in the sphere of the relative." Therefore the first great necessity of a modern architecture is this keen sense of order as integral. That is to say the *form* itself in orderly relationship with purpose or function: the *parts* themselves in order with the form: the materials and methods of work in order with both: a kind of natural integrity—the integrity of each in all and of all in each. This is the exacting new order.

Wherein, then, does the new order differ from the ancient? Merely in this—the ancient order had gone astray, betrayed by "culture," misled by the historian. But the organic simplicity to be thus achieved as new is the simplicity of the universe which is quite different from the simplicity of any machine, just as the art of being in the world is not the same thing as making shift to get about in it.

Internal disorder is architectural disease if not the death of architecture. Needed then, young man, by you who would become an architect, and needed as a very beginning, is some intellectual grasp, the more direct the better, of this radical order of your universe. You will see your universe as architecture.

An inspired sense of order you may have received as a gift— certainly the schools cannot give it to you. Therefore, to the young man in architecture, the word *radical* should be a beautiful word. Radical means "of the root" or "to the root" —begins at the beginning and the word stands up straight. Any architect should be radical by nature because it is not enough for him to begin where others have left off.

Traditions in architecture have proved unsafe. The propaganda of the dead which you now see in a land strewn with the corpses of opportunity, is no more trustworthy than the propaganda of the living. Neither can have much to do with organic architecture. No, the working of principle in the direction of integral order is your only safe precedent. So the actual business of your architectural schools should be to assist you in the perception of such order in the study of the various architec-

1941   Lloyd Burlingham house, project, *El Paso, Texas.* Plan. (Perspective on page 148.)

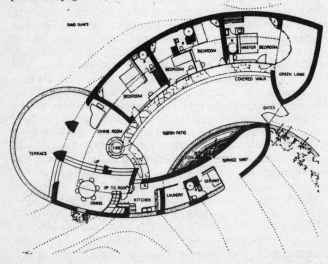

tures of the world—otherwise schools exist only to hinder and deform the young. Merely to enable you, young man, to make a living by making plans for buildings is not good enough work for any school. Thus you may see by this definition of order that the "orders" as such have less than nothing at all to do with modern, that is to say organic, architecture. And too, you may see how little any of the great buildings of the ages can help you to become an architect *except as you look within them* for such working of principle as made them new in the order of their own day. As a matter of course, the particular forms and details appropriate to them become eccentricities to you,—fatalities, should you attempt to copy them for yourselves when you attempt to build. This much at least, I say, is obvious to all minds as the machine-age emerges into human view, with more severe limitations than have ever been imposed upon architecture in the past, but these very limitations are your great, fresh opportunity.

Now, even the scribes are forced by inexorable circumstances to see old materials give way to new materials,—new industrial systems taking the place of old ones,—just as all see the American concepts of social liberty replace the feudal systems, oligarchies and hereditary aristocracies: and by force of circumstances too, all are now inexorably compelled to see that we have nothing, or have very little, which expresses, as architecture, any of these great changes.

Due to the very principles at work as limitations in our mechanical or mechanized products, today, you may see coming into the best of them a new order of beauty that, in a sense, *is* negation of the old order. In a deeper sense, a little later, you may be able to see it, too, as scientific affirmation of ancient order. But you, young man, begin anew, limited, though I hope no less inspired, by this sense of the new order that has only just begun to have results. Only a horizon widened by science, only a human sensibility quickened by the sense of the dignity and worth of the individual as an individual, only this new and finer sense of internal order, *inherent* as the spirit of architecture, can make you an architect now. Your buildings *must* be new because the law was old before the existence of heaven and earth.

You may see on every side of you that principle works in this spirit of cosmic change today just as it worked since the beginning. Lawless you cannot be in architecture, if you are for nature. And do not be afraid, you may disregard the laws, but you are never lawless if you are for nature.

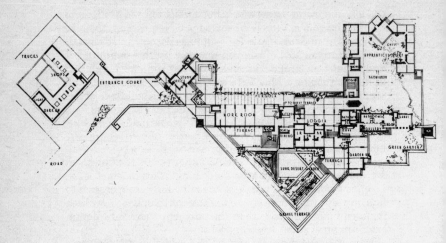

1938   Taliesin West, Frank Lloyd Wright's winter home, near *Scottsdale, Ariz.* Plan. (Photographs on pages 152–155.)

Would you be modern? Then it is the nature of the thing which you now must intelligently approach and to which you must reverently appeal. Out of communion with nature, no less now than ever, you will perceive the order that is new and learn to understand that it is old because it was new in the old. Again I say be sure as sure may be that a clearer perception of principle has to be "on straight" in your mind today before any architectural ways or any technical means can accomplish anything for you at all.

As to these technical ways and means, there are as many paths as there are individuals with capacity for taking infinite pains, to use Carlyle's phrase. All are found in the field itself, the field where all that makes the America of today is active commercial issue. An architect's office may be a near corner of that field. A school in which modern machinery and processes were seen at actual work would be your true corner of that field. If only we had such schools one such school would be worth all the others put together. But only a radical and rebellious spirit is safe in the schools we now have, and time spent there is time lost for such spirits. Feeling for the arts in our country, unfortunately for you, is generally a self-conscious attitude, an attitude similar to the attitude of the provincial in society. The provincial will not act upon innate kindness and good sense, and so tries to observe the other guests to do as

236

they do. Fear of being found ridiculous is his waking nightmare. Innate good sense, in the same way, forsakes the provincial in the realm of ideas in art. By keeping in what seems to him good company, the company of the "higher-ups," he thinks himself safe. This self-conscious fear of being oneself, this cowardly capitulation to what is "being done," yes, the architectural increment *servility* deserves,—this is your inheritance, young man!—your inheritance from the time when the architect's lot was cast "in between," neither old nor new, neither alive nor quite dead. Were this not so it would not be so hard for you to emerge, for you to be born alive. But as a consequence of the little modern architecture we already have, young architects, whatever their years, will emerge with less and less punishment, emerge with far less anguish, because the third generation is with us. That generation will be less likely to advertise to posterity by its copied mannerisms or borrowed "styles" that it was neither scholar nor gentleman in the light of any ideal of spiritual integrity.

It would be unfair to let those architects "in between" who served as your attitudinized or commercialized progenitors go free of blame for your devastating architectural inheritance. Where they should have led they followed by the nose. Instead of being arbiters of principle as a blessed privilege, they became arbiters or victims of the taste that is usually a matter of ignorance. When leisure and money came these progenitors of yours became connoisseurs of the antique, patrons and peddlers of the imitation. So with few exceptions it was with these sentimentalized or stylized architects: "Boy, take down Tudor No. 37 and put a bay window on it for the lady"; or, solicitous, "Madam, what style will you have?" A few held out, all honor to them. A tale told of Louis Sullivan has the lady come in and ask for a Colonial house—"Madam" said he, "you will take what we give you."

Except in a few instances (the result of some such attitude as this) the only buildings we have today approaching architecture are the industrial buildings built upon the basis of common sense: buildings built for the manufacturer who possessed common sense or buildings for residence built to meet actual needs without abject reference to the "higher-ups"—nor with foolish, feathered hat in hand to "culture." These sensible works we possess and the world admires, envies and emulates. This American of common sense, is today the only "way out" for America. He is still the only architectural asset America ever had or has. Give him what he needs when he needs it.

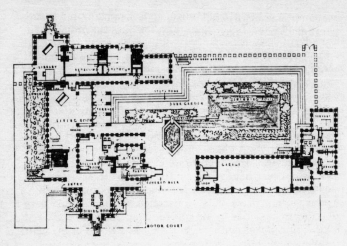

1929   Richard Lloyd Jones house, *Tulsa, Okla*. Plan. (Perspective on page 135.)

To find out what he needs go whenever and wherever you can to the factories to study the processes in relation to the product and go to the markets to study the reactions. Study the machines that make the product what it is. To acquire technique study the materials of which the product is made, study the purpose for which it is produced, study the manhood *in* it, the manhood *of* it. Keep all this present in your mind in all you do, because ideas with bad technique are abortions.

In connection with this matter of "technique" you may be interested to know that the Beaux Arts that made most of your American progenitors is itself confused, now likely to re-interpret its precepts, disown its previous progeny and disin-herit its favorite sons or be itself dethroned, since posterity is already declining the sons as inheritance: the sons who enabled the plan-factory to thrive, the "attitude" to survive in a sen-timental attempt to revive the dead. Yes, it is becoming day by day more evident to the mind that is a mind how shame-fully the product of this culture betrayed America. It is be-ginning to show and it shames America. At our architecture as "culture" quite good-naturedly the Old World laughs. Coming here expecting to see our ideals becomingly attired, they see us fashionably and officially ridiculous, by way of assumption of customs and manners belonging by force of nature and circumstances to something entirely different. They see us betraying not only ourselves but our country itself. But now by grace of freedom we have a little otherwise to show to command dawning respect. No, young man, I do not refer to the skyscraper in the rank and file as that something nor does the world refer to it, except as a stupendous adventure in the business of space-making for rent,—a monstrosity. I again refer you to those simple, sincere attempts to be ourselves and make the most of our own opportunities which are tucked away in out-of-the-way places or found in industrial life as homes or workshops. Our rich people do not own them. Great business on a large scale does not invest in them unless as straightforward business buildings where "culture" is no consideration and columns can give no credit

American great wealth has yet given nothing to the future worth having as architecture or that the future will accept as such unless as an apology. In building for such uses as she had, America has made shift with frightful waste.

Though half the cost of her buildings was devoted to making them beautiful as architecture, not one thought-built structure synthetic in design has American great-wealth, and even less American factotumized "learning," yet succeeded in giving to the modern world. American wealth has been "sold" as it has, itself, bought and sold and been delivered over by professions, or the Scribes, to the Pharisees. So, young man, expect nothing from the man of great wealth in the United States for another decade. Expect nothing from your government for another quarter of a century! Our government, too (helpless instrument of a majority hapless in art), has been delivered over to architecture as the sterile hang-over of feudal thought, or the thought that served the sophist with the slave. That is why the future of architecture in America really lies with the well-to-do man of business,—the man of independent judgment and character of his own, unspoiled by great financial success,—that is to say the man not persuaded, by winning his own game, that he knows all about everything else.

Opportunity to develop an architecture today lies with those sincere and direct people, who, loving America for its own sake, live their own lives quietly in touch with its manifold beauties,—*blessed by comprehension of the ideal of freedom that founded this country.* In our great United States notwithstanding alleged "rulers" or any "benign" imported cultural influences, these spontaneous sons and daughters are the soul of our country; they are fresh unspoiled life and therefore they are your opportunity in art, just as you, the artist are their opportunity. You will be their means to emerge from the conglomerate "in between."

And this brings us to the American "ideal." This American ideal must be in architecture what it is in life. Why obscure the issue by any sophisticated aesthetics or involution with academic formulae? The arts are only such media as we have for the direct expression of life reacting in turn with joy-giving force upon that life itself—enriching all human experience to come. The arts in America are on free soil, and therefore all-imperatively call for the creative artist.

The soul of that new life we are fond of calling American is liberty: liberty tolerant and so sincere that it must see all free or itself suffer. This freedom is the highest American ideal. To attain it, then, is inner-experience, because there is no "exterior" freedom. Freedom develops from within and is another expression of an integral order of the mind in high estate. Freedom is impossible where discord exists either within or without. So, perfect freedom no one has though all may aspire. But, to the degree freedom is attained, the by-product called "happiness," meaning, I suppose, innocent life, will be the consequence.

Very well,—take the American ideal of freedom from the realm of human consciousness to our specific expression of that consciousness we call architecture. Could any decorator's shop, even were it called a "studio," sell anything ready-made out of the world's stock of "styles" to do more than bedizen or bedevil this essential sentiment?—artificially dress it up for artificiality-making social occasion? No, it would be impossible to do more,—architecture like freedom *cannot be put on,* it must be worked out from within.

Could any school of architecture inculcating the culture of Greece or Rome fit the case any better with current abstractions of ancient culture as dedicated to the sophist and the slave? No, ancient culture produced nothing to fit the case of an individual freedom evolved by the individual from within. And this is justification,—(is it?) . . . for evolving nothing and going on with make-believe just because make-believe is organized and therefore the decorator has it in stock, the plan-factory sells it, and the schools provide it. The present tendency in architecture which we style modern says emphatically "NO" to this betrayal.

240

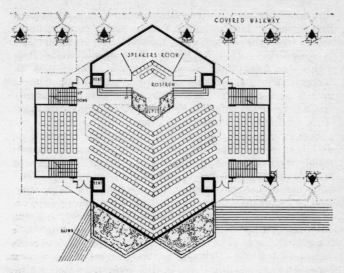

1940 Ann Pfeiffer Chapel, Florida Southern College, *Lakeland, Fla.* (Photographs on pages 150, 151.)

If we are determining ourselves as a free people (and we are), by what you build you will now say proudly "NO" to further menial treason of this academic type.

Are we a free people? Of course not. The question that is important however, is—do we have it in our hearts as it is written in our constitutional charter to be free? Is it sincerely and passionately our ideal to be free? Notwithstanding so much cowardly popular evidence to the contrary, I say it is our ideal. Those highest in the realm of freedom should build suitable buildings and build them now, for that spirit, first—and for America to ponder. There is no longer any doubt in the mind that eventually America will have a truly characteristic architecture,—that much is already written for you on the vanishing wall and the disappearing cave.

Young man in architecture, wherever you are and whatever your age, or whatever our job, we—the youth of America—should be the psychological shock-troops thrown into action against corruption of this supreme American ideal. It will be for youth, in this sense, to win the day for freedom in architecture.

That American architecture cannot be imitative architecture is self-evident in spite of false standards. It is self-evident that neither architect who imitates nor architecture imitative can be free,—the one is a slave, the other forever in bondage. It is as evident that free architecture must develop from within,—an integral, or as we now say in architecture, an "organic" affair. For this reason if for no other reason modern architecture can be no "mode" nor can it ever again be any "style." You must defend it against both or senility will again set in for another cycle of thirty years.

Specifically then, you may ask, what is truly "modern" in architecture? . . . The answer is *power,*—that is to say material resources,—*directly applied to purpose.* Yes, modern architecture is power directly applied to purpose in buildings in the same sense that we see it so applied in the airship, ocean liner or motor car. Therefore it is natural enough perhaps for newly awakened architects to make the error of assuming that, beyond accepting the consequences of directness and integral character, the building itself must resemble utensil-machines or flying-, fighting- or steaming-machines, or any other appliances. But there is this essential difference (it makes all the difference) between a machine and a building. A building is not an appliance nor a mobilization. The building as architecture is born out of the heart of man, permanent consort to the ground, comrade to the trees, true reflection of man in the realm of his own spirit. His building is therefore consecrated space wherein he seeks refuge, recreation and repose for body but especially for mind. So our machine-age building need no more look like machinery than machinery need look like buildings.

Certain qualities, humanly desirable qualities, I am sure you may obtain by means of machinery or by intelligent use of our mechanized systems without selling your souls to factotums by way of a factorialized aesthetic. There is rather more serious occasion for becoming ourselves in our environment, our architecture becoming more human, our dwelling-places becoming more imaginatively fresh and original in order to overcome not only the "cultured tag" but the deadly drag of mechanical monotony and the purely mechanical insignificance that otherwise characterizes us and that will eventually destroy us. But the "ites" of the "ism" and "ist" give signs of being so engrossed in a new machine-aesthetic that they will be unable to rise above themselves—sunk, and so soon, in the struggle for machine-technique. Already hectic architects' "modernistic" and the decorators' "modernism" obscure the simple issue. I would have you believe that to be genuinely new, the man must begin to win over the machine, and not the machine win over the man by way of the man.

We have already observed that whenever architecture was great it was modern, and whenever architecture was modern human values were the only values preserved. And I reiterate that modern architecture in this deeper sense is novelty only to novitiates, that the principles moving us to be modern now are those that moved the Frank and Goth, the Indian, the Maya and the Moor. They are the same principles that will move Atlantis recreated. If there is architecture in Mars or Venus, and there is, at least there is the architecture of Mars and Venus themselves,—the same principles are at work there too.

Principles are universal.

If you approach principles from within you will see that many of the traditions we flattered to extinction by emulation never were even on speaking terms with principle, but were bound up with education by way of impotence or deadly force of habit, or what not? Modern architecture knows them now for impositions, and is gaining courage to cast them out, together with those who insist upon their use and administer them. This in itself you should gratefully recognize as no small value of "the modern-movement," so-called.

Goethe observed that death was nature's ruse in order that she might have more life. Therein you may see the reason why there must be a new, and why the new must ever be the death of the old, but this tragedy need occur only where "forms" are concerned, if you will stick to principle. It is because we have not relied on principle that the genius of the *genus homo* is now to be taxed anew to find an entirely new kind of building that will be a more direct application of power to purpose than ever before has existed in history. But again let us repeat that to secure beauty of the kind we perceive in external nature in the inflexible standardization that characterizes that "power" today, we must not dramatize the machine but dramatize the man. You must work, young man in architecture, to lift the curse of the "appliance" either mechanical or sentimental from the life of today.

But this modern constructive endeavor is being victimized at the start by a certain new aesthetic wherein appearance is made an aim instead of character made a purpose. The "new" aesthetic thus becomes at the very beginning "old" because it is only another "appliance." The French with all the delicacy and charm they seem to possess as substitute for soul, and with French flair for the appropriate gesture at the opportune moment, have contributed most to this affix or suffix of the appliance. Initiators of so many "art movements" that prove ephemera, they recognize the opportunity for another "movement." The new world and the old world too had both already recognized a certain new order that is beauty in the clean-stripped, hard look of machines,—had admired an exterior simplicity due to the direct construction by which automatons were made to operate, move and stop. But certain aesthetes,—French by sympathy or association,—are trying to persuade us that this exterior simplicity *as a new kind of decoration,* is the appropriate "look" of everything in our machine age. French painting foolishly claims to have seen it first,—foolishly because we saw it first ourselves. But French Modernism proceeds to set it up flatwise in architecture in two dimensions,—that is to say to survey it in length and breadth. Although these effects of surface and mass were already well along in our own country (two dimensions, completed by surfaces parallel to the earth, as a third dimension to grip the whole building to the ground)—Paris nevertheless ignores this, with characteristic desire for "movement," and sets up characteristic machine-appearance in two dimensions (that is to say in the surface and mass effects with which Paris is familiar), and architecture thus becomes decoration. You may see it in the fashionable shops while France contemplates a fifty-four million dollar building to propagandize her arts and crafts in the American field while America is busy making enough motorcars to go around.

A certain inspiration characterized the first French recognition but uninspired emulation has become reiteration and in the end nothing will have happened unless another "mode," another aesthetic dictum gone forth to languish as superficial fashion. Another "istic," another "ism" comes to town to pass away,—this time not in a hansom cab but in a flying machine!

Yes, America is young, so healthy it soon wearies of negation. The negation we have here is stranger to mysterious depths of feeling. It is protestant. The protestant is useful but seldom beautiful. When he ceases to protest and becomes constructive himself,—some new protestant will arise to take his place and we may see this happening at the moment.

Yet for young America today a light too long diverted to base uses is shining again through all the propaganda and confusion. This light is the countenance of integral order, a more profound, consistent order than the world has fully realized before, wherein power is applied to purpose in construction just as mathematics is sublimated into music. By that light you may clearly see that, where there is no integral order, there is no beauty, though the order be no more obvious than mathematics in music is obvious.

Not so strange then that the novitiate takes the machine itself as the prophet of this new order, though you must not forget that although music is sublimated mathematics the professor of mathematics cannot make music. Nor can the doctor of philosophy nor the master of construction nor the enthusiastic antiquarian make architecture.

No rationalizing of the machine or factorializing of aesthetics can obscure the fact that architecture is born, not made, —must consistently grow from within to whatever it becomes. Such forms as it takes must be spontaneous generation of materials, building methods and purpose. The brain is a great tool with great craft; but in architecture you are concerned with our sense of the specific beauty of human lives as lived on earth in relation to each other. Organic achitecture seeks superior sense of use and a finer sense of comfort, expressed in organic simplicity. That is what you, young man, should call *architecture.* Use and comfort in order to become architecture must become *spiritual satisfactions* wherein the soul insures a more subtle use, achieves a more constant repose. So, architecture speaks as poetry to the soul. In this machine age to utter this poetry that is architecture, as in all other ages, you must learn the organic language of the natural which is *ever the language of the new.* To know any language you must know the alphabet. The alphabet in architecture in our machine age is the nature of steel, glass and concrete construction,—the nature of the machines used as tools, and the nature of the new materials to be used.

Now what language?

Poverty in architecture,—architecture the language of the human heart,—has grown by unnatural appropriation of artificiality, has grown wretched and miserable by the fetish of the appliance, whether by the appliance as mechanical or sentimental. Prevailing historical sympathy administered as standardized learning has confused art with archaeology. In this academic confusion we have been unable to cultivate the principles that grow architecture as a flower of the mind out of our own nature as flowers grow out of earth.

To make architectural growth, you must now perceive that

the essential power of our civilization can never be expressed or even capitalized for long in any shallow terms of any factorialized or merely mechanized art. If you would be true to the center of architecture wherever the circumference of architecture may be formed you will see the machine as a peerless tool but otherwise you will see any machine as sterility itself. Engrossed in the serious struggle for new technique, you may not override your love of romance, except such foolish abuse of romance as is our present sentimentality or senility,—our barren lot long since past.

I assure you that at least enough has appeared in my own experience to prove to me that the power of the man with the machine is really no bar at all to tremendously varied *imaginative* architecture.

Nor does any mind that is a mind doubt that the worthy product of our own industrialism should and would give us more digestible food for artistic enjoyment, than the early Italian, Italian pasticcio or the medieval ever gave us. But such artistic enjoyment should not, could not, mean that the machine-age commonplaces were accepted as worthy. It would mean these commonplaces transfigured and transformed by inner fire to take their places in the immense vista of the ages as human masterpieces. Such interpretation by inner fire as *character in the realm of nature* is the work of the young man in architecture.

Oh—America will have to go through a lot of amateurish experiments with you. We as Americans may have to submit to foolish experiments used in the American manner as "quick-turnover" propaganda. But we must be patient because architecture is profound.

Architecture is the very body of civilization itself. It takes time to grow,—begins to be architecture only when it is thought-built,—that is to say when it is a synthesis completed from a rational beginning and, naturally as breathing, genuinely *modern*.

America will factorialize and factotumize much more, and as many Americans will die of ornaphobia as of ornamentia by the wayside before any goal is reached. She will listen to much reasoning from all and sundry and will justly despise the poisonous fruits of most of the reasoning. She will see many little bands or cliques among you muddling about near-ideas, attempting to run with them and kick a goal for personal glory in what we already sufficiently know as "modern movements." And you yourselves will see exploitation of perfectly good ideals by every shade of every imported nationality on earth when the women's clubs of America wake to the great significance to the family of this rapidly changing order in which we live and which they are only now learning to call modern from the midst of antiques. And then in characteristic fashion America will be inclined to mistake abuse of the thing for the thing itself and kick the thing out. As a characteristic abuse we have already seen pseudo-classic architecture stripping off its enabling cornices, entablatures and columns, and fundamentally unchanged, hung up to us on a grand scale as "modern." We will soon see more of it on a grander scale. But washing pseudo-classic behind the ears cannot make architecture modern.

One abusive formula that enables the plan-factory to modernize overnight is that all architecture without ornament is modern. Another agonizing formula that gives the decorator "a break," is, that sharp angles cutting flat surfaces are modern. Never mind,—we will accept anything, just so recurrent senility does not again become a new aesthetic.

Yes, modern architecture is young architecture,—the joy of youth must bring it. The love of youth, eternal youth must develop and keep it. You must see this architecture as wise, but not so much wise as sensible and wistful,—nor any more scientific than sentient, nor so much resembling a flying machine as a masterpiece of the imagination.

Oh yes, young man; consider well that a house is a machine in which to live, but by the same token a heart is a suction-pump. Sentient man begins where that concept of the heart ends.

Consider well that a house is a machine in which to live but architecture begins where that concept of the house ends. All life is machinery in a rudimentary sense, and yet machinery is the life of nothing. Machinery is machinery only because of life. It is better for you to proceed from the generals to the particulars. So do not rationalize from machinery to life. Why not think from life to machines? The utensil, the weapon, the automaton—all are *appliances*. The song, the masterpiece, the edifice are a warm outpouring of the heart of man,—human delight in life triumphant: we glimpse the infinite.

That glimpse or vision is what makes art a matter of inner experience,—therefore sacred, and no less but rather more individual in this age, I assure you, than ever before.

Architecture expresses human life, machines do not, nor does any appliance whatsoever. Appliances only serve life.

247

Lack of appreciation of the difference between the appliance and life is to blame for the choicest pseudo-classic horrors in America. And yet our more successful "modern" architects are still busy applying brick or stone envelopes to steel frames in the great American cities. Instead of fundamentally correcting this error, shall any superficial aesthetic disguised as new enable this same lack of appreciation of the principles of architecture to punish us again this time with a machinery abstract which will be used as an appliance of the appliance of another cycle of thirty years? If so as between architecture as sentimental appliance and architecture as mechanical appliance or even the aesthetic abstract itself as an architectural appliance,—it would be better for America were you to choose architecture as the mechanical appliance. But, then, organic architecture would have to keep on in a little world of its own. In this world of its own the hard line and the bare upright plane in unimaginative contours of the box both have a place, —just as the carpet has a place on the floor, but the creed of the naked stilt, as a stilt, has no place. The horizontal plane gripping all to earth comes into organic architecture to complete the sense of forms that do not "box up" contents but imaginatively express space. This is modern.

In organic architecture the hard straight line breaks to the dotted line where stark necessity ends and thus allows appropriate rhythm to enter in order to leave suggestion its proper values. This is modern.

In organic architecture, any conception of any building as a building begins at the beginning and goes *forward* to incidental expression as a picture and does not begin with some incidental expression as a picture and go groping *backward.* This is modern.

Eye-weary of reiterated bald commonplaces wherein light is rejected from blank surfaces or fallen dismally into holes cut in them, organic architecture brings the man once more face to face with nature's play of shade and depth of shadow seeing fresh vistas of native creative human thought and native feeling presented to his imagination for consideration. This is modern.

The sense of interior space as reality in organic architecture coordinates with the enlarged means of modern materials. The building is now found in this sense of interior space; the enclosure is no longer found in terms of mere roof or walls but as "screened"—space. This reality is modern.

In true modern architecture, therefore, the sense of surface and mass disappears in light, or fabrications that combine it with strength. And this fabrication is no less the expression of principle as power-directed-toward-purpose than may be seen in any modern appliance or utensil machine. But modern architecture affirms the higher human sensibility of the sun-lit space. Organic buildings are the strength and lightness of the spiders' spinning, buildings qualified by light, bred by native character to environment—married to the ground. That is modern!

Meanwhile by way of parting moment with the young man in architecture—this he should keep—concerning ways and means:

1. Forget the architectures of the world except as something good in their way and in their time.

2. Do none of you go into architecture to get a living unless you love architecture as a principle at work, for its own sake—prepared to be as true to it as to your mother, your comrade, or yourself.

3. Beware of the architectural school except as the exponent of engineering.

4. Go into the field where you can see the machines and methods at work that make the modern buildings, or stay in construction direct and simple until you can work naturally into building-design from the nature of construction.

5. Immediately begin to form the habit of thinking "why"

1948   Adelman Laundry, project, *Milwaukee, Wis.*

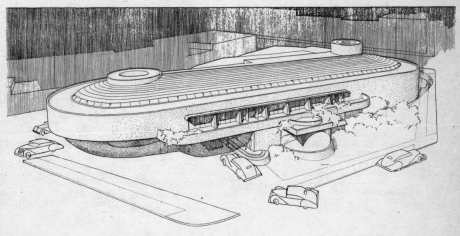

concerning any effects that please or displease you.

6. Take nothing for granted as beautiful or ugly, but take every building to pieces, and challenge every feature. Learn to distinguish the curious from the beautiful.

7. Get the habit of analysis,—analysis will in time enable synthesis to become your habit of mind.

8. "Think in simples" as my old master used to say,— meaning to reduce the whole to its parts in simplest terms, getting back to first principles. Do this in order to proceed from generals to particulars and never confuse or confound them or yourself be confounded by them.

9. Abandon as poison the American idea of the "quick turnover." To get into practice "halfbaked" is to sell out your birthright as an architect for a mess of pottage, or to die pretending to be an architect.

10. Take time to prepare. Ten years' preparation for preliminaries to architectural practice is little enough for any architect who would rise "above the belt" in true architectural appreciation or practice.

11. Then go as far away as possible from home to build your first buildings. The physician can bury his mistakes,—but the architect can only advise his client to plant vines.

12. Regard it as just as desirable to build a chicken-house as to build a cathedral. The size of the project means little in art, beyond the money-matter. It is the quality of character that really counts. Character may be large in the little or little in the large.

1948   Adelman Laundry. Longitudinal section.

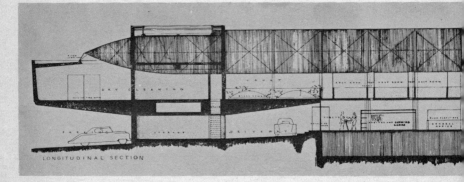

250

13. Enter no architectural competition under any circumstances except as a novice. No competition ever gave to the world anything worth having in architecture. The jury itself is a picked average. The first thing done by the jury is to go through all the designs and throw out the best and the worst ones so, as an average, it can average upon an average. The net result of any competition is an average by the average of averages.

14. Beware of the shopper for plans. The man who will not grubstake you in prospecting for ideas in his behalf will prove a faithless client.

It is undesirable to commercialize everything in life just because your lot happens to be cast in the machine-age. For instance, architecture is walking the streets today a prostitute because "to get the job" has become the first principle of architecture. In architecture the job should find the man and not the man the job. In art the job and the man are mates; neither can be bought or sold to the other. Meantime, since all we have been talking about is a higher and finer kind of integrity, keep your own ideal of honesty so high that your dearest ambition in life will be to call yourself an honest man, and look yourself square in the face. Keep your ideal of honesty so high that you will never be quite able to reach it.

Respect the masterpiece,—it is true reverence to man. There is no quality so great, none so much needed now.

from TWO LECTURES IN ARCHITECTURE, *1931*

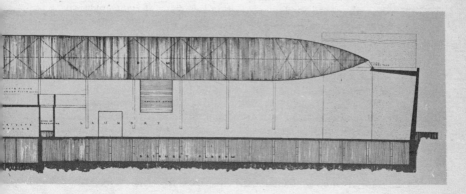

The Chicago Century of Progress

As skyscraperism characterizes the thought of the group characterizing the Chicago World's Fair—they themselves idealized the Fair as "New York seen from one of its own high buildings . . ."

Why not, then, the Fair itself apotheosis of the skyscraper?

Build a great skyscraper (in which the Empire State Building might stand free in a central court) devoted to all the resources of the modern elevator.

Instead of the old stage-props, the same old miles of picture-buildings faked in cheap materials, wrapped around a lagoon, a fountain or a theatrical waterfall—all to be eventually butchered —let there be, for once, a genuine modern construction.

If elevators handle the population of New York, they could handle the crowds at the Fair. Why not handle the crowds directly from several expansive tiers of mechanized parking space, great terraces from which the skyscraper itself would rise. The construction should be merely the steel itself designed as integral pattern in structural framing. Then concrete slabs for floors projecting as cantilever balconies, floor above floor— garden floors intervening as restaurants.

Instead of glass for enclosure—some light, transparent glass substitutes might be used; the multitudinous areas thus created would be let to exhibitors. The top stories could be garden observatories, pleasure places. A vast auditorium might join the skyscraper at the base to handle great aggregations of people on the ground. The tower construction might rise from triple-decked parking terraces, one corner of the terraces extending into the lake projecting two ways at right angles to make piers and harbors for water craft. Where the reflections of the tower would fall, powerful jets of the lake itself could be lifted by submerged power pumps to great height, all to be illuminated by modern light apparatus, projecting toward the tower and from it, the lake becoming thus at selected points a series of great fountains irradiated by light.

The Lake Front Park itself would be mere landscape adjunct to a great modern structure which might easily rise two hundred and forty-five stories, say two thousand five hundred feet above the lake level—or about a half mile high.

The clouds might naturally or artificially drift across its summit. Or effects be created by aeroplanes laying down colored ribbons of smoke to drift across it.

252

Such construction today would be no impossible feat, financially or structurally, in fact, entirely within reach.

And it could stay thus, a feature of the Chicago lake front beautiful as the Eiffel Tower never was (and the Eiffel Tower would reach only well below its middle).

Something accomplished worthy of a century of progress? The beacons from the top would reach adjoining states: the radio from the antennae lifting from the tower crown, would be in touch with all the world.

But if not skyscraper-minded and preferring to roam instead of to be lifted up on high ... then ...

A weaving characteristic of this age of steel in tension. Accept from pioneer constructor John Roebling the message of the Brooklyn Bridge.

Build noble pylons—the Fair commissioners seemed to like the word pylon—on the Lake Front five hundred feet apart each way until enough park, including threading waterways, has been covered to accommodate all exhibitors on park level and one balcony. A canopy would be anchored by steel cables to the outer series of pylons. Weave main and minor and intermediate cables, a network to support transparent glass substitutes, and thus make an architectural canopy more beautiful and more vast than any ever seen. The canopy could rise five hundred feet at the pylons, to fall between them to one hundred and fifty feet above the park. The fabric should fall at the sides as a screen to close the space against wind. Rain would wash the roof spaces or they could be flushed from the pylon tops as fountains, the water spouting through openings at the low points of the canopy into fountain basins, features of the lagoons that would wind and thread their way beneath the canopy through the greenery of the park.

All trees, foliage and waterways could be joined by moving walkways reaching individual plots allotted to exhibitors. Little footwork for the beholders. Each individual exhibitor would be free to set up his own show and ballyhoo it as he pleased.

The old fair spirit, exciting as of old—but made free to excite the sophisticated modern ego once more by great spans and wondrous spinning.

Well, this type of construction with appropriate illumination and hydroelectric effects should cost less in standardization thus extended and made beautiful than the pettifogging, picture-making, individualized buildings of so many architects, all only interfering with exhibits and exhibitions in order to say exactly nothing in the same old way. Tagged—publicity tagged only—as new. At least, the great pylons might remain as lighting features of Lake Front Park; whereas the hodge-podge of buildings faked in synthetic cardboard and painted, would all have to be thrown away some day.

Or ... more romantically inclined? Then why not—

There on the Lake Front is the Chicago harbor, already enclosed against the turbulence of Lake Michigan. Why not use that for a genuine holiday? A gay festival for the eye.

Why not a pontoon fair?

Make sealed, lightly reinforced metal cylinders, exhaust air from these like those of the catamaran; use them for floating foundations. Fabricate light thin tubes, some large, others not so large, some slender, and each in any desired length. Fabricate them in pulp to be very light, soaked and stiffened in waterproofing or in transparent synthetics. Use these "reeds" in rhythmic verticality, grouping them to get support for light roof-webbing. Again use the steel strand, anchored in metal drums, to get and hold the webbing for roof cover. Large pontoons for tall buildings, long buildings. Square for square buildings. All to be connected by interesting floating bridges. Floating gardens too could be connected to the buildings—the whole of the assembled floating units connected by characteristic link units, themselves attractive features, so that while all were joined, yet all might gently undulate with no harm.

Then introduce transparent colored glass tubing among the colored pulp tubing. Why not illuminate the glass and have, for once, airy verticality as a sheer legitimate modern fabrication, only aimed at as "a charm of New York" and there seen only at night in the rain?

The particolored opaque and transparent verticality would be doubled by direct reflections trembling in the water.

The water itself could again be thrown up to great heights and in enormous quantity by inserted force-pumps, effects costing nothing but power. Fair a whole world of illumination, irradiating and irradiated light—an iridescent fair or a fair of iridescent, opalescent "reeds."

The great whole would be a picturesque, pleasurable float.

Modern pageantry, this, and genuine in itself. Space could easily be created for specific purposes and adapted to suit each commercial need: these varied units linked together as a continuous, varied, brilliant modern circumstance.

Then, after the Fair was over, appropriate units could be

detached and floated to an anchorage in the lagoons of the various parks and waterways of the Lake Front to serve as restaurants or good-time places, concessions rented from the city.

If there are these three ideas, genuine and practical as modern architecture, there could be as easily three hundred to choose from for the Fair.

from AN AUTOBIOGRAPHY, *1932*

The City

Illusion

And yet, coming to the greatest of them, New York, for the first time, one has the illusion that we must be a great people to have raised this heavy barrage of relentless commercial mantraps so high; to have grandly hung so much book-architecture upon cumbrous old-fashioned steel framing, so regardless. Inhabited at such enormous cost not alone in money but in all human values as well.

Such frantic energy pours through this haphazard money-mountain made by the mile to pile up and confuse men and materials, haphazard; here and there ruthless; drenched by what relentless ambition has wrung from our abounding national resources. Well, what of it—if everywhere these resources are wasted by foolish attempts at establishment by the nation and we end in some form of bad surface-decoration? What if one arrogant skyscraper does outrun or ram another, and crams the horizon with harsh haphazard masses—upended, crowding on the bewildered wistful eye, peering up from black shadows cast upon the man down there below on hard pavement? What, if so? We have seen crowding, greater if similar, as destructive drama wherever irresistible physical force has violated mankind or tilted up and broken through earth's crust. So—see in this volcanic crater of confused energy bred by money-power, no wise control of enormous mechanical forces, pushing up to crowd and be crowded, to grind against each other with a blind force moved by common greed. Crowded exploitation, as only the Machine can crowd and exploit, forcing *anxiety* upon all modern life. Is astonishment at all this akin to admiration? But consider—this is never a *noble* expression of life; it is again and again only the apotheosis by the gregarious expedient of overmastering Rent.

The shadows of these haphazard skyscrapers cast down below are significant. Their shadows are the surviving shadow-of-the-ancient-wall of the cave-dweller.

The skyscraper if considered as independent achievement in itself may be justifiable: a prideful thing! A tall building may be very beautiful, economical and desirable in itself—provided always that it is in no way interference with what lives below, but looking further ahead than the end of the landlord's ruse—by inhabiting a small green park. That park is humane now. The skyscraper is no longer sane unless in free green space. In the country it may stand beautiful for its own sake.

Exaggerated perpendicularity has no such bill-of-health. It is now the terrible stricture of our big city. Whatever is perpendicular casts a shadow: shadows of the skyscraper fall aground and where crowded are an utterly selfish exploitation. Because, if the civic rights of the neighbor down there below, in the shadows, were to be exercised, there would be no "skyscraping" at all. There would be only a general rise in urban floor-level. Without much sense and with no distinction, cramping and swamping all tenantry in artificial light and forced ventilation, all would congest and be congestion unbearable even to the herd-struck morons our present skyscraperism has cultivated.

The Light of Day

So to the urban skyscraper-builder in overcrowded cities the very insolence of the urban skyscraper-feat is no small measure of its attraction? Although skyscraperism fits so well into the primitive psychology of the "rugged individualist" of the industrial revolution—he who from an office fifty stories above the man in the street casts his ominous shadow below upon the man he directs in some great money-making enterprise— he *is* "success?" He is at last picturesque in the way he likes to be. The tall silk hat and gold-tipped stick of the past had only a little something to gratify his old-fashioned equivalent —but now? What a hallmark, the very tallest building in the big city outcrowding the already overcrowded, based upon commercial success! Ancient titles? Mere nicknames! Here he is—the tangible proof of the "greatness" of modern business. In the city, is this skyscraper shadow his own shadow? But what does that matter or mean to his place in Time? He will never know.

Now move him and his shadow into the open spaces and he becomes truly splendid: a contribution to the glory and dignity of our era. The difference?

Simple. As material things stand with us today the sky-scraper might be ultimate expression of the individuality fairly expected from the freedom of democracy to signify what we have so painstakingly prophesied and now discourage. But in the overcrowded big city it is no exalted order of merit. See it there as conspicuous proof of the cultural lag and a fine example of our conspicuous waste.

In the present era's future (if it has one) the skyscraper will be considered *"ne plus ultra* of the *e pluribus unum"* capital-istic centralization. The New York skyscraper will be seen as the prancing of this great iron horse—the industrial revolu-tion. The iron horse rearing high hoofs in air for the plunge before the runaway—the runaway to oblivion by way of the atom bomb—or we go to the country!

Thus enforced upon our understanding by the non-under-standing in overgrown urban life, skyscraping is not merely a falsity but a moral, economic, aesthetic, ethical monstrosity!

This exaggeration of privilege among us is already far out of democratic scale. Owing to social, collegiate, and commer-cial pride of exploitation going hand in hand with miseduca-tion—if properly citified, "well mechanized," that is to say standardized by commerce, the citizen is now so far gone that he easily mistakes the pig-piling and crowding of big business for eminence of excellence: mistakes the pushbutton powers of the machine age for his own powers and finds hectic excite-ment in urban uproar and the vertigo of verticality. The more citified he becomes the less civilized he is; the more this racing of the iron-horse into the inferiority of conformity grows characteristic of his weakness. Roaring tumults of congestion emphasize terrific collisions of power; explosions of grinding mechanical forces in this whirling vortex, urban exaggeration; in these the rich whirling-dervish thinks he sees *his own* greatness. In the whirl the citizen is satiated—his "greatness" something wholly vicarious. But his shadow too is the shadow cast by the sun.

And yet—seen at night, heedless of stampede, the haphazard

monster has myriad beauties of silhouette; light streaming—
the light punctuated by reflected or refracted lights. In human
terms yet undefined, the nocturnal monster yields rhythmical
perspectives, glowing spotted walls of light, dotted lines, a
world of fascinating reflections hung upon other reflections
ranging along vistas of the street or pendent as the wisteria
hangs its violet racemes on a trellis or the trees. Then the
skyscraper is, in the dusk, a shimmering, prismatic verticality;
gossamer veil of a festive scene, hanging there against the
backdrop of a black night sky to dazzle, entertain, and amaze,
in great masses. Lighted interiors come through the veil with
a sense of life and well-being. The City then seems alive. It
does live as illusion lives.

The light of day? Streams of more and more insignificant
facades and dead walls rise and pour out of hard faced masses
behind and above human beings all crawling on hard pavements like ants to "hole in" somewhere or find their way to
this or that cubicle. Beings packed into the roar, rush and
danger of a new kind of the old voracity—speed. And out of
other holes everywhere elsewhere pour these sordid reitera-
tions, rent, rented, or in pursuit of rent! Overpowering emphasis everywhere of the cell in upended stricture; continual
slicing, edging, inching in all the crowding. Tier above tier
rises the soulless habitation of the shelf. Interminable empty
crevices run up and down the winding ways of windy un-
healthy canyons. Heartless, this now universal grip of grasp-
ing, unending stricture. Box to box on box boxing, glassed in
boxing looking into other glass-boxing. Black shadows falling
on glass fronts with artificial lights burning behind them day
long. Millions upon millions of little cavities, cells squared by
the acre, acreage spread by the mile. This a vast prison with
glass fronts.

Above this avaricious aggregation which cruel ambition has
built and now patronizes are haphazard odd insignificant sky-
lines: like the false ambitions below making it all more human
by lying about it. Elaborate ornamentation is all spasmodic.
Here goes and comes to go again the to-and-fro, anxiety,
satiety of life in the machine age. Incessant the wear of the
cities, always to stop-and-go, go-and-stop only to crisscross
again. Every human movement made is made to be broken!
Every human being's interest, private interest, is entangled
and in danger everywhere. Every heart that beats—beaten
soon or late.

Streets? All too narrow channels jammed and jamming

traffic. When available they are all, at best, only half effective owing to the ubiquitous crisscross of the gridiron. Always the gridiron! Forever a bedlam of harsh, torturing shrieks and roars. This wasteful spasm of racing movement to and fro in the crisscross. Down erstwhile narrow old village lanes one is deep in dark shadows cast by distorted forces. Therein lurk the ambitions and frustrations of the human being urbanized out of scale with its own body. Here see defeat of all aspirations of the human heart. The sense of humane proportion lost.

Incongruous mantrap of monstrous dimensions! Enormity devouring manhood, confusing personality by frustration of individuality? Is this not Anti-Christ? The Moloch that knows no God but *more?*

The agonizing traffic problem is here seen forced upon the city originally made and now aggravated by the persistent landlord with his skyscraper. The present city is yet only about one-tenth the motor car city it must become within the next fifteen years unless the citizen abandons his car. But dutiful devotion to advantages of our machine age now means to every citizen either a motor car—or two or three—(comparative flight) a helicopter; or else a frustrated moron for a citizen. Or a maniac? Every citizen will have a car or two or already dreams of having more, meantime envying the neighbor his four. Three, two or one—observe if the new freeway or the gridiron congestion is not already crucifixion. Then what comes, as average success multiplies and relentlessly multiplies the excess of our already excessive mechanical leverage?

Roughly calculate the mass of public conveyances, taxicabs, buses, private cars and trucks that success will bring to any overgrown village consisting of one hundred thousand to several million people: add half that number of private cars and add, perhaps one twenty-fifth as many delivery machines; add one fiftieth as many buses to displace streetcar tracks and carry children to school; and add unwholesome subways. You will find that—with room enough for each incidental transient coming into town from the suburbs (or going out), in order to function at all lengthwise, to say nothing of around about or crosswise—the surging maniacal mass inextricable would pigpile in the narrow channels of the city well above the seventh story!

Allowing now for the established urban crisscross (the gridiron making every city street only half-time efficient) the struggling mass would again double; pile up and submerge even the ten-story buildings? Call this exaggeration: cut it in two. Then, if you like, cut it in two again. There will still be enough cars pounding along the streets and pouring carbon monoxide into them to put Manhattan and all its kind completely out of commission, starved for oxygen.

Now consider the fact that motorcar traffic has just begun within this resurrection of ancient Bedlam. Then why deck, double-deck, or triple-deck city streets or burrow in holes below them at a cost of billions only to invite further increase and eventually inevitable defeat? Now see these new imitations of old feudal cities as total loss to modern times.

Why not then allow the citizenry to keep the billions they would have to pay for decking and burrowing? They could buy more and better cars and perhaps soon safe flying machines, eventually bailing out of the urban mantrap into the more natural life of the small town fruitfully expanded in the country. As the freedom of our democracy dawns genuine in the citizen's heart, the present prison-city vanishes by way of its own senseless excess. Hazardous machine power built the excess and, if left haphazard, will ruin it. A City should now be the planned consequence of better understanding of what the nature of the machine may mean to the man with a conscience; and this must now be made constructive. Without this integrity on our part our boasted democratic freedom is going—going—something soon doomed entirely by its own foolish extravagant ignorance—and gone.

So no longer manifest is any clear thought or sane feeling for humane good in urban exaggeration. Humane elements are sterilized by it or demoralized. Lurking in sinister urban shadows cast by these prideful urban strictures, lie the legalised impositions of today; and no less in our libraries, museums, colleges and in institutions of learning and especially of authority —a terrifying make-believe. The abortion we see in street facades has become a general frown. This surviving shadow of the ancient wall itself sinister. Savage or unsane as the convulsions caused by the overgrown city are—we see in them as valid an example of deterioration by "advantages" as has existed in all time.

Just because we have some little thriving village of yesterday (port perhaps) driven thus mad by excess—why is it so conveniently mistaken for principles? Success creative would seldom if ever know! The abnormality the city breeds is nothing more

than much more of the already much-too-much in all the hell
there is right now!

from THE LIVING CITY, *1958*

Democracy in Overalls

The dream of the free city is to establish democracy on a
firmer basis. . . . Is it a dream? A vision certainly. Ideas
always precede and configure the facts. But I am here writing
no more than the too specific outline of a practical ideal perceiving Change as already upon us. Old phases as well as
phrases must come to an end. Graphic and plastic arts and fine
art come in at this point to aid in showing just what the universal city and its buildings might be. The different buildings here
described have already been given either graphic (the drawing)
or three-dimensional (the model) form. To begin, I believe that
a general outline of any ideal is better than specific plan or
model of its particular features. An ideal once clearly fixed in
mind—and the plan will come naturally enough. Fresh under-
takings then appear and proceed from generals to particulars
with the necessary techniques peculiar to each. True ideas
must develop their own technique afresh: The higher the ideal
at first the more important and difficult the technique.

To the impatient, critical reader and all architectural eclectics who have come along thus far, these all too broad outlines
of the coming free city may seem only one more "Utopia" to
join so many harmless dreams that come and go like glowing
fireflies in July meadows. But I am not trying to prove a case.
My interest lies in sincerely appraising, in our own behalf, elemental changes I see existing or surely coming. There is
plenty of evidence now at hand to substantiate all the changes
I outline. At least here you have an earnest architect's conscientious study of organic structure ahead based upon manifest circumstances and the experience of a lifetime trying to
get organic architecture to come alive as the true-form-of-
building for American Democracy. An architect's struggle (so
it is) in these United States lies in trying to get any profound
study of any sort in the Arts into good form. I am seeing and
saying that organic architecture is the only true architecture

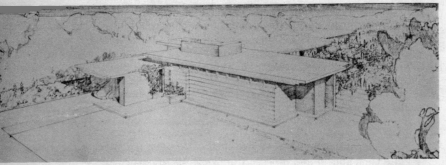

1937   Herbert Jacobs house, Westmorland, near *Madison, Wis.* Preliminary sketches.

for our democracy. Democracy will some day realize that life
is itself architecture organic, or else both architecture and
mankind will become in vain together.

As a people no doubt we are busy sacrificing the greater
usefulness and the only happiness we can ever know in our own
name to put our all into the cheaper, lesser "efficiencies," expedient as I see them. It is useless to go on further working for the
senseless mechanisms of mere machinery for the landlord, the
machine lord and his lady (as they stand) hoping for any
sound general profit for the great future culture of this nation
—and for the culture of this world. Noble life demands a noble
architecture for noble uses of noble men. Lack of culture means
what it has always meant: ignoble civilization and therefore
imminent downfall.

The true center (the only centralization allowable) in Usonian democracy, is the individual in his true Usonian family

home. In that we have the nuclear building we will learn how to build. Integration is vitally necessary to that normal home. Natural differentiation just as necessary. Given intelligent, free, individual choice the home should especially cherish such free choice—eventually based upon a greater range of possible freedom, range for such individual choice in the specific daily cultivation of principles in Architecture as well as in the daily uses we make of Science and Art. In Religion? No less!

Luxury (it, *too,* is primarily a matter of individual quality) would enter the democratic social sense as gratification of

1937 Herbert Jacobs house. Plan. First house with gravity heat. Steam pipes in the floor slab.

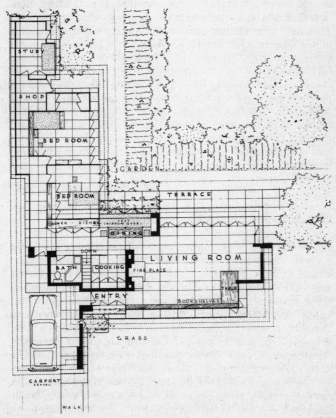

more and more developed humane *sensibility,* beauty the concern. Exuberance is beauty but not excess. Yes. Liberty is not license, exaggeration is not exuberance. Every true home should be actually bound to grow from within to dignity and spiritual significance: *grow* by the right concept and practice of building into a pervasive social circumstance: *grow* out of one's own good ground and better self into everybody's light, not in everybody's nor anybody's way. Every man's home his "castle!" No, every man's home his sphere in space—his appropriate place to live in spaciousness. On his own sunlit sward or in wood or strand enhancing all other homes. No less but more than ever this manly home a refuge for the expanding spirit of man the individual. This home is for the citizen of Usonian democracy, our teenager. In *his own home* thus the Broadacre citizen would be not only impregnable. He would be inviolate. This nation indestructible! He would be true exponent of a man's true relationship to his fellow-men because he *is* his fellow-man. He *is* his country. So he would naturally inculcate high ideals in others by practicing them himself. He would insist upon opportunity for others to do no less. External compulsions, personal or official, were never more than weakness continually breeding weaknesses or weaklings. Usonian homemakers of Broadacres would first learn to know all this so well that the citizen would practice this knowledge instinctively in his every public act, not only to the benefit of others who come in contact with him but to gratify something deep in his very nature.

The Awakened Citizen

Improvements. Well, "improvements" in the sense of this sense of self are not only on but *of* the ground. Actually they belong to those who make the improvements and learn to use them as features of their own life; use them well in relation to other lives. It would make sound economic sense for the home-owner to surround himself with all such ideal expressions as might seem square with his ideal. He could no longer be compelled to pay unjust penalties for so doing. Advantages flow naturally in upon the enlightened and enlightening democratic unit in this new humane stronghold. Well aware of these, the significance of much that he knew but never realized comes clear. In worldly situations, radical changes necessarily due to fundamental realizations of freedom would render obsolete most

(a) 1934   **Malcolm M.** Willey house, *Minneapolis, Minn.* Plan.
(b) 1937   Wingspread, *Wind Point, Wis.* Plan.

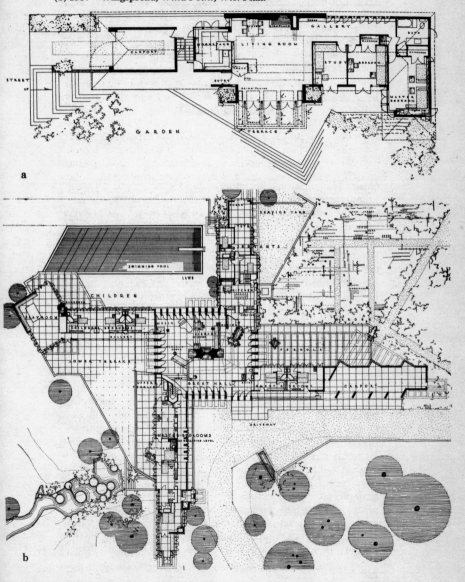

a

b

265

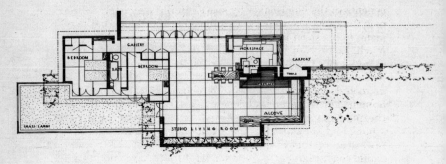

1939   Winkler-Goetsch house, *Okemos, Mich.* Plan. (Photograph on page 142.)

of his old educational paraphernalia: destroy nearly all the so-called "traditions" once cherished by his teachers. He *knew* this, but now he *realizes* it. Then to what may he hold fast as he finds himself able to go forward to new life in this new way on his own ground? Power is now to become his own responsibility—power never dreamed of until he thus began to live as a free man. Power now is perpetually renewed from within himself, power appropriate to his new circumstances.

Production with a capital *P* has previously battened and fattened upon the homemaker. At exorbitant rent he has painfully acquired utilitarian conveniences by debt and such modern sanitation as the homemaker may have in this present day of the runaway industrial revolution. But all these and more may now be made from the bottom up and from inside out into one single unit *for him.* Convenience, ten to one in point of economy and true beauty (they are one now) may be his and do for him what he could not ask of "conveniences" heretofore: Electrification, sanitation, gadgetry of the kitchen complete, all utilities lacking individuality, to be delivered to him as is his car, in prefabricated units. Composing the characteristic Usonian abode, great variety of individual choices exists. Choice would naturally *increase* as the new materials—glass, steel, sheet metal, and the new plastics—let his life expand, *understood.* Vision comes into grounds surrounding and he places appropriate gardens around him. Vistas of the landscape become part of his house and life just as his house becomes integral part of neighborhood landscape. The machine properly disciplined by good design brings tangible, fruitful benefits to the homemaker by space interior and exterior—the new time-space concept, as described earlier. What that may mean to his spirit as well as his comfort lies easily within his reach. Luxury for him will consist in his new sense of a harmony—space free is his. However simple this house, it will be well designed and planned *with him for him:* good materials in good design, well executed. To be himself, the Broadacres homemaker will exercise his new sense in the ground plan of the place he is to live in, as well as the scheme of things around him, the spirit that made it free will maintain it so. The reward and refuge of such life as this would be in the free city would consist largely in fresh opportunity to have and to hold his own shelter secure by his own effort in his own atmosphere, free to go, stay or come. And whenever, however, he pleases to go, there is always something nearby worth seeing—a pleasure to go to.

Every man's new standard of space-measurement (we have said it is the man seated in his car) affects him everywhere he goes, and he can go anywhere. But, most of all, the new sense of space affects him where and how he may live. New breadths, increased depths, not only in the simple reaches of the new building he proudly calls home but into the very makeup of his faith in freedom. A feature of his philosophy realized. Thus inner sense of security defends him against imposition leading eventually to "repossession." And it will be just as hard to scare this Usonian out of his sense or his home as to scare him out of himself. The Usonian citizen will find new faith in himself, on his own acreage no longer a man to be afraid or to be afraid of. He will not "huddle." Nor will he run with the pack! Ask him. His faith is in—what?

Now because the American citizen will learn how expanded light, spacious openness and firm cleanliness of significant line in oneness of the whole may be his own, and how all may add to his stature as a man among men, he will not be stampeded. More chary than ever of grandomania, either at home or abroad: to this richly animated, awakened citizen's imagination quiet repose appeals most because beauty is concerned with him and he with beauty. With a sense of rhythmic quality in the appropriateness of plane to quiet length of line, he is able to trace the flowing simplicity of melodious contours of structure as he sees them in what he does to the land itself. Learns from it. The grace of native flowers in garden or meadow or by the roadside—he truly sees—the trees in teeming life of the wood or landscape. Naturally all will be a refreshing feeling of intimacy with Nature; grateful for space to be lived in; the new spaciousness understood, deeply enjoyed. In his new life the truth is he himself "belongs!" Even as hill-slopes, or the beautiful ravines and forests themselves belong and as bees and trees and flowers in them belong so *he* belongs. While at home, the citizen is pleased and pleasing lord of space. He has integrity. Spacious interior freedom becomes him and is the *new reality*. Romantic: he is both introvert and extrovert. No longer is his faith placed in arbitrary hangovers of Roman law because he goes deeper to the organic law beneath. There in Nature is where his new faith in himself is founded and can be defended.

Both physical and spiritual significance his, oneness of life lies in this new more natural sense of himself. The citizen is bound to see and find tremendous spiritual consequences come alive in him. For all of life, love, and the pursuit of happiness is no longer a phrase. It is the architecture of his soul.

Why, then, should citizenry ever be small, dishonest or mean? Why should the citizen deny to others what he has learned to value so highly within himself? Out of independence such as his a new idea of man emerges. He co-operates because it is for him to say either "Yes" or "No" and say so *as his own conscience dictates!*

Romance

This interior sense of space in spaciousness is romantic and growing throughout the world. Well understood, it is the true machine age triumph, a true luxury. And as this sense of space in spaciousness becomes innate to mankind, I believe the American citizen will develop a more concrete freedom than a Greek or a Roman ever knew or even the Goth felt in the Middle Ages. Or any freedom to which West or East has subscribed or aspired. Perhaps greater in range of freedom interior, to go with freedom exterior, than man ever believed could be unless, perhaps, some adventurer like the ancient Arab or American Indian, some romantic like Francois Villon, or people of the earth-loving East sensed, "once upon a time." In sweep, simplicity (especially *in quality*), architecture never surpassed in significance and beauty what may be this awakened citizen's architecture—that of the free City that is a Nation. Again—that new city is nowhere unless everywhere.

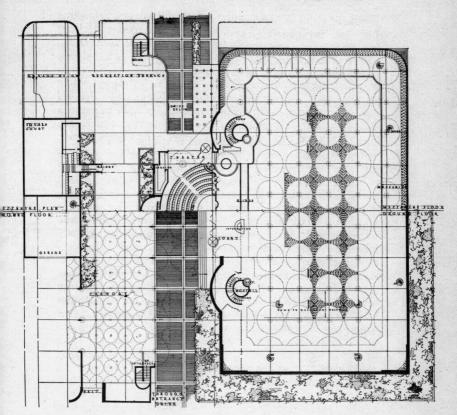

1936   S. C. Johnson and Son, administration building, *Racine, Wis.*
Plan. (Photographs on pages 138–141.)

Space comes alive, to be enjoyed and lived in, characteristic
of this age of the machine. This is our growth, spiritual integration with everyday life. Simple because it is universal conservation of life, happiness is inevitable consequence.

Architecture

Such practice of life lies in the province of organic architecture: architecture sure to react upon every practical homemaker's sense of himself. Modern man cannot fail to grow in

health of mind as he becomes aware of himself as free. He *is* freedom! Freedom at home makes all men doubly democratic in spirit: Any man now demands the freedom for other men and their nations that he asks for himself because only so may he demand freedom as his "inalienable" *right?* It will not now be too difficult for the Broadacre citizen to see "his" right as no more than "their" right. When the meaning of the word "organic" dawns within the mind of the man, he will demand integrity and significance in everything he has to live with or that he does to others. His awakened eye will see boldly and he will not hesitate to search habitual forms everywhere, rejecting forms he once took for granted when he was only educated not cultured. He now challenges all form. The Usonian of Broadacres will have truth of form or he will have none! This goes out from him to his familiars and to establish better economic and social relations with other nations. It goes out from him to characterize American life—no curse put upon the world by insane exhortations of business to increase private "production" for greater public waste.

The citizen of Broadacres would see political science too as something organic—"the science of human happiness." And see economics that way too. He would reject state department banking and trading as likely to be vicious. Broadacres citizens would also regard philosophy as organic. The simplicities of Laotze and those of Jesus would dawn afresh. To practice them he would learn to find them concrete, effective *forces* that really work. At last the citizen would see that the inner forces at work in his life are organic and therefore prophetic.

Discipline

So *interior discipline of an Ideal* thus set up in the citizen will go to work. Undreamed of potentialities show in the work of the workman as he becomes responsible to *himself* for himself. He is the only *safe* man because he is the man now disciplined not by government (the police) but from within by himself! Herein lies the great social potential worthy of the greatest of human works of art and science. Democracy itself.

So free men will soon walk abroad in modern times, nobler men among nobler-minded manhood—more than ever potent in making a fairer-minded world. A better sense of proportion now to go with his sense of humor and his true sense of himself.

As world citizen the Usonian's power no longer lies in ped-

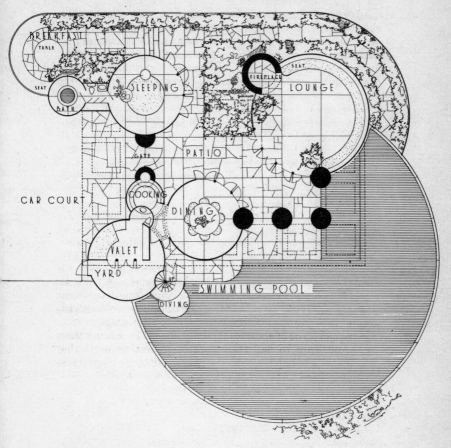

1938   Ralph Jester house, project, *Palos Verdes, Cal.* Plan.

dling or meddling or borrowing or lending or becoming stupidly mischievous with money "abroad." Power no longer in the control of vicarious officialism at public expense. Individual aspiration would never consist in or subsist on imitating anything. First of all—for all—quality. Only because of well-founded confidence in his own strength will man be eager to *share* in the work of the world. The world will be invigorated by his happiness because it will have the vitality of good sense. His actual practice of the democracy we preach will be no less inspiring. Were the world to see this citizen, results would become ideal for all the world. Exemplar in his own life in his own home, feet on his own ground! See a man free, alive.

from THE LIVING CITY, *1958*

Fallingwater

For the first time in my practice, where residence work is concerned in recent years, reinforced concrete was actually needed to construct the cantilever system of this extension of the cliff beside a mountain stream, making living space over and above the stream upon several terraces upon which a man who loved the place sincerely, one who liked to listen to the waterfall, might well live. Steel sash came within reach also for the first time. In this design for living down in a glen in a deep forest, shelter took on definite masonry form while still preserving protection overhead for extensive glass surface. These deep overhangs provide the interior, as usual, with the softened diffused lighting for which the indweller is invariably grateful, I have found ...

This building is a late example of the inspiration of a site, the cooperation of an intelligent, appreciative client and the use of entirely masonry materials except for an interlining of redwood and asphalt beneath all flooring. Again, by way of steel in tension this building takes its place and achieves its form. The grammar of the slabs at their eaves is best shown by a detail. But the roof water is caught by a lead strip built into the concrete above near the beginning of the curve ... It is not the deluge of water in a storm that hurts any building: it is ooze and drip of dirty water in thawing and freezing, increased by slight showers.

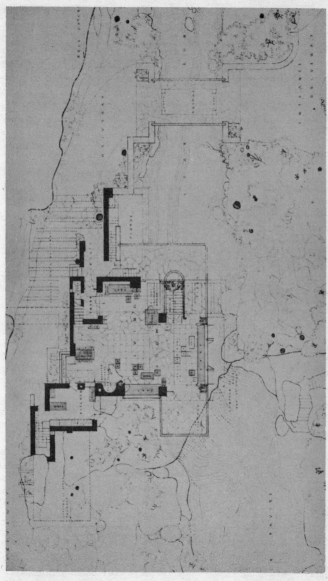

1936   Fallingwater, on *Bear Run, Pa*. Site and main-floor plan.

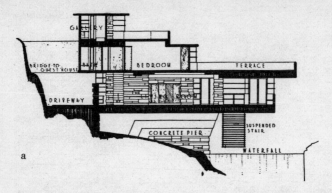

a

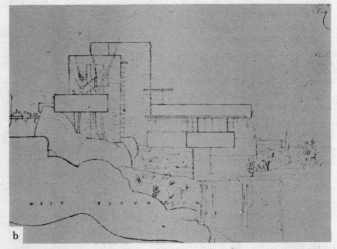

b

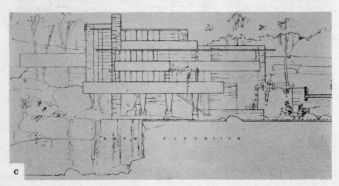

c

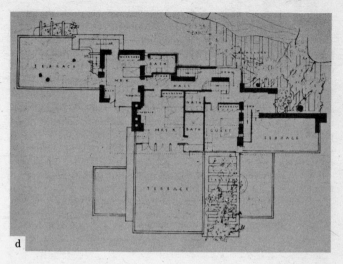

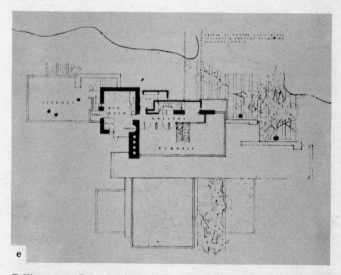

Fallingwater, *Bear Run, Pa.* (Photographs on pages 136, 137.) (a) Section. (b) West elevation. (c) South elevation. (d) Second-floor plan. (e) Third-floor plan.

The cantilever slabs here carry parapets and the beams. They may be seen clutching big boulders. But next time, I believe, parapets will carry the floors—or better still we will know enough to make the two work together as one, as I originally intended.

This structure might serve to indicate that the sense of shelter—the sense of space where used with sound structural sense—has no limitations as to form except the materials used and the methods by which they are employed for what purpose. The ideas involved here are in no wise changed from those of early work. The materials and methods of construction come through them, here, as they may and will always come through everywhere. That is all. The effects you see in this house are not superficial effects.

from THE ARCHITECTURAL FORUM, *1938*

St. Mark's-in-the-Bouwerie

This skyscraper planned to stand free in an urban park and thus fit for human occupancy, is as nearly organic as steel in tension and concrete in compression can make it, doing for tall building what Lidgerwood made steel do for the long ship. The ship had its keel: this building has its concrete core. A shaft of concrete rises through the floors engaging each slab at eighteen levels. Each floor proceeds outward as a cantilever slab extended from the shaft. The slab, thick at the shaft, grows thinner as it goes outward in an overlapping scale pattern until at the final leap to the screen wall it is no more than 3 inches thick. The outer enclosing screen of glass and copper is pendent from these cantilever slabs; the inner partitions rest upon the slabs.

With four double-decked apartments to each floor, each apartment unaware of the other as all look outward, the structure eliminates the weight and waste space of masonry walls. The central shaft standing inside, away from lighted space, carries elevators and entrance hallway well within itself. Two of the exterior walls of every apartment are entirely of glass set into sheet-copper framing. But the building is so placed that the sun shines on only one wall at a time and narrow upright blades, or mullions, project 9 inches so that as the sun moves, shadows fall on the glass surfaces.

The building increases substantially in area from floor to floor as the structure rises, in order that the glass frontage of each story may drip clear of the one below, the building thus cleaning itself. Also, areas become more valuable the higher (within limits) the structure goes. The central shaft extending well into the ground may carry with safety a greatly extended top mass. This building, earthquake, fire and soundproof from within, by economics inherent in its structure weighs less than half the usual tall building and increases the area available for living by more than 20 per cent.

It is a logical development of the idea of a tall building in the age of glass and steel, as logical engineering as the Brooklyn Bridge or an ocean liner. But the benefits of modernity such as this are not merely economic. There is greater privacy, safety, and beauty for human lives within it than is possible in any other type of apartment building.

A one-two triangle is employed, because it allows flexibility of arrangement for human movement not afforded by the rectangle. The apparently irregular shapes of the rooms would not appear irregular in reality; all would have great repose because all are not only properly in proportion to the human figure but to the figure made by the whole building.

from ARCHITECTURAL FORUM, *1938*

What is Architecture

What is architecture anyway? Is it the vast collection of the various buildings which have been built to please the varying taste of the various lords of mankind? I think not. No, I know that architecture is life; or at least it is life itself taking form and therefore it is the truest record of life as it was lived in the world yesterday, as it is lived today or ever will be lived. So architecture I know to be a Great Spirit. It can never be something which consists of the buildings which have been built by man on earth . . . mostly now rubbish heaps or soon to be. . . . Architecture is that great living creative spirit which from generation to generation, from age to age, pro-

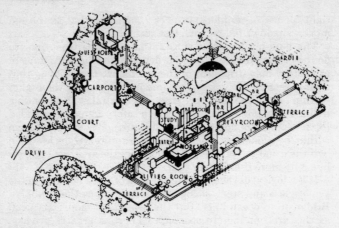

1937   Paul R. Hanna house, *Palo Alto, Cal.* Plan.

ceeds, persists, creates, according to the nature of man, and his
circumstances as they change. That is really architecture.

. . . I declare, the time is here for architecture to recognize its
own nature, to realize the fact that it is out of life itself for life
as it is now lived, a humane and therefore an intensely human
thing; it must again become the most human of all the expressions of human nature. Architecture is a necessary interpretation of such human life as we now know if we ourselves are to
live with individuality and beauty.

Out of the ground into the light—yes! Not only must the
building so proceed, but we cannot have an organic architecture unless we achieve an organic society! We may build some
buildings for a few people knowing the significance or value of
that sense of the whole which we are learning to call organic,
but we cannot have an architecture for a society such as ours
now is. We who love architecture and recognize it as the great
sense of structure in whatever is—music, painting, sculpture,
or life itself—we must somehow act as intermediaries—maybe
missionaries.

. . . Let our universities realize and teach that *the law of
organic change is the only thing that mankind can know as
beneficent or as actual!* We can only know that all things are
in process of flowing in some continuous state of becoming.
Heraclitus was stoned in the streets of Athens for a fool for
making that declaration of independence, I do not remember
how many hundreds of years ago.

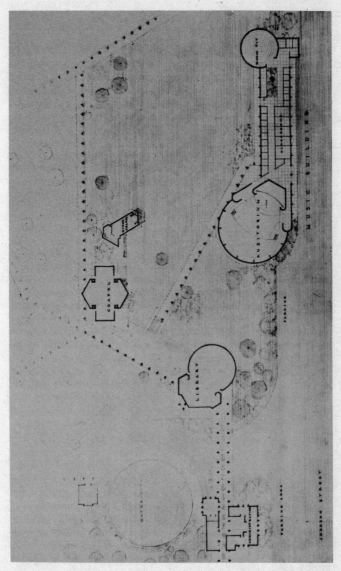

1938 Florida Southern College, *Lakeland, Fla.* (Continued through 1959.) Campus plan. (Photographs on pages 150, 151.)

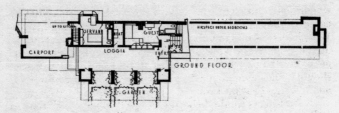

1940   Lloyd Lewis house, *Libertyville, Ill.* Ground floor plan. (Photograph on page 145.)

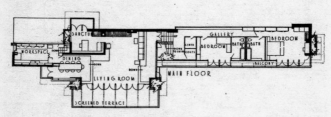

1940   Lloyd Lewis house. Main-floor plan.

... So modern architecture rejects the major axis and the minor axis of classic architecture. It rejects all grandomania, every building that would stand in military fashion heels together, eyes front, something on the right hand and something on the left hand. Architecture already favors the reflex, the natural easy attitude, the occult symmetry of grace and rhythm affirming the ease, grace, and naturalness of natural life. Modern architecture—let us now say *organic* architecture —is a natural architecture—the architecture of nature, for nature.

... Architecture which is really architecture proceeds from the ground and somehow the terrain, the native industrial conditions, the nature of materials and the purpose of the building, must inevitably determine the form and character of any good building.

... No man can build a building for another who does not believe in him, who does not believe in what he believes in, and

280

who has not chosen him because of this faith, knowing what he can do. That is the nature of architect and client as I see it. When a man wants to build a building he seeks an interpreter, does he not? He seeks some man who has the technique to express that thing which he himself desires but cannot do. So, should a man come to me for a building, he would be ready for me. It would be what I could do, that he wanted.

... Architects would do better and well enough were they to stick to their own last and do their own work quietly in their own way. I do not suppose that I myself have much right to be standing here preaching and talking to you of all this except as I have done this thing for a lifetime and swear never to try to tell you of something that I myself have not practiced and so do not really know.

from AN ORGANIC ARCHITECTURE, *1939*

World Architecture

After World War II Frank Lloyd Wright enjoyed a unique position in modern architecture. The idiosyncrasies of his romantic art and of his occasionally caustic tongue were clearly less important than his fertile, fundamental genius. 1947 was another year of great projects: the vast country club for Huntington Hartford, the Pittsburgh Point schemes, the Rogers Lacy Hotel for Dallas, even the smaller funeral chapels for San Francisco and the suburban shopping center near Phoenix are all superb. Then followed the balloon-roofed Milwaukee laundry, the Meteor Crater tourist center, the San Francisco second bay crossing—bold if less elaborate projects. Three buildings of quality were built, the gift shop for V. C. Morris in San Francisco with its closed front and spiral ramp; the Madison Unitarian Church with its eloquent roof and rich window; and the crisp, almost classic, Walter house at Quasqueton, Iowa. Some small homes followed—the Laurent, Carr, and Berger, all with extraordinary, suitable forms. A few, more elaborate, remained unbuilt: the Chahroudi, the Bloomfield, the second Winkler-Goetsch, the lavish and inventive Bailleres scheme for Acapulco. But three masterly homes followed, the

*William Palmer and the Herman Mossberg in the Midwest, the
Walker at Carmel—all built and all evidence of Wright's una-
bated creativity in his mid-eighties. Before 1950 Wright had
designed a circular house for his son David and in 1953 he produced another equal tour de force combined with livability for
another son, Llewellyn; both were built, as was the serene Zim-
merman house. The Price Tower arose in Oklahoma, realizing
in new form the old dream for St. Mark's-in-the-Bouwerie.
In Italy, Venice rejected a beautiful marble palazzino designed
for the Grand Canal and miraculously in tune with the ancient architecture it would have augmented. The interfaith
project of the mid-twenties sired a bold triangular descendant
in the Beth Sholom Synagogue, at the edge of Philadelphia,
sharply faceted, a gleaming gem of faith. The Price family
also built a magnificent desert pavilion in Phoenix. And for
Madison Frank Lloyd Wright designed a new and splendid
civic center (proposed before, in 1939) that has been a center
of controversy and politicking ever since the citizens voted to
build it.*

*By now, in the mid 1950s, Frank Lloyd Wright could be
publicized as "the world's most honored architect." In the
1940s and 50s a score of official honors from all over the
world had been bestowed on him. A stream of books and articles again issued from the architect, culminating in A TESTA-
MENT, published 1957. In the last four years of his life Wright
produced such truly unprecedented designs as the Mile High
skyscraper, five hundred stories tall for Chicago; the lush
magnificence of the Baghdad Opera House; the grill-shaded
authority of the Arizona State Capital; the elegant prolonga-
tion of the Price Tower into the Chicago Golden Beacon.
Only a mature genius could produce such enchanting challenges. Fortunately some were put into construction—the big,
bold government buildings for Marin County, west of San
Francisco, the music building on the Florida Southern campus, the Christian Science church in California, and the
unique, vigorous, graceful Greek Orthodox Church for Milwaukee. In 1959, before his death on April ninth, Frank Lloyd
Wright signed and sent the joyous drawings of the Donahoe
houses to the client. No curb was ever set on the vision and
powers of the American genius; his achievements, disturbing
as are those of every original artist, may be expected to seem
more amazing and more rewarding as generations learn to
understand them by living with them.*

The Destruction of the Box

I think I first *consciously* began to try to beat the box in the Larkin Building—1904. I found a natural opening to the liberation I sought when (after a great struggle) I finally pushed the staircase towers out from the corners of the main building, made them into free-standing, individual features. Then the thing began to come through as you may see.

I had *felt* this need for features quite early in my architectural life. You will see this feeling growing up, becoming more apparent a little later in Unity Temple: there perhaps is where you will find the first real expression of the idea that the space within the building is the reality of that building. Unity Temple is where I thought I had it, this idea that the reality of a building no longer consisted in the walls and roof. So that sense of freedom began which has come into the architecture of today for you and which we call organic architecture.

You may see, there in Unity Temple, how I dealt with this great architectural problem at that time. You will find the sense of the great room coming through—space not walled in now but more or less free to appear. In Unity Temple you will find the walls actually disappearing; you will find the interior space opening to the outside and see the outside coming in. You will see assembled about this interior space, screening it, various free, related features instead of enclosing walls. See, you now can make features of many types for enclosure and group the features about interior space with no sense of *boxing* it. But most important, after all, is the sense of shelter extended, expanded overhead, and which gives the indispensable sense of protection while leading the human vision beyond the walls. That primitive sense of shelter is a quality architecture should always have. If in a building you feel not only protection from above, but liberation of interior to outside space (which you do feel in Unity Temple and other buildings I have built) then you have one important secret of letting the interior space come through.

Now I shall try to show you why organic architecture is the architecture of democratic freedom. Why? Well . . .

Here—say—is your box: big hole in the box, little ones if you wish—of course.

What you see of it now is this square package of containment. You see? Something not fit for our liberal profession of democratic government, a thing essentially anti-individual.

Here you may see (more or less) the student architecture of almost all our colleges.

I was never ambitious to be an engineer. Unfortunately I was educated as one in the University of Wisconsin. But I knew enough of engineering to know that the outer angles of a box were not where its most economical support would be, if you made a building of it. No, a certain distance in each way from each corner is where the economic support of a box-building is invariably to be found. You see?

Now, when you put support at those points you have created a short cantileverage to the corners that lessens actual spans and sets the corner free or open for whatever distance you choose. The corners disappear altogether if you choose to let space come in there, or let it go out. Instead of post and beam construction, the usual box building, you now have a new sense of building construction by way of the cantilever and continuity. Both are new structural elements as they now enter architecture. But all you see of this radical liberation of space all over the world today, is the corner window. But, in this simple change of thought lies the essential of the architectural change from box to free plan and the new reality that is *space* instead of matter.

1950   David Wright house, *Phoenix, Ariz.* (Completed 1952.) Ground-floor plan. (Perspective on page 162.)

1950   David Wright house. Main-floor plan.

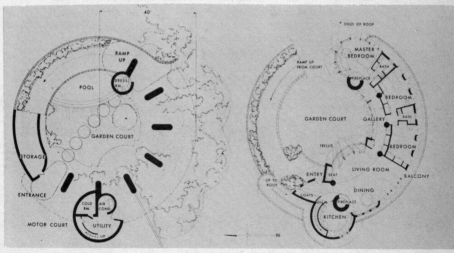

From this point we can go on to talk about organic architecture instead of classic architecture. Let's go on. These unattached side walls become something independent, no longer enclosing walls. They're separate supporting screens, any one of which may be shortened, or extended or perforated, or occasionally eliminated. These free-standing screens support the roof. What of this roof? Overhead it becomes emphasized as a splendid sense of shelter, but shelter that hides nothing when you are inside looking out from the building. It is a shape of shelter that really gives a sense of the outside coming in or the inside going out. Yes, you have now a wide-spreading overhead that is really a release of this interior space to the outside: a freedom where before imprisonment existed.

You can perfect a figure of freedom with these four screens; in any case, enclosure as a box is gone. Anything becoming, anything in the nature of plan or materials is easily a possibility. To go further: if this liberation works in the horizontal plane why won't it work in the vertical plane? No one has looked through the box at the sky up there at the upper angle, have they? Why not? Because the box always had a cornice at the top. It was added to the sides in order that the box might not look so much like a box, but more classic. This cornice was the feature that made your conventional box classic.

Now—to go on—there in the Johnson Building you catch no sense of enclosure whatever at any angle, top or sides. You are looking at the sky and feel the freedom of *space*. The columns are designed to stand up and take over the ceiling, the column is made a part of the ceiling: continuity.

The old idea of a building is, as you see, quite gone. Everything before these liberating thoughts of cantilever and conti-

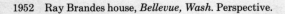

1952   Ray Brandes house, *Bellevue, Wash.* Perspective.

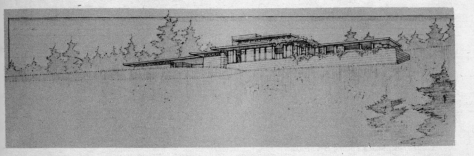

1954 Beth Sholom Synagogue, Elkins Park, near *Philadelphia, Pa.*
(Completed 1959.) Section.

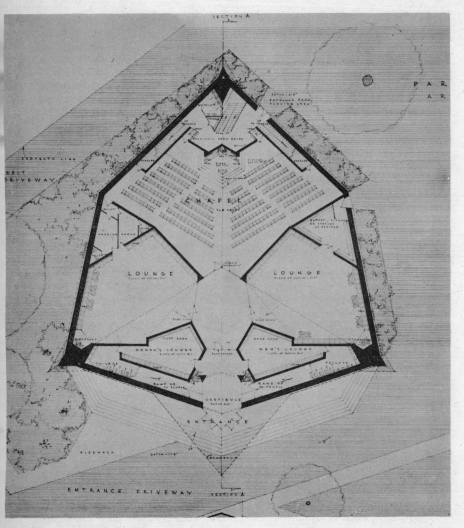

1954   Beth Sholom Synagogue. Lower-floor plan.

nuity took effect, was post and beam construction: super-imposition of one thing upon another and repetition of slab over slab, always on posts. Now what? You have established a natural use of glass according to this new freedom of space. Space may now go out or come in where life is being lived, space as a component of it. So organic architecture is architecture in which you may feel and see all this happen as a third dimension. Too bad the Greeks didn't know of this new use for steel and glass as a third dimension. If they had known what I am trying to describe here, you wouldn't have to think much about it for yourselves today, the schools would long ago have taught these principles to you.

Be that as it may, this sense of space (space alive by way of the third dimension), isn't that sense, or *feeling* for architecture, an implement to characterize the freedom of the individual? I think so. If you refuse this liberated sense of building haven't you thrown away that which is most precious in our own human life and most promising as a new field for truly creative artistic expression in architecture? Yes, is there anything else, really? All this, and more, is why I have, lifelong, been fighting the pull of the specious old *box*. I have had such a curious, controversial and interesting time doing it that I myself have become a controversial item. Suspicion is always in order.

Now, to go back to my own experiences: after this building of Unity Temple (as I have said) I thought I had the great thing very well in hand. I was feeling somewhat as I imagine a great prophet might. I often thought, well, at least here is an essentially new birth of thought, feeling and opportunity in this machine age. This is the modern means. *I* had made it come true! Naturally (I well remember) I became less and less tolerant and, I suppose, intolerable. Arrogant, I imagine, was the proper word. I have heard it enough.

> *From an address to the Junior Chapter of the American Institute of Architects, New York City, 1952. Taped and typed; corrected by Frank Lloyd Wright.*

The New Theatre

We do not intend to explain here technical details of the design for the New Theatre. Controversy is inevitable to the new and therefore unfamiliar ways of achieving greater impact of actor upon audience. But the main ideas of such a theatre are clear enough.

Free the legitimate stage from its present peep-show character and scenery loft, establishing a simple, workable basis for presenting plays in the round, performers and audience together in one room, allowing staging more like sculpture than like painting: now a frame (or proscenium) places performance in one room, audience in another.

Playwright and stage designer when familiar with this new freedom will discover fascinating realms of expression open to them; and no doubt the best of them will be inspired to create new dramatic effects.

Actors will find the acoustics of the New Theatre so sensitive that the slightest nuance of tone, or shade of expression, will register with ease and far greater effect than under present conditions.

Lighting and music are provided for. Lighting is such that make-up is more effective; less will be needed.

A production is reduced to simple mechanical means; several men can do work now done by dozens.

Sets are all prepared below stage and rise by way of tracks and dollies on the ramps to become scenery on the revolving stage. By dropping the dividing screen, a great depth may be added to the revolving stage. Scenes can succeed one another almost instantly. A set rises on one ramp and goes back down on the one opposite. If desired, a continuous performance may be staged.

The entire atmosphere of effect of the auditorium and stage taken together dramatizes the performance itself and serves to heighten artistic values by concentration and contrast.

Building construction and arrangements within are fireproof and made with regard to safety and comfort. Entrance is from one side, egress from the other. Directed exits are directly behind the audience, coat rooms and toilets conveniently on main level.

The New Theatre is excellent for orchestral concerts. Lectures or solo performances of every kind.

The technical equipment of the New Theatre may be as desired, more and more detailed until almost automatic. Costs of production could not only be cut but effects made possible that are now impossible.

By means of these simple organic changes in technique and traditions a new life for the theatre is likely.

from THE NEW THEATRE, *catalogue of the Wadsworth Athenaeum, 1949*

On the Johnson Laboratory

When the matter of a new research laboratory came up at the S. C. Johnson Wax Co., Herbert Johnson said, "Why not go up in the air, Frank?"

"That's just it," I said. I had seen several of the meandering, flat piles called laboratories, ducts running here, there and everywhere and a walkaround for everybody. I knew we would get twice the sunlight and twice the net working area, dollar for dollar, in a tall building.

So we went up in the air around a giant central stack with floors branching from it, having clear light and space all around each floor. All laboratory space was then clear and in direct connection with a duct-system cast in the hollow reinforced-concrete floors, connecting to the vertical hollow of the stack itself.

This seemed to me a natural solution . . . affording all kinds of delightful sunlit, directly related work space. Cantilevered from the giant stack, the floor slabs spread out like tree branches, providing sufficient segregation of departments vertically. Elevator and stairway channels up the central stack link these departments to each other. All utilities and the many intake and exhaust pipes run in their own central utility grooves, arranged like the cellular pattern of the tree trunk.

From each alternate floor slab an outer glass shell hangs firm. This glass shell, like that of the original administration building, is formed of glass tubes held in place by small vertical cast aluminum stanchions sealed horizontally by plastic. Inside, for temperature insurance, a second screen of plate glass was clipped to the aluminum stanchions and made movable for cleaning.

from ARCHITECTURAL FORUM, *1951*

291

On the Price Tower

The building has a complete standardization for prefabrication; only the concrete core and slabs need be made in the field. Our shop-fabricating industrial system could function at its best here with substantial benefits to humanity. Owing to the unusual conformations the furniture would have to be a part of the building, as the metal (copper) furniture is designed to be. Here again is the poise, balance, lightness, and strength that may characterize the creations of this age.

The first expression of a treelike mast structure was in a project for St. Mark's-in-the-Bouwerie in 1929. The skyscraper was indeed the product of modern technology, but it was not suitable if it increased congestion, which it inevitably would unless it could stand free in the country. There was one planned as a feature of Broadacre City—so those from the city wouldn't feel lost in that vision of the country, and the Johnson laboratory tower is another such. But it was an idea that had to wait over thirty years for full realization. It is actually being built now by H. C. Price in Bartlesville, Okla. The total weight of the building will be about 6/10 of the conventional structure of the Rockefeller Center type, due to cantilever and continuity. Now the skyscraper will come into its own on the rolling plains of Oklahoma.

from THE NEW YORK TIMES, *1953*

Integrity

What is needed most in architecture today is the very thing that is most needed in life—Integrity. Just as it is in a human being, so integrity is the deepest quality in a building; but it is a quality not much demanded of any building since very ancient times when it was natural. It is no longer the first demand for a human being either, because "Success" is now so immediately necessary. If you are a success, people will not want to "look the gift horse in the mouth." No. But then if "success" should happen today something precious has been lost from life.

Somebody has described a man of this period as one through the memory of whom you could too easily pass your hand. Had there been true *quality* in the man the hand could not so easily pass. That quality in the memory of him would probably have been "Integrity."

In speaking of integrity in architecture, I mean much the same thing that you would mean were you speaking of an individual. Integrity is not something to be put on and taken off like a garment. Integrity is a quality *within* and *of* the man himself. So it is in a building. It cannot be changed by any other person either nor by the exterior pressures of any outward circumstances; integrity cannot change except from within because it is that in you which is *you*—and due to which you will try to live your life (as you would build your building) in the best possible way. To build a man or building from within is always difficult to do because deeper is not so easy as shallow.

Naturally should you want to really live in a way and in a place which is true to this deeper thing in you, which you honor, the house you build to live in as a home should be (so far as it is possible to make it so) integral in every sense. Integral to site, to purpose, and to you. The house would then be a home in the best sense of that word. This we seem to have forgotten if ever we learned it. Houses have become a series of anonymous boxes that go into a row on row upon row of bigger boxes either merely negative or a mass nuisance. But now the house in this interior or deeper organic sense may come alive as organic architecture.

We are now trying to bring *integrity* into building. If we succeed, we will have done a great service to our moral nature—the psyche—of our democratic society. Integrity would become more natural. Stand up for *integrity* in your building and you stand for integrity not only in the life of those who did the building but socially a reciprocal relationship is inevitable. An irresponsible, flashy, pretentious or dishonest individual would never be happy in such a house as we now call organic because of this quality of integrity. The one who will live in it will be he who will grow with living in it. So it is the "job" of any true architect to envision and make this human relationship—so far as lies in his power—a reality.

Living within a house wherein everything is genuine and harmonious, a new sense of freedom gives one a new sense of life—as contrasted with the usual existence in the house indiscriminately planned and where Life is *contained* within a series of confining boxes, all put within the general box. Such life is bound to be inferior to life lived in this new integrity—the Usonian Home.

In designing the Usonian house, as I have said, I have always proportioned it to the human figure in point of scale; that is, to the scale of the human figure to occupy it. The old idea in most buildings was to make the human being feel rather insignificant—developing an inferiority complex in him if possible. The higher the ceilings were then the greater the building was. This empty grandeur was considered to be human luxury. Of course, great, high ceilings had a certain utility in those days, because of bad planning and awkward construction. (The volume of contained air was about all the air to be had without violence.)

The Usonian house, then, aims to be a *natural* performance, one that is integral to site; integral to environment; integral to the life of the inhabitants. A house integral with the nature of materials—wherein glass is used as glass, stone as stone, wood as wood—and all the elements of environment go into and throughout the house. Into this new integrity, once there, those who live in it will take root and grow. And most of all belonging by nature to the nature of its being.

Whether people are fully conscious of this or not, they actually derive countenance and sustenance from the "atmosphere" of the things they live in or with. They are rooted in them just as a plant is in the soil in which it is planted. For

1949   Kenneth Laurent house, *Rockford, Ill.* (Completed 1951; enlarged 1959.) Plan. (Perspective on page 162.)

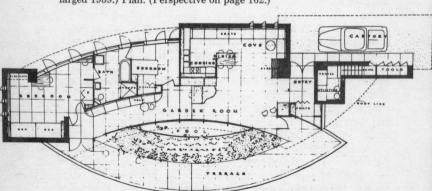

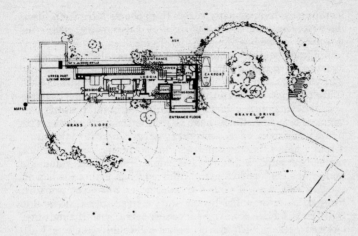

1945   Douglas Grant house, near *Des Moines, Iowa*. (Completed
1951.) Entrance-floor plan. (Perspective on page 146.)

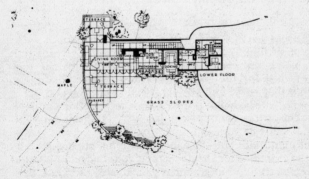

1945   Douglas Grant house. Lower-floor plan.

instance, we receive many letters from people who sing praises for what has happened to them as a consequence; telling us how their house has affected their lives. They now have a certain dignity and pride in their environment; they see it has a meaning or purpose which they share as a family or feel as individuals.

We all know the feeling we have when we are well-dressed and like the consciousness that results from it. It affects our conduct and you should have the same feeling regarding the home you live in. It has a salutary effect morally, to put it on a lower plane than it deserves, but there are higher results above that sure one. If you feel yourself becomingly housed, know that you are living according to the higher demands of good society, and of your own conscience, then you are free from embarrassment and not poor in spirit but rich—in the right way. I have always believed in being careful about my clothes; getting well-dressed because I could then forget all about them. That is what should happen to you with a good house that is a *home*. When you are conscious that the house is right and is honestly becoming to you, and feel you are living in it beautifully, you need no longer be concerned about it. It is no tax upon your conduct, nor a nag upon your self-respect, because it is featuring you as you like to see yourself.

from THE NATURAL HOUSE, *1954*

The Grammar of Architecture

Every house worth considering as a work of art must have a grammar of its own. "Grammar," in this sense, means the same thing in any construction—whether it be of words or of stone or wood. It is the shape-relationship between the various elements that enter into the constitution of the thing. The "grammar" of the house is its manifest articulation of all its parts. This will be the "speech" it uses. To be achieved, construction must be grammatical.

Your limitations of feeling about what you are doing, your choice of materials for the doing (and your budget of course) determine largely what grammar your building will use. It is largely inhibited (or expanded) by the amount of money you

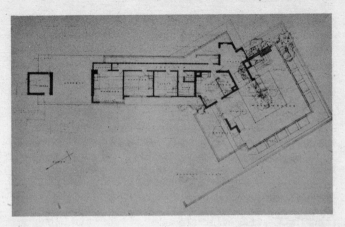

1949   Lowell Walter house, *Quasqueton, Iowa.* Plan. (Photograph on page 143.)

have to spend, a feature only of the latitude you have. When the chosen grammar is finally adopted (you go almost indefinitely with it into everything you do) walls, ceilings, furniture, etc., become inspired by it. Everything has a related articulation in relation to the whole and all belongs together; looks well together because all together are speaking the same language. If one part of your house spoke Choctaw, another French, another English, and another some sort of gibberish, you would have what you mostly have now—not a very beautiful result. Thus, when you do adopt the "grammar" of your house—it will be the way the house is to be "spoken," "uttered." You must be consistently grammatical for it to be understood as a work of Art.

Consistency in grammar is therefore the property—solely—of a well-developed artist-architect. Without that property of the artist-architect not much can be done about your abode as a work of Art. Grammar is no property for the usual owner or the occupant of the house. But the man who designs the house must, inevitably, speak a consistent thought-language in his design. It properly may be and should be a language of his own if appropriate. If he has no language, so no grammar, of his own, he must adopt one; he will speak some language or other whether he so chooses or not. It will usually be some kind of argot.

from THE NATURAL HOUSE, *1954*

Organic Architecture and the Orient

Many people have wondered about an Oriental quality they see in my work. I suppose it is true that when we speak of organic architecture, we are speaking of something that is more Oriental than Western. The answer is: my work *is*, in that deeper philosophic sense, Oriental. These ideals have not been common to the whole people of the Orient; but there was Laotse, for instance. Our society has never known the deeper Taoist mind. The Orientals must have had the sense of it, whatever may have been their consideration for it, and they instinctively built that way. Their instinct was right. So this gospel of organic architecture still has more in sympathy and in common with Oriental thought than it has with any other thing the West has ever confessed.

The West as "the West" had never known or cared to know much about it. Ancient Greece came nearest—perhaps—but not very close, and since the later Western civilizations in Italy, France, England and the United States went heavily—stupidly—Greek in their architecture, the West could not easily have seen an indigenous organic architecture. The civilizations of India, Persia, China and Japan are all based on the same central source of cultural inspiration, chiefly Buddhist, stemming from the original inspiration of his faith. But it is not so much the principles of this faith which underlie organic architecture, as the faith of Laotse—the Chinese philosopher—his annals preserved in Tibet. But I became conscious of these only after I had found and built it for myself.

And yet the West cannot hope to have anything original unless by individual inspiration. Our culture is so far junior and so far outclassed in time by all that we call Oriental. You will surely find that nearly everything we stand for today, everything we think of as originated by us, is thus old. To make matters in our new nation worse, America has always assumed that culture, to be culture, had to come from European sources—be imported. The idea of an organic architecture, therefore, coming from the tall grass of the Midwestern American prairie, was regarded at home as unacceptable. So it went around the world to find recognition and then to be "imported" to its own home as a thing to be imitated everywhere, though the understanding of its principles has never yet really caught up with the penetration of the original deed at home.

It cannot truthfully be said, however, that organic architec-

1957   State Capitol, project, near *Phoenix, Ariz.* Plan. (Perspective on page 159.)

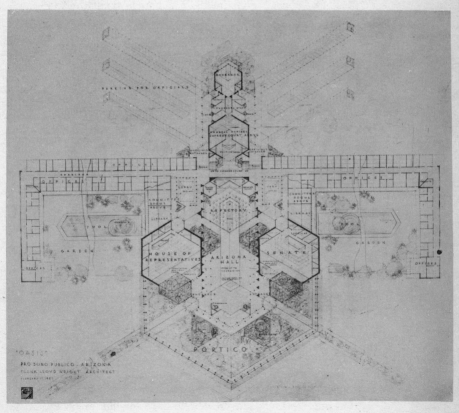

ture was derived from the Orient. We have our own way of putting these elemental (so ancient) ideals into practical effect. Although Laotse, as far as we know, first enunciated the philosophy, it probably preceded him but was never built by him or any Oriental. The idea of organic architecture that the reality of the building lies in the space within to be lived in, the feeling that we must not enclose ourselves in an envelope which is the building, is not alone Oriental. Democracy, proclaiming the integrity of the individual *per se,* had the feeling if not the words. Nothing else Western except the act of an organic architecture had ever happened to declare that Laotsian philosophic principle which was declared by him 500 years before our Jesus. It is true that the wiser, older civilizations of the world had a quiescent sense of this long before we of the West came to it.

For a long time, I thought I had "discovered" it, only to find after all that this idea of the interior space being the reality of the building was ancient and Oriental. It came to me quite naturally from my Unitarian ancestry and the Froebelian kindergarten training in the deeper primal sense of the form of the interior or heart of the appearance of "things." I was entitled to it by the way I happened to come up along the line—perhaps. I don't really know. Chesty with all this, I was in danger of thinking of myself as, more or less, a prophet. When building Unity Temple at Oak Park and the Larkin Building in Buffalo, I was making the first great protest I knew anything about against the building coming up on you from the outside as enclosure. I reversed that old idiom in idea and in fact.

When pretty well puffed up by this I received a little book by Okakura Kakuzo, entitled *The Book of Tea,* sent to me by the ambassador from Japan to the United States. Reading it, I came across this sentence: "The reality of a room was to be found in the space enclosed by the roof and walls, not in the roof and walls themselves."

Well, there was I. Instead of being the cake I was not even dough. Closing the little book I went out to break stone on the road, trying to get my interior self together. I was like a sail coming down; I had thought of myself as an original, but was not. It took me days to swell up again. But I began to swell up again when I thought, "After all, who built it? Who put that thought into buildings? Laotse nor anyone had consciously *built* it." When I thought of that, naturally enough I thought, "Well then, everything is all right, we can still go along with head up." I have been going along—head up—ever since.

from THE NATURAL HOUSE, *1954*

Influences and Inferences

Genuine expressions as essence of the great art itself cannot be taught or imitated. Nor can they in any way be forced. If the quality of vision we call inspiration is lacking, all is lacking; and inspiration comes in its own good time in its own way, from within—comes only when all is ready, and usually must wait.

Great art has always, at first, been controversial. Now that our means of communication have multiplied, how much more so today? Any moot point soon becomes every man's controversy. Specialists in controversy, numerous and vociferous, sprout on every branch. And the pressure toward conformity leaves young minds weak with the uncertainty that cleaves, for reassurance, to the static in some form.

Resemblances are mistaken for influences. Comparisons have been made odious where comparison should, except as insult, hardly exist. Minds imbued by the necessity of truth, uttering truths independently of each other and capable of learning by analysis instead of comparison are still few. Scholarly appraisals? Only rarely are they much above the level of gossip. So, up comes comparison, to compare organic architecture to the Crystal Palace of London, for instance—Horatio Greenough, *Art Nouveau,* Emerson, Whitman, Sullivan, Coleridge, Thoreau, etc.

Those adversaries of truth who claim its discovery are invariably traitorous. Contemporary criticism is mostly posture, at the back door or at best side entrance, therefore a mere guess as to what the affair really looked like from the front. Every now and then one of the so-dedicated writes a book about a book written by a man who did the same, to win the "take away" prize in this game; never actually to be won because it was lost before it started.

To cut ambiguity short: there never was exterior influence upon my work, either foreign or native, other than that of Lieber Meister, Dankmar Adler and John Roebling, Whitman and Emerson, and the great poets worldwide. My work is original not only in fact but in spiritual fiber. No practice by any European architect to this day has influenced mine in the least.

As for the Incas, the Mayans, even the Japanese—all were to me but splendid confirmation. Some of our own critics could be appreciated—Lewis Mumford (*Sticks and Stones*),

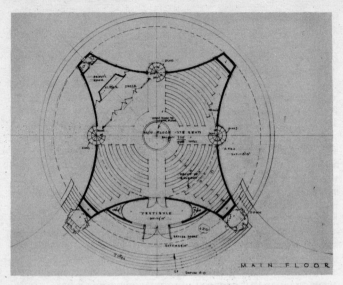

1956   Greek Orthodox Church, *Wauwatosa, Wis.* (In construction.)
Plan. (Perspective on page 162.)

early Russell Hitchcock, Montgomery Schuyler and a few
others.

While admiring Henry Hobson Richardson, I instinctively
disliked his patron Henry Adams as our most accomplished
(therefore most dangerous) promoter of eclecticism. I believed
Adams, Boston Brahmin, would dislike Louis Sullivan and
Walt Whitman. His frame of reference was never theirs, or
mine. My enthusiasm for "sermons in stones and books in running brooks" was not "fascination frantic for ruins romantic—
when sufficiently decayed."

At that early day I was thrilled by Mayan, Inca and Egyp-
tian remains, loved the Byzantine. The Persian fire-domed,
fire-backed structures were beautiful to me. But never anything Greek except the sculpture and the Greek vase—the
reward of their persistence in search of the elegant solution.
My search was more for the exception that went to prove the
rule, than for the rule itself.

As for inspiration from human nature, there were Laotze,
Jesus, Dante, Beethoven, Bach, Vivaldi, Palestrina, Mozart.
Shakespeare was in my pocket for the many years I rode the

302

morning train to Chicago. I learned, too, from William Blake (all of his work I read), Goethe, Wordsworth, Dr. Johnson, Carlyle (*Sartor Resartus* at the age of fourteen), George Meredith, Victor Hugo, Voltaire, Rousseau, Cervantes, Nietzsche, Unamuno, Heraclitus, Aristotle, Aristophanes.

I loved the Byzantine of San Sophia—a true dome in contrast to Michelangelo's bastard. I loved the great Momoyama period in Japanese painting and the later Ukiyoe as I found it in the woodblock prints of the periods. These prints I collected with extravagant devotion and shameful avidity, and sat long at the inspiring series of Hokusai and Hiroshige; learned much from Korin, Kenzan, Sotatz and always the primitives. The Ukiyoe and the Momoyama, Japanese architecture and gardening, confirmed my own feeling for my work and delighted me, as did Japanese civilization which seemed so freshly and completely of the soil, organic.

Gothic soared for me, too; but seldom if ever the Renaissance in architecture, outside the original contributions of the Italians. I read, being a minister's son, much of the Bible; and inhabited, now and then, all the great museums of the world, from America to London, across the globe to Tokyo.

I read and respected many of our own poets and philosophers, among them: Emerson, Thoreau, Melville, William James, Charles Beard, John Dewey, Mark Twain, our supreme humorist-story-teller; especially the giver of the new religion of democracy, Walt Whitman. I cared little for the great pragmatists in philosophy and less for the Greek sophists. Historicism always seemed equivocal to me; the best of the histories Gibbon's *Rome;* my respect for Frederick Froebel always high owing to my mother's kindergarten table. Soon I turned away from the Greek abstraction via Oxford or elsewhere. Of all the fine arts, music it was that I could not live without, and—as taught by my father (the symphony an edifice of sound)—found in it sympathetic parallel to architecture. Beethoven, and Bach too, were princely architects in my spiritual realm.

I liked Beethoven's great disciple, Brahms. Italy was to me and is still so ever the beating heart of art creative, manifest in Vivaldi, the Italian troubadours and Palestrina. They came along with Giotto, Mantegna, Leonardo, etc.

My mother taught me, in my childhood as described, the kindergarten "gifts" of Frederick Froebel—a true philosopher. At the age of eleven I was confided by my mother to her brother, my uncle James, on the farm in "the Valley" to practice both edifice and gifts as I might, and did. Never a thought in politics as other than profane until I was past fifty-five.

Again: I found repeatedly confirmed that the inferior mind not only learns by comparison, but loosely confers its superlatives, while the superior mind which learns by analysis refrains from superlatives. I have learned about architecture by root, by world-wide travel and by incessant experiment and experience in the study of nature. In the midst of sensible experiment based always upon preliminary experiments, I never had the courage to lie. Meantime I lived with all the expressions of beauty I could see. And all those that I could acquire and use for study and enjoyment I acquired as my library, but living with them all as I might. I never had much respect for the collector's mind.

from A TESTAMENT, *1957*

The New Architecture: Principles

I   The Earth Line

At last we come to the analysis of the principles that became so solidly basic to my sense and practice of architecture. How

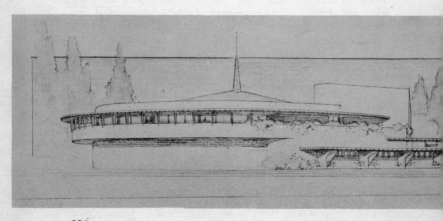

do these principles, now beginning to be recognized as the centerline of American democracy, work?

Principle one: Kinship of building to ground. This basic inevitability in organic architecture entails an entirely new sense of proportion. The human figure appeared to me, about 1893 or earlier, as the true *human* scale of architecture. Buildings I myself then designed and built—Midwest—seemed, by means of this new scale, to belong to man and at the moment especially as he lived on rolling Western prairie. Soon I had occasion to observe that every inch of height there on the prairie was exaggerated. All breadths fell short. So in breadth, length, height and weight, these buildings belonged to the prairie just as the human being himself belonged to it with his gift of speed. The term "streamlined" as my own expression was then and there born.

As result, the new buildings were rational: low, swift and clean, and were studiously adapted to machine methods. The quiet, intuitional, horizontal line (it will always be the line of human tenure on this earth) was thus humanly interpreted and suited to modern machine-performance. Machine-methods and these new streamlined, flat-plane effects first appeared together in our American architecture as expression of new ways to reach true objectives in building. The main objective was gracious appropriation of the art of architecture itself to the Time, the Place, and Modern Man.

1957   Florida Southern College, *Lakeland, Fla.* Music Building. (Campus plan on page 279; photographs on pages 150, 151.)

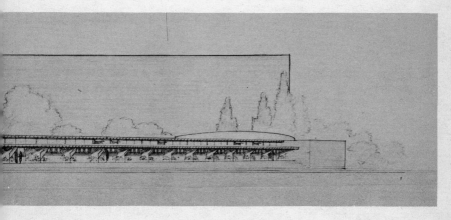

What now is organic "design"? Design appropriate to modern tools, the machine, and this new human scale. Thus, design was opportune, and well within the architect's creative hand if his mind was receptive to these relatively new values: moving perception at this time with reverential spirit toward the understanding of the "nature of nature." The nature of the machine, studied by experiment and basically used in structural design, was still to be limited to a tool, and proved to be a powerful new medium of expression. Buildings before long were evidencing beautiful simplicity, a fresh exuberance of countenance. Originality.

Never did I allow the machine to become "motif"—always machine for man and never man for the machine. Ever since, in organic architecture I have used the machine and evolved a system of building from the inside out, always according to the nature of both man and machine—as I could see it—avoiding the passing aspects now characteristic of urban architecture. The machine I found a better means to broaden the humane interest in modern architecture. Nor, in point of style, have I once looked upon the machine as in itself an end, either in planning or building or style. Quantity has never superseded quality.

The Modular of the Kindergarten Table

Kindergarten training, as I have shown, proved an unforeseen asset: for one thing, because later all my planning was devised

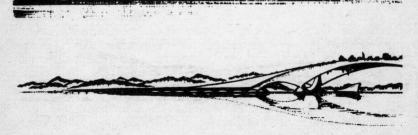

on a properly proportional unit system. I found this would keep all to scale, ensure consistent proportion throughout the edifice, large or small, which thus became—like tapestry—a consistent fabric woven of interdependent, related units, however various.

So from the very first this system of "fabrication" was applied to planning even in minor buildings. Later, I found technological advantages when this system was applied to heights. In elevation, therefore, soon came the vertical module as experience might dictate. All this was very much like laying warp on the loom. The woof (substance) was practically the same as if stretched upon this predetermined warp. This basic practice has proved indispensable and good machine technique must yield its advantages. Invariably it appears in organic architecture as visible features in the fabric of the design—insuring unity of proportion. The harmony of texture is thus, with the scale of all parts, within the complete ensemble.

II   Impulse to Grow

Principle two: Decentralization. The time for more individual spaciousness was long past due. 1893. I saw urban-decentralization as inevitable because a growing necessity, seeking more space everywhere, by whatever steps or stages it was obtainable. Space, short of breath, was suffocating in an airless situation, a shameful imposition upon free American life. Then, as

1949   The San Francisco Bay Crossing, project, *San Francisco, Cal.*

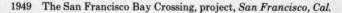

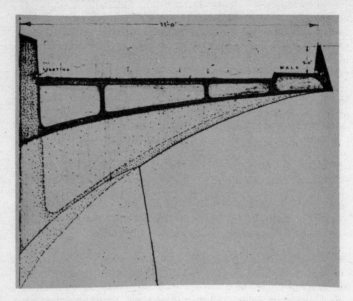

1949   The San Francisco Bay Crossing. Section of curved slab spring-
ing out from pier and supporting the roadway.

now, the popular realtor with his "lot" was enemy of space; he
was usually busy adding limitation to limitation, rounding up
the herd and exploiting the ground for quick profit.

Indigestible competition, thus added to the big city, despoiled
the villages. Over-extended verticality then congested to hold
the profits of congestion was added to the congestion already
fashioned on the ground.

To offset the senselessness of this inhuman act, I prepared
the Broadacre City models at Taliesin in 1932. The models
proposed a new space concept in social usage for individual and
community building. But the whole establishment was laid out
in accordance with the conditions of land tenure already in
effect. Though the centers were kept, a new system of subdivi-
sion was proposed.

Later, this model of the broader use of ground for a new idea
of a new city was carefully studied in detail in a series of
smaller tributary models, all as described in *When Democracy
Builds,* a book I later wrote on the suggestion of Robert
Hutchins. Buildings, roads, planting, habitation, cultivation,
decoration, all became as architectural as they were in Umbria

in Italy in the Middle Ages; qualities of ancient sort in modern form for modern times, considered in terms of modern humane utility. Thus broadened, the view of architecture as basic now in service to society came as relief and gave a preview of primary form facing the law of the changes inevitable.

Therefore quantity—the machine source—was in no way, nor anywhere, at any time, to be used to hinder the quality of new resources for human profit and delight in living. Living was to be a quality of man's own spirit.

Science, the great practical resource, had proceeded to date itself and magnify the potential sacrifice of man as menial, now wholesale destruction of democracy. Congested in cities by continually bigger mechanical means to avoid labor, man was to be given a new freedom. The ground plan of Broadacre City was bound together in advantageous, interactive relationship to the new resources of human life under protected freedom, our own if only we would reach out and take it.

Convenient, inspiring continuity appeared in this plan for a new community (still called a city), inevitable to the survival of human individuality. But I have learned that a new pattern can never be made out of the old one: only palliation is possible —and is soon inefficient. These initial Broadacre City models, still to be seen at Taliesin, were exhibited at Rockefeller Center, New York, 1934, and many times since, elsewhere in our country and abroad. Notwithstanding the A.I.A. and the critics, this complete group-model, new in concept and pattern, showing the new life of agrarian-urbanism and urbanized-agrarianism, virtually the wedding of city and country, reappeared to travel around the world in the exhibition "Sixty Years of Living Architecture." After being shown in Philadelphia, Florence, Paris Beaux-Arts (where I was told this was the only one-man exhibition since the one accorded to James McNeill Whistler), Zurich Art Institute, Munich Art Palace, Rotterdam Civic Center, University of Mexico, it returned to a special exhibition building in New York City, and later to a special extension of Olive Hill in Los Angeles by the Municipal Art Society.

III   *Character is a Natural*

Three: Appropriate "character" is inevitable to all architecture if organic. Significance of any building would clearly express its objective, its purpose—whether store, apartment building, bank, church, hotel or pie-club, factory, circus or school. Fun-

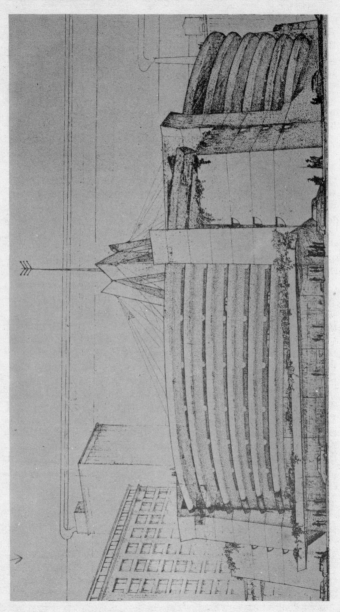

1947   Self-service garage, project for Pittsburgh, Pa.

damental requirement, this should apply to all building, in ground-planning and, especially, relative to human life and its site. This means sane appropriation of imaginative design to specific human purposes, by the natural use of nature-materials or synthetics, and appropriate methods of construction. Our new resources already evolved by science, especially glass and steel wrought by the machine, are bound continually to develop new forms. Continually new ways and shapes of building will continue to give fresh character and true significance to all modern structure.

Poetic tranquility instead of a more deadly "efficiency," should be the consequence in the art of Building: concordant, sane, exuberant, and appropriate to purpose. Durable, serviceable, economical. Beautiful. In the ever-changing circumstances of complex modern existence all this is not too easy to accomplish and the extent of these evolving changes may not yet be fully seen but as architects we may thus reconstitute architecture in our hearts and minds and act to re-write our dated "codes" and refrain from disfiguring our American landscape by buildings or "service" systems.

IV Tenuity Plus Continuity

Four: Completely new character by these simple means came to architecture; came to view, not by haphazard use, but by organic interpretation, of steel and glass. Steel gave rise to a new property: I call it *tenuity*. Tenuity is simply a matter of tension (pull), something never before known in the architecture of this world. No building could withstand a pull. Push it you might and it would stay together but pull on it and it would fall apart. With tensile strength of steel, this pull permits free use of the cantilever, a projectile and tensile at the same time, in building-design. The outstretched arm with its hand (with its drooping fingers for walls) is a cantilever. So is the branch of a tree.

The cantilever is essentially steel at its most economical level of use. The principle of the cantilever in architecture develops tenuity as a wholly new human expression, a means, too, of placing all loads over central supports, thereby balancing extended load against opposite extended load. This brought into architecture for the first time another principle in construction—I call it *continuity*—a property which may be seen as a new, elastic, cohesive *stability*. The creative architect finds here a marvelous new inspiration in design. A new freedom involving far wider spacings of more slender supports. Thus

1959   Mrs. D. J. Donahoe, project of three connected houses, near *Scottsdale, Ariz.* Central unit. (Perspective on page 169.) (b) Smaller unit, connecting with main house by reinforced concrete bridge.

b.

architecture arrived at construction from within outward rather than from outside inward; much heightening and lightening of proportions throughout all building is now economical and natural, space extended and utilized in a more liberal planning than the ancients could ever have dreamed of. This is now prime characteristic of the new architecture called organic.

Rigid box shapes, outsides steel-framed, belong strictly to the nineteenth century. They cannot be twentieth century architecture. Support at rigid corners becomes mere obstruction: corners themselves now insignificant become extravagant waste, mere accents of enclosure. Construction lightened by means of cantilevered steel in tension, makes continuity a most valuable characteristic of architectural enlightenment. Our new architectural freedom now lies within this province. In the character of this new circumstance buildings now may proceed *from within outward:* Because push or pull may be integral to building design.

V   The Third Dimension: Interpretation

Five: To sum up, organic architecture sees the third dimension never as weight or mere thickness but always as *depth*. Depth an element of space; the third (or thickness) dimension transformed to a *space* dimension. A penetration of the inner depths of space in spaciousness becomes architectural and valid motif in design. With this concept of depth interpenetrating depths comes flowering a freedom in design which architects have never known before but which they may now employ in their designs as a true liberation of life and light within walls; a new structural integrity; outside coming in; and the space within, to be lived in, going out. Space outside becomes a natural part of space *within* the building. All building design thus actually becomes four-dimensional and renders more static than ever the two-dimensional effects of the old static post and girder, beam and box frame type of construction, however novel they seem to be made. Walls are now apparent more as humanized screens. They do define and differentiate, but never confine or obliterate space. A new sense of reality in building construction has arrived.

Now a new liberation may be the natural consequence in every building exterior. The first conscious expression of which I know in modern architecture of this *new reality*—the "space within to be lived in"—was Unity Temple in Oak Park. True harmony and economic elements of beauty were consciously planned and belong to this new sense of space-within. The age-old philosophy of Laotze is alive in architecture. In every part of the building freedom is active. Space the basic element in architectural design.

This affirmation, due to the new sense of "the space within" as reality, came from the original affirmative negation (the great protestant) 1904, the Larkin Building of Buffalo—now demolished. Here came the poetic principle of freedom itself as a new revelation in architecture. This new freedom that was first consciously demonstrated in Unity Temple, Oak Park (1906) as written in 1927 for AN AUTOBIOGRAPHY. With this new principle at work in our American architecture came a new sense of style as innate. A quality natural to the act and art of modern habitation: no longer applied by "taste." (Again: "Such as the life is, such is the form"—Coleridge gives us perhaps a better slogan than Form Follows Function.) For Americans as for all shades and shapes of human beings everywhere "style" becomes generic: poetic expression of character. Style is intrinsic—or it is false. As a characteristic of "the space within to be lived in"—the life of style is perpetually fresh.

VI Space

Six: Space, elemental to architecture, has now found architectural expression. Glass: air in air, to keep air out or keep it in. Steel, a strand slight and strong as the thread of the spider spinning, is able now to span extraordinary spaces. By new products of technology and increased inventive ingenuity in applying them to building-construction many superlative new space-forms have already come alive: and, because of them, more continually in sight. Some as a matter of course will be novel but insignificant; some will be significant and really new. But more important, modern building becomes the solid creative art which the poetic principle can release and develop. Noble, vital, exuberant forms are already here. Democracy awakes to a more spiritual expression. Indigenous culture will now awaken. Properly focused upon needs of twentieth century life, new uses of livable space will continually evolve, improved; more exuberant and serene. A new security and a new tranquility. Enlightened enjoyment of fresh beauty is here or due. As for the future: encouraging to me are the many letters, coming continually, country-wide, from teen-agers now in high

1953   Masieri Memorial Building, students' library and dwelling, project for the Grand Canal, *Venice, Italy.*

school, asking for help with the term theses they have chosen to write upon organic architecture. This widening of the awareness of the coming generation's interest in architecture can only mean a new American architecture. When these youngsters become fathers and mothers, say a generation hence, they are going to demand appropriate space-homes on these modern terms. We will soon see the house as a work of art and because of its intrinsic beauty more a home than ever.

VII   Form

Seven: Anyone anything of an architect will never be content to design a building merely (or chiefly) for the picture it makes —any more than a man would buy a horse merely by its color. What kind of intellect must the critic have who seeing a building judges it by "the look of it," ignorant of the nature of its construction?

For the first time in 500 years a sense of architectural form appears as a new spiritual integrity.

Heavy walls, senseless overheads and overloads of every sort, vanish—let us be glad. Light and thin walls may now depend from cantilever slabs supported from the interior on shallow, dry-wall footings, walls themselves becoming slender screens, entirely independent of use as support. Centralized supports may stand isolated, balancing load against load— seen not as walls at all, but as integral pattern; walls may be slender suspension from point to point, in fascinating pendant forms. In general, structure now becomes an affair from the inside outward instead of from the outside inward. Various geometrical forms (circular especially) in planning structure become more economical than the square of the box. Building loads may be suspended, suspension supported by slender, isolated uprights. Glass or light plastics may be used to fill in and make the whole habitable. Sheet metal and light metal castings afford a permanent material for the exteriors of such structures. Enclosures extremely light in weight combined with such structural elements relieve all modern building of surplus static; structure no longer an obesity or likely to fall of its own weight. Walls require little or no floor space. Spaces hitherto concealed or wasted or made impossible by heavy walls are revealed and made useful. Arrangements for human occupation in comfort may be so well aimed that spaciousness becomes economical as well as beautiful, appearing where it was never before thought to exist. Space now gives not only charm and character to practical occupation but beauty to the countenance and form of a valid new kind of habitation for mankind. Buildings, at long last—like their occupants—may be themselves free and wear the shining countenance of principle and directly say honestly, by free expression, yet becomingly, what they really are, what they really mean. The new sense of interior space as reality may characterize modern building. Style will be the consequence of integral character. Intellect thus reinforces and makes Spirit effective. An art as flexible, as various, as infinite in its possibilities as the spirit of man.

Organic Unit

Thus environment and building are one: Planting the grounds around the building on the site as well as adorning the building take on new importance as they become features harmonious with the space-within-to-be-lived-in. Site, structure, furnishing—decoration too, planting as well—all these become as one in organic architecture. What was once called "decorating"—landscaping, lighting, etc.—and modern gadgetry (mechanical fixtures like air-conditioning) all are within the building structure as features of the building itself. Therefore all are elements of this synthesis of features of habitation and harmonious with environment. This is what *posterity* will call "modern architecture."

VIII   Shelter: Inherent Human Factor

Eight: As interior space to be lived in becomes the reality of building so shelter thus emphasized becomes more than ever significant in character and important as a feature. Shelter is still a strange disorder when reduced to a flat lid—though a common desire on account of economy. *To qualify this common-sense desire for shelter* as most significant feature of architecture is now in organic architecture of greatly increased importance. Witness, for instance: The new sense of spaciousness requires, as inherent human factor, significant cover as well as shade. Cover therefore now becomes in itself a feature more important as architectural form: Solidity of walls vanishing to reappear as imaginative screens involving light, and as inevitable consequence leaving more responsibility

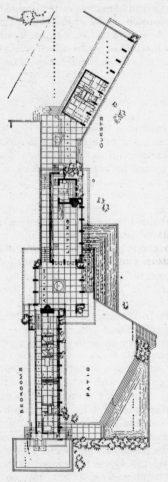

1955 H. C. Price house, *Phoenix, Ariz.* Plan. (Photograph on page 165.)

to the shapes and shaping of the whole building "overhead" with direct reference to the elements. Radical structural changes too now make the overhead lighter, less an imposition, more graceful, more harmonious feature of environment. Organic architecture sees shelter not only as a quality of space but of spirit, and the prime factor in any concept of building man into his environment as a legitimate feature of it. Weather is omnipresent and buildings must be left out in the rain. Shelter is dedicated to these elements. So much so that almost all other features of design tend to lead by one another to this important feature, shelter, and its component shade. In order to complete the building, protecting all within it from every changing circumstance of light, of cold and heat, of wear and tear and usage, we require shelter. The occupants of a building readily discover greater opportunity for comfort and more gracious, expanded living wherever shelter is becoming shade. By shade, charm has been added to character; style to comfort; significance to form.

The Client

Thus modern architecture implies far more intelligent cooperation on the part of the client than ever before. New rewards being so much greater in a work of art than by any "good taste" of the usual client, the wisdom of human investment now lies in "the home as a work of art." Correspondingly, the architect becomes more important than ever. The dwelling "as-a-work-of-art" is a better place in which to be alive, to live with, and live for and by in every sense. Therefore, why not a better "investment"? The interests of architect and owner are thus mutual and binding upon both.

IX Materials

Nine: I told my story of the nature of materials in building-construction in a series of articles written for Dr. Mikkelsen when he was editor of *The Architectural Record* of New York —about 1928. The good Doctor saved my economic life while I was getting a worm's eye view of society by calling me in to commission me to do a series of articles on "any subject I liked." I chose "The Nature of Materials," astonished to learn when starting research on the subject that nothing in any

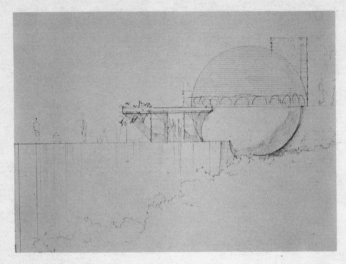

1947   Huntington Hartford house, part of project for country club, *Hollywood, Cal.* (Perspective of cottage center, also part of this project, on page 161.)

language had ever been written upon the subject.

All the materials usable in building-construction are more than ever important. They are all significant: each according to its own peculiar nature.

Old or new materials have their own lively contributions to make to the form, character and quality of any building. Each material may become a happy determinant of style; to use any one material wrongly is to abuse the integrity of the whole design.

Style

There is no such thing as true style not indigenous. Let us now try to evaluate style. "Style *is* the man." Yes, style is, as should be, largely a matter of innate *character*. But style only becomes significant and impressive in architecture when it is thus integral or organic. Because it is innate it is style genuine—or not at all. Style is now a quality natural to the building itself. Style develops from *within*. Great repose—serenity, a new tranquility —is the reward for proper use of each or any material in the true forms of which each is naturally most capable.

Ownership

In the hands of any prophetic architect the building is far more the owner's building than ever it was when built for him only by way of his, or her, own taste or whim. His building is the owner's now by his knowledge of the knowledge involved. So it is in the nature of architecture organic, that there can no longer be reason to deny any man his own way with his house if he really knows what he wants. The house may be designed to suit his preferences or his situation in his own way of life: but there is a difference between his preferences and his taste. If by his preferences, he reveals awareness of the principles involved and here touched upon, that will make his building genuinely his. If he seeks to understand *how* they involve, and evolve, his freedom *as individual* in this, his own, particular case his new home will declare his sovereignty as an enlightened individual. Homes of the new American *aristoi* may be as they must eventually become: one's own, not chiefly nor even ever "for sale." But this individual supremacy will come to the owner only with the knowledge of what it is that establishes this work of art as his own. "Taste" will now amount only to a certain discrimination in his approval of means to ends and appear once and for all in his choice of an architect. New light on both sides is indispensable to this new relationship, owner and architect.

Again, the *style* of each house may be much more than ever individual. Therefore the necessity for a new *cultural integrity* enters: individual sensitivity and personal responsibility are now essential. So comes a man-sized chance to choose a place not only in which to be alive, but in which to live as a distinguished entity, each individual owner genuinely a contributor to the indigenous culture of his time. Within the spirit of this wider range of individual choice, it becomes the home-owner's responsibility to be well aware of the nature of his choice of an architect. What he does now will not only surround him and represent him for life; it will probably be there for several hundred years. Integrity should appear in his life by his own choice. In our democracy the individual should rise to the higher level of aristocracy *only by his own perception of virtue*.

What is Natural

As the consequence of these basic principles of design, wood and plaster will be content to be and will look as well as wood and plaster, will not aspire to be treated to resemble marble. Nor will concrete buildings, reinforced with steel, aim to resemble cut-stone or marble. Each will have a grammar of its own, true to materials, as in the new grammar of "Fallingwater," my first dwelling in reinforced concrete. Were this simple knowledge of the grammar, the syntax, of organic design to become actual performance, each building would show its nature with such honest distinction of form as a sentient architect might afford to the awakened, appreciative owner. Building is an organism only if in accord outside with inside and both with the character and nature of its purpose, process, place and time. It will then incorporate the nature of the site, of the methods by which it is constructed, and finally the whole—from grade to coping, ground to skyline—will be becoming to its purpose.

A lady does not wear diamonds to market nor appear in shorts in the hotel lobby. Why then should she live with disregard for parallel good sense in the conduct of her own home environment? Building as organism is now entitled to become a cultural asset.

This is all merely the common-sense of organic architecture.

New materials in construction and methods of good building slowly remake the aspect of the world. A new grammar of design in the use of materials, all capable of characteristic effects, should enrich the building of the world without over-emphasis or ignorant abuse, should never become a cliché. However, not many such buildings are in evidence as thoroughbred.

Furniture

Furnishings should be consistent in design and construction, and used with style as an extension in the sense of the building which they "furnish." Wherever possible all should be natural. The sure reward for maintaining these simple features of architectural integrity is great serenity. What makes this whole affair of house-building, furnishing and environment so difficult to come by is the fact that though a good sense of proportion, which is the breadth and essence of organic design, may find adequate response from good "taste," good taste is not a substitute for knowledge. A sense of proportion cannot be taught; a sense of proportion is born. Only so gifted can it be trusted as an affair of culture. Knowledge not only of the philosophy of building but its constitution is necessary. But there is no true understanding of any art without some knowledge of its philosophy. Only then does its meaning come clear.

The Camera Eye

If one would get the essential character of an organic building, it could not be by camera, inasmuch as it is wholly a matter of experience. One must be *in* the building before he can understand what makes it what it is. To write about it otherwise is false. Its pictorial aspects are purely incidental—but integral. Pictures of the buildings of the old two-dimensional school (nineteenth century) are most meaningful because they were seen as pictorial when conceived. But the building living before us now as an organism (twentieth century) may only be seen *by experience within* the actual structure. Since the depth-planes so characteristic of these structures are inevitable to their effects and are, chiefly, edgewise to the camera, any true sense of the whole edifice is seldom if ever found in a photograph. The depth-plane defies the flat camera-eye. Profoundly natural, these buildings are never dull or monotonous because this subtle quality of integrity due to "the each in each and the each in all" is continually there although not tangible to any superficial view. The essence of organic building is space, space flowing outward, space flowing inward (not necessarily by the use of the picture-window). Both plan and construction are

1956   Lenkurt Electric Company, project, *San Carlos, Cal.* Typical work area.

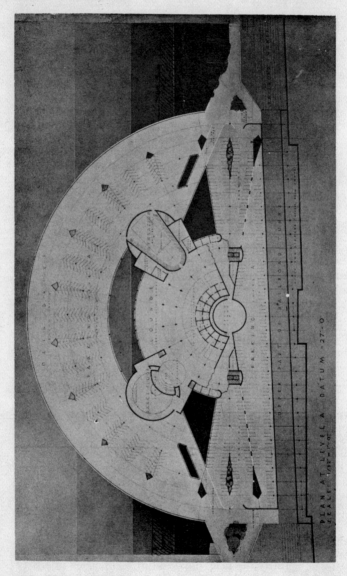

1955   Monona Terrace, civic center project, *Madison, Wis.* Plan.
(Perspective on page 164.)

seen to be inspired from within. For this important reason also, photographic views of these buildings are seldom satisfactory on the record. Only when the buildings are comprehended from within and each in its place a feature of its own special environment—serving its own appropriate purpose with integrity—are they really seen. If trees or mountains are round about, they will come to join and enrich the building by their natural sympathy. Architecture will become more charming because of this affinity. *The people in it gain the same distinction they would gain by being well-dressed.*

The character of the site is always fundamental to organic design. But fortified enclosure is no longer needed nor is it now often desirable. The old sense of fortification may still be with us as a more or less "monumental" weakness, as is any mere wall left standing alone. But ponderous though monumentality usually is, a monument often has its place: still serves some human purpose, as an emphasis of some chronic egotism or as true respect for the memorable, but usually abused as the dressiness of some exaggerated sentimentality.

The Profession

Architects today seem to have left but this one thing in common—something to sell: to be exact, themselves. Eventually, as a matter of course what *is* sold is chiefly themselves. Architecture is not on their minds.

But is degradation to the level of salesmanship and its profits a criterion to be tolerated by American society, either coming or going, in architecture? To take as earnest of our American future any cliché or endeavor to be international, this monotonous range of the commonplace which much of the architectural profession is now busy making of our present, is too fantastic, pessimistic egotism. Is there to be no true vision of whatever superior possibilities may exist for us in our new world besides these abortive boxes endeavoring to look tall?

Can it be that the ultimate chapter of this new era of democratic freedom is going to be deformed by this growing drift toward conformity encouraged by politics and sentimental education? If so then by what name shall our national American character be justly called? Doomed to beget only curiosities or monstrosities in art, architecture and religion by artists predominant chiefly by compliance with commercial expediency?

Machine standardization is apparently growing to mean little that is inspiring to the human spirit. We see the American workman himself becoming the prey of gangsterism made official. Everything as now professionalized, in time dies spiritually. Must the innate beauty of American life succumb or be destroyed? Can we save truth as beauty and beauty as truth in our country only if truth becomes the chief concern of our serious citizens and their artists, architects and men of religion, independent of established authority?

Nevertheless I realize that if all false or unfriendly forces (due to ignorance or so conditioned as here described) inimical to culture, were to become less and less, many long years would still be needed to overcome the deep habituations that have been built into the American scene by inroads upon the American character; wholly against natural grain and against our glorious original aim. If this twentieth century architecture, true to the principles of construction and more in line with our democratic faith, were to be more widely acknowledged by established authority; even if it were to be proclaimed from the housetops by cinema, television, press, politics, government and society as "the right thing" to be studied and practiced—there would still be controversy. Controversy would, even then, continue for the coming half-century at least, would perhaps never cease. Democracy knows only too well the senseless weight and conflicts of irresponsible public opinion, the chronic oralism, the dead weight of ignorance, the prejudices of conditioned minds siding right or left with selfish interests of hearts hardened—instead of the deep faith in Man necessary to inspire enlightenment by generosity of motive, which democracy meant to our forefathers and must yet mean to us. The common sense of the simple truth in this new-old philosophy, *from within outward*, if awakened in our society as now in our architecture, would ensure the true uses of technology for human shelter and reverential harmonious environment, both socially and politically. It would soon get into politics.

Meanwhile we continue to hope that the Comic Spirit in which we as a people do excel may survive long enough to salt and savor life among us long enough for our civilization to present us to the world as a culture, not merely as an amazing civilization. The basic distinction between the curious and the beautiful, in which culture really consists, will make all the difference between a society with a creative soul and a society with none.

from A TESTAMENT, *1957*

General Locations of
Frank Lloyd Wright Buildings

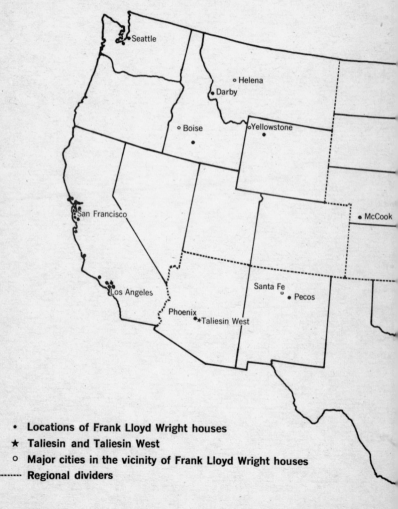

- • **Locations of Frank Lloyd Wright houses**
- ★ **Taliesin and Taliesin West**
- ○ **Major cities in the vicinity of Frank Lloyd Wright houses**
- ------- **Regional dividers**

Minneapolis

Madison
Taliesin
Milwaukee
Chicago
So. Bend
Canton

Grand Rapids
Detroit

Rochester
Buffalo

Manchester
Worcester

Bridgeport
New York

Des Moines
maha

Springfield

Philadelphia
Pittsburgh
Arlington

Trenton
Wilmington
Baltimore

Kansas City
St. Louis

Frankfort

Norfolk

Wichita

Tulsa

Chattanooga

Columbia

Dallas

Birmingham

Yemassee

Jackson

Houston

Lakeland

Palm Beach

Frank Lloyd Wright's Executed Works

1893-1959, *a list of structures standing—1960—arranged geographically*

This list was developed from several sources dealing with Wright's architecture including Henry-Russell Hitchcock's exhaustive catalogue for the period 1887 to 1941 published in his In the Nature of Materials, *and much of the post-war domestic work which has been collected in a list compiled by Bernard Pyron to whom special thanks are due. The author's own knowledge of Wright's work has also filled several gaps. While the list is largely complete, additional buildings doubtlessly exist and some designed shortly before Mr. Wright's death are presently in various stages of construction. The problem of assigning accurate dates to many of the recent buildings has been a singularly knotty one. Where possible, the final design date is given as the most meaningful, but in some cases this is not known and dates of completion have been substituted.*

It should be emphasized that this list is presented as a catalogue of Frank Lloyd Wright's buildings and obligates the owners in no way whatsoever nor even implies they know of its existence. Their privacy, of course, should be respected. In many cases the owners of houses listed above will have changed since the date of their construction.

Bruce F. Radde

I Eastern States: North to South

A NEW HAMPSHIRE
    1. *Manchester*
        Toufic H. Kalil, Heather Street, 1957
        Isadore Zimmerman, Heather Street, 1950

B MASSACHUSETTS
    1. *Amherst*
        Theodore Baird, Shays Street, 1940

C CONNECTICUT
    1. *New Canaan*
        John L. Rayward, Frogtown Road, 1956–8
    2. *Stamford*
        Frank S. Sander, Springbough, Woodchuck Rds., completed
          1955

D NEW YORK (West to East)
    1. *Derby*
        Darwin D. Martin, "Graycliff," 1927
    2. *Buffalo*
        George Barton, 118 Summit Avenue, 1903
        Darwin D. Martin, 125 Jewett Parkway, 1904
        W. R. Heath, 76 Soldiers Place, 1905
        Walter V. Davidson, 57 Tillingham Place, 1908
        Martin Blue Sky Mausoleum (Reported in construction by
          Hitchcock, 1941)
    3. *Rochester*
        E. E. Boynton, 16 East Boulevard, 1908
    4. *Lake Mahopac*
        A. K. Chahroudi, Petra Island, 1952
    5. *Pleasantville*
        Sol Friedman, Usonia Homes, 1950
        Ed Serlin, Usonia Homes, 1950
        Roland Reisley, Usonia Homes, 1954
    6. *Rye*
        Maximilian Hoffman, North Manursing Island, 1954
    7. *New York City*
        Guggenheim Museum, 5th Avenue and E. 88th Street, 1956–9
        Mercedes-Benz Show Room, 430 Park Avenue, 1955
    8. *Great Neck, L. I.*
        Ben Rebhuhn, Great Neck Estates, Myrtle Avenue and Mag-
          nolia Drive, 1938
    9. *Staten Island*
        First Pre-Fab, 1959

E NEW JERSEY
  1. *Waldwick*
     Stuart Richardson, 1951 (Hitchcock reports the house being
       built in Livingstone, N.J. in 1941)
  2. *East Caldwell*
     William Guenther, 1941
  3. *Bernardsville*
     James B. Christie, Jockey Hallow Road, 1940
  4. *Merchantville*
     J. A. Sweeton, Kings Highway, 1950
  5. *Millstone*
     Abraham Wilson, Main Street, 1956

F PENNSYLVANIA. East to West
  1. *Elkins Park* (near Philadelphia)
     Beth Sholom Synagogue, Old York Road, 1956–9
  2. *Ardmore*
     Tod Company, "Suntop Homes," Sutton Road near Spring
       Avenue, 1939
  3. *Uniontown*
     I. N. Hagan, Chalk Hill, Ohiopyle Road, 1954
  4. *Bear Run*
     Edgar J. Kaufmann, "Fallingwater," 1936
     Kaufmann guest house, 1939
  5. *Pittsburgh*
     Edgar J. Kaufmann, Office, First National Bank Building, 1937

G MARYLAND
  1. *Baltimore*
     Joseph Euchtman, 6807 Cross Country Boulevard, 1940
  2. *Bethesda*
     R. L. Wright, 7929 Deepwell Road, 1955

H DELAWARE
  1. *Wilmington*
     Dudley Spencer, 619 Shiply Road, 1956

II Southern States: North to South

A VIRGINIA
  1. *Falls Church*
     Loren Pope, 1005 Locust Street, 1940
  2. *Virginia Beach*
     Andrew B. Cooke, 403 Crescent and 41st Sts., 1958–9

3. *McLean*
Louis Marden, 4413 Chainbridge Road, 1952

B SOUTH CAROLINA
1. *Greenville*
Gabrelle Austin, 19 W. Avondale Drive, 195?
2. *Yemassee*
Leigh Stevens, "Auldbrass Plantation," 1940

C FLORIDA
1. *Lakeland*
Florida Southern College
Ann Pfeiffer Chapel, 1940; Three Seminar Buildings, 1940;
T. R. Roux Library, 1941; Administration Building, 1946–50;
Industrial Arts, 1950–5; Science Building, 1952; Danforth
Chapel, 1955; Music Building, 1959–?
2. *Palm Beach*
House, name and location unknown, 1913
3. *Tallahassee*
George Lewis, 3117 Okeeheepkee Road, 1954

D ALABAMA
1. *Florence*
Stanley Rosenbaum, Riverview Drive, 1937 (expanded, 1948)

E MISSISSIPPI
1. *Jackson*
Willis J. Hughes "Fountainhead," 1951–6
2. *Ocean Springs*
James Charnley, 1890
Louis Sullivan, 1890
3. *Pass Christian*
W. L. Fuller, completed 1953

F TENNESSEE
1. *Chattanooga*
Seamour Shavin, 334 N. Crest Road, 1952

G KENTUCKY
1. *Frankfort*
Rev. J. R. Ziegler, 509 Shelby Street, 1910

III   Great Lakes States: East to West

A OHIO
1. *Madison*
Karl A. Staley, Lake Road, 1955

    2. *Willoughby*

       Louis Penfield, River Road, 1955

    3. *Canton*

       John J. Dobkins, 5120 Plain Center Road, completed 1955
       Ellis A. Feiman, 452 Santa Clara Drive, N.W., completed 1955
       Nathan Rubin, 518 44th Street, N.W., 1953

    4. *Oberlin*

       C. E. Weltzheimer, Morgan Street, 1950

    5. *Springfield*

       Burton J. Westcott, 1340 E. High Street, 1907

    6. *Dayton*

       Dr. Kenneth Meyer Clinic, 1958–9

    7. *Cincinatti*

       Cedric Boulter, 1 Rawson Wood Circle, completed 1956
       William Boswell, 1958–9
       Gerald B. Tonkins, 6880 Knoll Amby, 195?

B INDIANA

    1. *Marion*

       Dr. Richard Davis, Shady Hills, 1954

    2. *Lafayette*

       Prof. John E. Christian, Woodland Ave. & US 52, 195?

    3. *South Bend*

       K. C. deRhodes, 715 W. Washington Street, 1906
       H. T. Mossberg, 1405 Ridgedale Road, 1951

    4. *Ogden Dunes* (near Gary)

       Andrew F. H. Armstrong, 1939

C MICHIGAN: North to South

    1. *Northport*

       Mrs. W. C. Alpaugh, 1948–9

    2. *Manistee*

       George Dlesk, completed 1958

    3. *Whitehall*

       Walter Gerts, Birch Brook, 1902
       George E. Gerts, Birch Brook, 1902
       Mrs. Thomas H. Gale, Birch Brook, 1921

    4. *Grand Rapids*

       Meyer May, 450 Madison Avenue, S.E., 1909
       J. H. Amberg, 505 College Avenue, 1910

    5. *Lansing*

       Stanley Hartman, 1958–9

6. *Okemos*

   Katherine Winkler-Alma Goetsch, Hulett Road, 1939
   James Edwards, 2504 Arrowhead Road, 1951
   Erling Brauner, 2527 Arrowhead Road, 1946-7
   Donald Schaberg, 1155 Wrightwind Drive, completed 1958

7. *Milford Village*

   Oscar Miller, 1958–9

8. *Bloomfield Hills*

   Gregor Affleck, 1941
   Melwyn Maxwell Smith, 5045 Pon Valley Road, 1951

9. *Detroit*

   Dorothy Turkel, 2760 W. Seven Mile Road, completed 1958

10. *Plymouth*

    Carl Wall, 12305 Beck Road, 1941-7 (?)
    Lewis H. Goddard, 12221 Beck Road, 1955

11. *Ann Arbor*

    William Palmer, 227 Orchard Hills Drive, 1951

12. *Galesburg Village* (ten miles east of Kalamazoo)

    David Weisblatt, 11185 Hawthorne Drive, 1951
    Samuel Eppstein, 11098 Hawthorne Drive, 1953
    Curtis Meyer, 11108 Hawthorne Drive, 1951
    Eric Pratt, 11036 Hawthorne Drive, 1951

13. *Kalamazoo* (Parkwyn Village)
    Ward Greiner, 2617 Taliesin Drive, 1951
    Ward McCartney, 2662 Taliesin Drive, 1955
    Eric V. Brown, 2806 Taliesin Drive, 1951
    Robert Levin, 2816 Taliesin Drive, 1951
    Robert D. Winn, 2822 Taliesin Drive, 1951

14. *Benton Harbor*

    Howard Anthony, 1150 Miami Road, 1951
    Carl Schultz, 1958–9

15. *St. Joseph*

    Ina Morriss Harper, Lake Shore Road, 1951

16. *Grand Beach*

    Ernest Vosburgh, Crescent Road, 1916
    W. S. Carr, Lakeview and Pine Avenue, 1916
    Joseph J. Bagley, Lakeview and Cedar Avenue, 1916

17. *Marquette* (Upper Peninsula)

    Mrs. Abby Beecher Roberts, "Deertrack," R.F.D. 1 (unsupervised) 1936
    Arthur Heurtley, "Les Chenaux Club," Marquette Island, 1902

18. *Grosse Ile*

    Allen Zieger, 1958–9

337

FRANK LLOYD WRIGHT'S EXECUTED WORKS

D WISCONSIN: North to South

1. *Wausau*
   Charles L. Manson, 1224 Highland Boulevard, 1940
   Duey Wright, Highway 51, south side of town, 1957–8
2. *Stevens Point*
   First Pre-Fab, 1958
3. *Oshkosh*
   Stephen Hunt, 685 Algona Avenue, 1917
4. *Two Rivers*
   Bernard Schwartz, Still Bend, 1939
5. *Bayside* (north of Milwaukee)
   First Pre-Fab, 1959–60, Joseph Mollica, Builder
6. *Fox Point*
   Albert Adelman, 7111 N. Barnett, 1948–9
7. *Milwaukee*
   F. C. Bogk, 2420 N. Terrace Avenue, 1916
   Arthur L. Richards houses and apartments, 1835 S. Layton
     Blvd., 2714–2732 W. Burnham Street, 1916
   Arthur Munkwitz Apartments, 1102–1112 N. 27th Street,
     1916
8. *Wauwatosa*
   Annunciation Greek Orthodox Church, N. 92nd and W. Congress Streets, 1956
9. *Dousman*
   Dr. Maurice Greenberg, 2 miles south, Highway 67, 1955 (?)
10. *Jefferson*
    Richard Smith, 801 Linden Street, 1951
11. *Columbus*
    Clark Arnold, 954 Line Road, 1955
12. *Madison*
    Robert M. Lamp, 22 N. Butler Street, 1904
    E. A. Gilmore, 120 Ely Place, 1908
    Herbert Jacobs, 441 Toepfer Street, 1937
    Arnold Jackson, 3515 Beltline Highway, 1957–8
    Unitarian Meeting House, 900 University Bay Drive, 1951
    Erdman Co., First Pre-Fab, Rosa Road, near Crestwood, 1957
    Erdman Co. Second Pre-Fab, 1959
13. *Shorewood Hills* (*near Madison*)
    John Pew, 3650 Mendota Drive, 1940
14. *Middleton*
    Herbert Jacobs, Old Sauk Road, 1948–9

338

15. *Spring Green* (Route 23 on the east bank of the Wisconsin River)

    Hillside Home School, 1902
    Taliesin Farm Group, 1938
    Romeo & Juliet Windmill, 1896
    Taliesin III, 1925
    Andrew T. Porter, "Tany-Deri," 1907
    Riverview Terrace Restaurant, under construction, 1950's

16. *Wyoming Valley*

    Wyoming Valley School, Route 23, 1957

17. *Richland Center*

    A. D. German Warehouse, 1915, incomplete

18. *Lancaster*

    Patrick Kinney, 1952–3

19. *Delavan Lake*

    A. P. Johnson, South Shore Road, 1905
    George W. Spencer, South Shore Road, 1902
    Dr. H. Goodsmith, South Shore Road, 1900
    Charles S. Ross, South Shore Road, 1902
    Fred B. Jones, "Penwern," South Shore Road, 1902

20. *Lake Geneva*

    Hotel Geneva, 1912

21. *East Troy*

    Rainbow Springs Lodge (private), 1940(?), largely destroyed, 1958

22. *Racine*

    S. C. Johnson & Son, Administration Building and Research Tower, 1525 Howe Street, 1936–9; 1947–50
    Herbert F. Johnson, "Wingspread," Wind Point, 1937
    Thomas P. Hardy, 1319 South Main, 1905
    Willard H. Keland, Valley View Drive, 1956

E   ILLINOIS: North to South

1. *Rockford*

    Kenneth Laurent, Spring Brook Road, 1951

2. *Belvidere*

    W. H. Pettit Chapel, Belvidere Cemetery, 1906

3. *Libertyville*

    Lloyd Lewis, Little St. Mary's Road, 1940

4. *Lake Bluff*

    Herbert Angster, 605 Blodgett Road, 1911

5. *Lake Forest*

    Charles F. Glore, 170 North Mayflower, 1955

6. *Highland Park*

Ward W. Willitts, 1445 Sheridan Road, 1902
Mary M. W. Adams, 103(?) Lake Ave., 1905
George Madison Millard, 1689 (410) Lake Ave., 1906

7. *Glencoe*

E. D. Brigham, 790 Sheridan Road, 1915
Sherman M. Booth, 265 Sylvan Road, 1915
W. A. Glasner, 850 Sheridan Road, 1905
Ravine Bluffs Development, 272 Sylvan Road, 1023–1031
  Meadow Road, 1915

8. *Kenilworth*

Hiram Baldwin, 205 Essex Road, 1905

9. *Wilmette*

Frank J. Baker, 507 Lake Avenue, 1909

10. *Evanston*

Charles E. Brown, 2420 Harrison Avenue, 1905

11. *Glenview*

John C. Carr, 1544 Portage Run, 1951

12. *Barrington*

Lewis B. Frederick, County Line Road, 1957–8
First Pre-Fab, Donlea Road, 1957–8

13. *Plato Center*

Robert Muirhead, S.W. of Village, 1952

14. *Geneva*

P. D. Hoyt, 318 S. Fifth, 1906
Col. Geo. Fabyan, Batavia Road, 1907
A. W. Gridley, North Batavia Avenue, 1906

15. *Aurora*

Wm. B. Green, 1300 Garfield Avenue, 1912

16. *Hinsdale*

Frederick Bagley, 121 County Line Road, 1894
W. H. Freeman, 106 N. Grant Street, 1903

17. *La Grange*

Stephen M. B. Hunt, 345 S. 7th Avenue, 1907
Peter Goan, 108 S. 8th Avenue, 1894
Robert G. Emmond, 109 S. 8th Avenue, 1892

18. *Riverside*

Coonley Playhouse, 350 Fairbanks Road, 1912
Avery Coonley, 300 Scottswood Road, 1908
F. F. Tomek, 150 Nuttell Road, 1907
Gardener's Cottage, 1911

19. *Elmhurst*

F. B. Henderson, 301 S. Kenilworth Avenue, 1901

20. *River Forest*—West to East

Wm. H. Winslow, Auvergne Place, 1893
Chauncey L. Williams, 530 Edgewood Place, 1895
Isabel Roberts, 603 Edgewood Place, 1908
J. Kibben Ingalls, 562 Keystone Avenue, 1909
E. Arthur Davenport, 559 Ashland Avenue, 1901
River Forest Tennis Club, 615 Lathrop Avenue (at Quick St.), 1906

21. *Oak Park*—West to East

George W. Smith, 404 Home Ave. (South of railroad tracks), 1898
Francis Woolley, 1030 Superior Street, 1894
Walter Gale, 1031 Chicago Avenue, 1893
R. P. Parker, 1027 Chicago Avenue, 1892
Thomas H. Gale, 1019 Chicago Avenue, 1892
Frank Lloyd Wright House and Studio, 428 Forest Avenue; 951 Chicago Avenue, 1889; 1895
Dr. W. H. Copeland, 408 Forest Avenue, 1909
Arthur Heurtley, 318 Forest Avenue, 1902
E. R. Hills, 313 Forest Avenue, 1901
Nathan G. Moore, 333 Forest Avenue, 1895, 1924
P. A. Beachy, 238 Forest Avenue, 1906
Frank Thomas, 210 Forest Avenue, 1901
Mrs. Thos. H. Gale, 6 Elizabeth Court, 1909
O. B. Balch, 611 N. Kenilworth Avenue, 1911
Unity Church, Lake Street & Kenilworth, 1906
Scoville Park Fountain, Lake Street
Charles E. Roberts Stable, 317 N. Euclid Avenue, 1896
George Furbeck, 223 N. Euclid Avenue, 1897
Harry S. Adams, 710 Augusta Avenue, 1913
W. E. Martin, 636 N. East Street, 1903
H. C. Goodrich, 534 N. East Avenue, 1896
Edwin H. Cheney, 520 N. East Avenue, 1904
William G. Fricke, 540 Fair Oaks Avenue, 1902
Rollin Furbeck, 515 Fair Oaks Avenue, 1898

22. *Chicago—West Side*

J. J. Walser Jr., 42 N. Central Avenue, 1903
E-Z Polish Factory, 3005-7 W. Carroll Street, 1905
Edward C. Waller Apartments, 2840-58 W. Walnut Street, 1895
Francisco Terrace Apts., 253-7 Francisco Avenue, 1895
Chicago—North Side
Oscar Steffens (Kings Arms Restaurant), 7631 Sheridan Road, 1909
Emil Bach, 7415 Sheridan Road, 1915
Chicago—Downtown
Rookery Building, Remodeling of LaSalle & Adams Street lobbies, 209 S. LaSalle Street, 1905

Chicago—South Side
Robert Roloson, 3213–19 Calumet, 1894
Abraham Lincoln Center (Perkins), Oakwood Boulevard at
   Langley Avenue, 1903
Francis Apartments, 4304 Forestville Avenue, 1895
Dr. Allison Harlan, 4414 Greenwood Avenue, 1892
Warren McArthur, 4852 Kenwood Avenue, 1892
George Blossom, 4858 Kenwood Avenue, 1892 (garage, 1907)
Isidor Heller, 5132 Woodlawn Avenue, 1897
Frederick C. Robie, 5757 Woodlawn Avenue, 1908–9
William Adams, 9326 South Pleasant Avenue, 1900
Robert W. Evans, 9914 Longwood Drive, 1908
S. A. Foster, 12147 Harvard Avenue, 1900

23. *Flossmoor* (south of Chicago)

Frederick Nicholas, Brassie Avenue (east of Illinois Central
   railroad tracks), 1906

24. *Kankakee*

B. Harley Bradley, 701 S. Harrison Avenue, 1900
Warren Hickox, 687 S. Harrison Avenue, 1900

25. *Dwight*

First National Bank (Frank L. Smith Bank), 1906

26. *Peoria*

Francis W. Little, 603 Moss Avenue, 1903

27. *Springfield*

Susan Lawrence Dana, Lawrence Avenue at 4th Street, 1903
   (library, 1905)

28. *Decatur*

E. P. Irving, Millikin Place, 1910 (executed by von Holst)

IV Middle Western States

A MINNESOTA: North to South

1. *Cloquet*

R. W. Lindholm, 1955
Lindholm Filling Station, 1957–8

2. *Stillwater*

Donald Loveness, Route 3, Woodpile Lake, 1954

3. *Minneapolis*

Malcolm M. Willey, 255 Bedford Street, 1934
Henry J. Neils, 2815 Burnham Boulevard, 1951

4. *Wayzata*

Francis W. Little, "Northome," R.F.D. 3, 1913

5. *Rochester*

Dr. A. H. Bulbulian, Skyway Drive, 1951
Thomas E. Keyes, Skyway Drive, 1951

6. *Austin*

S. P. Elam, 107 Eastwood Road, 1951

B IOWA: North to South

1. *Mason City*

Dr. G. C. Stockman, 311 First Street S.E., 1908
City National Bank & Hotel, West State Street & S. Federal, 1909

2. *Charles City*

Dr. A. L. Miller, 701 E. Blount Street, 1951

3. *Quasqueton*

Lowell E. Walter, 1949–50

4. *Cedar Rapids*

Douglas Grant, Carroll Drive and Adel Street, 1951

5. *Marshalltown*

Robert Sunday, 1958–9

6. *Des Moines*

Paul Trier, 1958–9

7. *Oskaloosa*

Carroll Alsop, 1907 A Avenue E., completed 1951
Jack Lamberson, 117 N. Park, completed 1951

C MISSOURI: East to West

1. *St. Louis*

T. A. Pappas, 846 Pennsylvania Avenue, 195?

2. *Kirkwood*

Russell M. Kraus, 120 N. Ballas Road, 1953

3. *Kansas City*

Kansas City Community Church, 4601 Main Street, 1940 (unsupervised)
Clarence Sondern, 3600 Bellview Avenue, 1940 (expanded 1949)

D KANSAS

1. *Wichita*

Henry J. Allen, 255 Roosevelt Boulevard, 1917

E NEBRASKA

1. *McCook*

Harvey P. Sutton, 602 Main Street, 1907

343

V Southwestern States: East to West

A OKLAHOMA

    1. *Bartlesville*

    Price Tower, 1953–6
    Harold C. Price, Jr., Country Club Terrace, 1956

    2. *Tulsa*

    Richard Lloyd Jones, 3700 Birmingham Road, 1929

B TEXAS

    1. *Dallas*

    John Gillin, 9400 Rockbrook, 1957–8
    Dallas Theater Center, 1958–9

    2. *Houston*

    W. L. Thaxton, Jr., 12024 Tall Oaks, completed 1955

C NEW MEXICO

    1. *Pecos*

    Arnold Friedman, Pecos National Forest, 1947–8

D ARIZONA

    1. *Phoenix*

    Arizona Biltmore Hotel Cottages, 1926 (with Albert McArthur)
    Rose Pauson, Orange Road, 1940 (largely destroyed)
    Benjamin Adelman, 5710 N. 30th Street, 1953
    Jorgine Boomer, 5804 N. 30th Street, 1953
    Raymond Carlson, 1123 W. Palo Verde Drive, 1950

    2. *Paradise Valley* (near Scottsdale)

    Frank Lloyd Wright: Taliesin West, Maricopa Mesa, 1938
    David Wright, 1952
    Harold C. Price, Sr., 1956

VI Northwest and Pacific Coast States: North to South

A WYOMING

    1. *Cody*

    Quentin Blair, 3 miles east on U.S. 16, 1953

B MONTANA

    1. *Darby*

    Como Orchards Summer Colony, Bitter Root Township, 1910
    (partly demolished)

C IDAHO

    1. *Bliss*

    Archie Boyd Teater, Hagerman Valley, 1955

D WASHINGTON: North to South

1. *Seattle*
   W. B. Tracy, 18971 Edgecliff Drive, 1956
2. *Tacoma*
   Chauncey Griggs, 78 John Dower, Chambers Creek, 1943–53

E CALIFORNIA: North to South

1. *San Anselmo*
   Robert Berger, 259 Redwood Road, 1952–59
2. *San Francisco*
   V. C. Morris Shop, 140 Maiden Lane, 1948
3. *Orinda*
   Maynard Beuhler, Great Oak Circle, 1948–9
4. *Hillsborough*
   Sidney Bazett, 101 Reservoir Road, 1940
5. *Atherton*
   Arthur Matthews, 83 Wisteria Way, Lindenwood Estates, 1952
6. *Palo Alto*
   Paul R. Hanna, 737 Frenchmans Road, 1937
7. *Carmel*
   Mrs. Clinton Walker, Scenic Drive, 1952
8. *San Luis Obispo*
   Dr. Karl Kundert, Medical Building, 1106 Pacific Street, 1955
9. *Montecito*
   George C. Stewart, 166 Summit at Hot Springs Road, 1909
10. *Eagle Rock*
    Arch Oboler, Ventura Boulevard, 1941–
11. *Brentwood Heights*
    George D. Sturges, 449 Skyway Road, 1939
12. *Los Angeles*
    Anderton Court Center, Rodeo Drive (Beverly Hills), 1953–4
    Dr. John Storer, 8161 Hollywood Boulevard, 1923
    Charles Ennis, 2607 Glendower Road, 1924
    Samuel Freeman, 1962 Glencoe Way, 1924
    Aline Barnsdall, "Hollyhock," 1920
    Barnsdall: Studio Residence A, Hollywood and Edgemont Boulevards, 1920
    Exhibition Building for Frank Lloyd Wright architectural exhibit; contiguous with "Hollyhock" house 1956 (now a gallery for the Municipal Art Center of Los Angeles)

13. *Pasadena*

Mrs. George Madison Millard, "La Miniatura," 645 Prospect Crescent, 1923

VII Buildings Outside United States:

A CANADA

1. *Desbarats*

E. H. Pitkin, Sapper Island, near Kensington Point, 1900

2. *Montreal, P. Q.*

C. Thaxter Shaw, 3466 Peel Street, 1906 (remodeling)

B JAPAN

1. *Tokyo*

Imperial Hotel, 1915–22
Imperial Hotel Annex, 1916
Aizaku Hayashi house, Komazawa, 1917
Jiyu Gakuen Girls' School of the Free Spirit, 1921

2. *Hakone*

Fukuhara House, 1918 (damaged by quake, 1923)

3. *Ashiya*

Yamamura house, 1918

FRANK LLOYD WRIGHT
The distinguished American architect Frank Lloyd Wright was born in Richland Center, Wisconsin, on June 8, 1869. He died in Phoenix, Arizona, on April 9, 1959.

EDGAR KAUFMANN
For fifteen years Edgar Kaufmann was on the staff of the Museum of Modern Art, part of that time as director of the Department of Industrial Design. He has also been editor for applied arts at the ENCYCLOPAEDIA BRITANNICA. *Mr. Kaufmann is the author and editor of a number of books, among them* WHAT IS MODERN DESIGN? *and* AN AMERICAN ARCHITECTURE, *and is, as well, a contributor to many periodicals.*

BEN RAEBURN
Mr. Raeburn was Frank Lloyd Wright's publisher, editor, and friend for many years.